AN AMERICAN IDEA

John K. Hillers, 1871-78
ZION NATIONAL PARK, UTAH

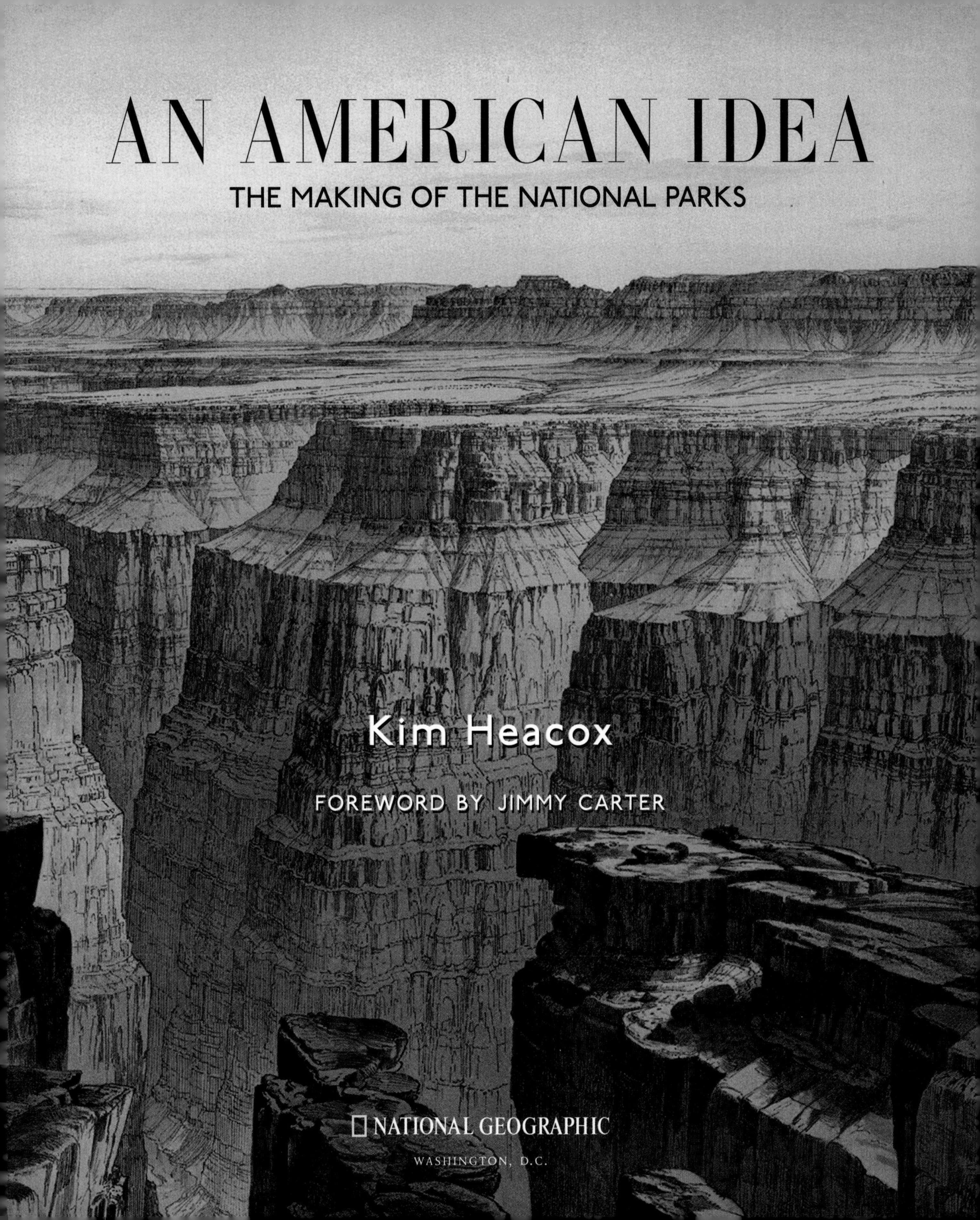

AN AMERICAN IDEA

THE MAKING OF THE NATIONAL PARKS

Kim Heacox

FOREWORD BY JIMMY CARTER

NATIONAL GEOGRAPHIC
WASHINGTON, D.C.

THE OLD WILDERNESS SCENERY AND THE OLD WILDERNESS LIFE

ARE TO BE KEPT UNSPOILED FOR THE BENEFIT

OF OUR CHILDREN'S CHILDREN.

President Theodore Roosevelt, 1903

At the turn of the century, President Teddy Roosevelt stands with conservationist John Muir at Glacier Point above Yosemite Valley, California. Ardent believers in the importance of protecting our natural landscape, the two worked tirelessly to preserve America's wild lands.

1364. The Magnificent New Virginia Canyon Road and
Virginia Falls, Yellowstone National Park.
Copyrighted, 1905, by T. W. Ingersoll.

Stagecoach in Yellowstone National Park, Wyoming, 1905

CONTENTS

FOREWORD

The Finest Legacy

by Jimmy Carter

NATURE HAS ALWAYS BEEN MY INSPIRATION—and my solace. Growing up in rural Georgia during the Great Depression, I hunted, fished, explored, experienced solitude and independence, and absorbed the values that continue to guide me. In several books, I have shared the restful, invigorating, and spiritual renewal that I still find in the outdoors.

When I was President, Camp David and the surrounding Maryland countryside was my favorite haven. Rosalynn and I often hiked the Catoctin Mountains, skied the pristine snowy trails, cast a fly for trout in nearby crystal-clear streams, or simply watched the magical change of seasons. I remember the thrill of making the first tracks of winter, gliding through the cold and elegant silence. In *An Outdoor Journal,* I confessed that "I have never been happier, more exhilarated, at peace, rested, inspired and aware of the grandeur of the universe and the greatness of God than when I find myself in a natural setting not much changed from the way He made it."

National parks give each of us an opportunity to treasure what Henry David Thoreau called those "little oases of wildness in the desert of our civilization." In fact, *An American Idea: The Making of the National Parks* demonstrates how much of our culture, art, and philosophy grew out of an almost sacred relationship with the land, and describes how vast portions of our magnificent country came to be set aside in its natural state for the enjoyment of all. It is a story line that runs throughout American history: the transcendental words of Ralph Waldo Emerson and Thoreau; the courageous commitment by Meriwether Lewis and William Clark to serve President Thomas Jefferson (who never went west of Harpers Ferry); the inspiring paintings of George Caleb Bingham and George Catlin; the photographs of William Henry Jackson and Ansel Adams; the pulpits of John Muir and Gifford Pinchot; and the efforts of many others of uncommon dedication and vision.

Politically, the creation of national parks has never been easy. Powerful forces have opposed setting aside land, calling it an impediment to the progress of science and commerce. Yellowstone was our first national park, and the Yellowstone Park Act passed by Congress and signed by President Ulysses S. Grant in 1872 actually had the approval of the railroads to attract tourists on their new transcontinental line. But many of the other parks created over the next 125 years did not enjoy local or national political support.

A personal high point in my own Presidency came in December 1980 when I signed the Alaska National Interest Lands Conservation Act, which more than doubled the size of our national park system. Getting to this point was a long and difficult struggle that at the time angered many Alaskans and powerful politicians. I remember that during a refueling stop in Anchorage, en route to Tokyo, the Secret Service suggested that I not leave the plane. They had heard that a group of angry Alaskans might create a serious disturbance.

Twenty years later, I visited Alaska for the anniversary of the lands act and received an enthusiastic reception. The *New York Times* reported that "instead of burning Mr. Carter in effigy and shouting obscenities as Alaskans have done in past visits, the crowds that greeted him in the twilight of summer hailed Mr. Carter as a hero and visionary for what has been called the greatest conservation act in American history." The best part of our Alaska visit was watching almost 100,000 caribou surge around us in the vast expanse of the Arctic National Wildlife Refuge in their annual migration from the Arctic slope. I am proud to have helped make that sacred journey possible – hopefully, forever.

Rosalynn and I have had the privilege of visiting other wondrous and healing places throughout our country: Yellowstone and Yosemite, Denali and Death Valley, Grand Canyon and Great Smoky Mountains, Shenandoah and Sequoia, Crater Lake and Carlsbad Caverns, Mount Rainier and Mammoth Cave, Everglades and Virgin Islands, Lake Clark and Haleakala. They are all part of a land ethic that gives us national parks, refuges, sanctuaries, and historic sites.

But as reflected in this history, America's "best idea" is still an unfinished one. Our national parks have not always been managed properly, and the millions of excited tourists who visit them each year make the task of good stewardship even more difficult. We must never forget the fundamental links between past and future, conservation and progress – and the fundamental differences between exploration and exploitation.

My hope is that this knowledge will help guide our actions in this new millennium. Many people with long-term vision have contributed to the creation and the protection of these parks. But today and every day, we must continue to defend the parks against those who would neglect or despoil them. Nothing would please me more than to know that my youngest grandson, who is now two years old, will have the privilege of experiencing these places just as they are today. That is a legacy of which we all can be proud.

PREFACE

Seeking the Parks

by Paul Pritchard

President, National Park Trust

WHEN I WAS A YOUNG MAN, I LEARNED THAT THE SEARCH FOR WISDOM STARTS with one word. I was on a scout outing in Kansas. It was cold and snowy, and we were sitting around a campfire near a creek – about ten senior scouts and five fathers. A special feast had been prepared to recognize our leadership in helping the younger "tenderfoot" scouts. I still can see the pot of steaming stew and smell the cherry cobbler baked by one of the old hands at camping.

After satisfying our hunger and doing a quick cleanup, we settled around the fire to talk. The conversation moved from light humor to an invitation from the fathers to discuss our concerns about life. It was a simple statement – "So, what's on your minds, boys?" – but it opened a world of uncertainties. As I think back, I'm reminded that campfire discussions may well be one of the most significant venues for intellectual exchange created by our species. When it was my turn, like most young men, I set out to impress the adults by asking, "If you could ask only one question in any situation, what would it be?" One of the fathers looked up from the fire and replied without hesitation, as if he had considered this question for a long time. "It would be one word: Why." I immediately liked his answer. It gave strength to someone like me, a young man who enjoyed intellectual challenges with others, especially adults. The question "why?" implied that we not only must seek an answer, we should also take nothing in life for granted.

Later, as a young journalist, I found that one word – why – to be the most thought-provoking and empowering question journalists learn to ask. And now as a conservationist devoting my life to parklands, this word is the ultimate issue as I consider their creation and existence.

Illustrations depicting Yellowstone National Park, 1872

Why did the United States "invent" the idea of national parks? Why are they unique when compared to the landscapes protected by other nations before the establishment of Yellowstone National Park in 1872? And why should parks survive from generation to generation?

National parks are an expression of public investment, of different degrees of public protection, even of different perceptions of political image. Therefore, park antagonists have questioned – even challenged – their existence. "Why shouldn't we sell parks to pay off the national debt?" one famous opponent opined. Others questioned, "Why should we have as many parks as we have?" Or, "Why can't we develop them to pay for themselves and for other public needs?"

At the core of these questions and answers are the values of American society. Any expenditure of public funds, any commitment of public protection, any planning for future expansion, I have learned, must be prefaced with a clear and commonly accepted justification by society. And so I have learned that I must be able not just to ask the question "why" but also to answer it.

It was with these thoughts and experiences that I began to explore the question of why these protected lands are such a staple of America's public agenda. Many books have dealt with the leaders of the park movement subsequent to the creation of the National Park Service in 1916. However, one unanswered question has remained – "Why were the parks created in the first place?" Was it the call of one person or the upwelling of the spirit of a nation?

So it is that this work is placed before the reader, to address the critical question of "Why our parks?" To savor the question and sample the sources of the answer.

Thomas Cole, 1827-28, EXPULSION FROM THE GARDEN OF EDEN, *oil on canvas*

PROLOGUE

The King's Forest

ONE BY ONE THE PEOPLE ARRIVED AT THE MEADOW ON THE EDGE OF THE FOREST. DAWN LEAKED ACROSS THE EASTERN SKY AND THE AIR GREW WARM. THEY TRAVELED ON FOOT – A STEADY PROCESSION OF MEN, WOMEN, AND CHILDREN – AND WORE THEIR SUNDAY FINERY. BACK IN TOWN, THE LITTLE STONE CHURCH, HAVING FALLEN INTO DISREPAIR, WAS CLOSED THIS EASTER. THE PEOPLE WERE HARD-WORKING COM-MONERS WHO DESPITE THEIR POVERTY FELT RICH THIS morning, as spokes of amber light spilled through long shadows in the trees, and the sun felt like ambrosia on their pallid brows. Spring had arrived with uncommon kindness this year of 1633 in southern England, and the planting season was filled with promise. Even the birds seemed to sing with extra exuberance.

The dour-faced pastor, apparently unmoved by the benevolent weather, delivered a sermon on predestination and original sin, and required that his congregation stand while the children squirmed in their mothers' arms. Later, the women spread blankets on the earth and opened baskets of prepared food. Everybody ate while the children played and climbed trees. A few of the older boys vaulted through the grass, while the girls played tag. A stranger among them, a young man with unruly blond hair and rimless spectacles, pulled a flute from a burlap bag and played sweet music.

Up the long road a horse approached, a sway-backed gelding as unimpressive as its rider – the sheriff. Everybody turned to watch him cross the creaky wooden bridge, climb the gentle slope, and rein his less-than-noble steed to a stop. There, among the picnickers, he announced that this was the King's Forest, and everybody had to leave. If they did not, he would issue an edict closing the meadow and forest forever. It was, after all, the exclusive property of Charles I, monarch of all England and Scotland, and not a public gathering place or pleasuring ground. Courtiers from Windsor had been seen not far away, and the monarch himself could arrive any day, to use His Forest as he wished – to hunt, to graze sheep, to do anything he chose.

Nobody moved.

The sheriff unrolled a parchment scroll and read aloud in a croaking voice: "There shall be no meeting of the people [in the King's Forest] or out of their own Parishes on the Lord's day (or Sunday) for any sport or pastimes whatsoever: nor any Bear-baiting, Bull-baiting, Enterludes, common Playes, or other unlawful pastimes, used by any within their own parishes, upon pain that every person offending...do forfeit for every offence three shillings four pence, to be imployed to the use of the poor of the same Parish where the offence shall be committed."

This was, in effect, an eviction the townspeople must accept. From the time of Nebudchanezzar's Hanging Gardens of Babylon, 600 years before Christ, royalty had enjoyed private parks at the expense of common folk. The Greek soldier Xenophon called such places *paradeisos,* and described them as vast enclosures that included fruit and ornamental trees, flowers, birds, and animals. They inspired awe and gave rise to the Latin word *paradisus,* which translated into the Bible as paradise, a place of perfect contentment and happiness.

Alexander the Great brought the idea of Persian gardens and private reserves west. The Romans adopted them, and centuries later the Normans of France established parks as "unruffled hunting estates" for the feudal nobility. Prior to the Norman Invasion of 1066, Saxon England had practiced folk law and a village community system, whereby certain lands belonged to everyone as "rights of the common," and could be used to take firewood and building materials, and to gather in ceremony and play. But Norman lords took many of these Saxon forests and meadows as their private deer parks, and in 1235 the Statute of Merton decreed that "the common" was henceforth "the Lord's waste" to do with as he pleased. Half a century later the Statute of Westminister granted the king or a favored lord the right to enclose common lands for limited entry, and to have anybody fined – in some cases arrested – who violated the law.

So it was that the people of the meadow gathered their belongings and prepared to leave. The stranger with the flute approached the sheriff and asked if he knew the right road to Plymouth.

Of course, the sheriff said. He gave the young man instructions and inquired as to his name and occupation. A name of no consequence, the young man said. As for his occupation, he was a winged seed who would blow west to Virginia, across the Big Pond, and there make a bright future.

Virginia? America? The New World?

That's right, the stranger said.

The sheriff regarded him with suspicion and told him he wanted no trouble. He reminded everybody of their transgression, then turned his horse and rode back down the road and across the creaky bridge into town.

Virginia, somebody said. What must it be like?

A hideous, howling wilderness, replied one man, a respected stonemason with seven children.

Not true, the stranger said. He spoke about Capt. Arthur Barlowe and Sir Walter Raleigh, Elizabethan mariners who 50 years earlier had found in America a garden of incredible abundance. The soil, according to Barlowe, was "the most plentifull, sweete, fruitfull, and wholesome of all the worlde." Virgin forests of the "highest and reddest Cedars of the world."

The stonemason shook his head and said, Remember what became of Raleigh's colony on Roanoke Island, founded on the coast of North Carolina in 1585? And the second colony founded just two years after that? Both disappeared, with all inhabitants gone, probably killed by Indians, or taken hostage.

Others nodded as the stonemason, a guildsman and obvious civic leader, gathered his children around him.

The stranger smiled.

The stonemason's eldest daughter, a pretty girl with willowy arms, broke free of her father and asked the stranger if it was true that in America there lived a beautiful Indian princess who married an Englishman.

It's true, the stranger said. The princess was named Pocahontas, and she married John Rolfe, the first Englishman to export tobacco out of Virginia. Yes, Roanoke failed, he added. Many first ventures do. But look now at Jamestown, and at Williamsburg. Look at Plymouth. Just three years ago, in 1630, some 20,000 English men and women sailed to America, to freedom and open land and towns without sheriffs who tell you where you can and cannot have a picnic.

Somebody said, Life in America is hard.

So is life in England, another person answered.

People crowded around the stranger as he reached into his burlap bag and pulled out a small book, a thin wafer compared to the pastor's Bible. Few around him could read, yet all were fascinated by this young man with bright eyes who played the flute and wore spectacles and carried books and spoke with magnetism. This particular book, tattered and torn, was a copy of *The Tempest,* a play by William Shakespeare who, although dead now for 17 years, seemed more alive than ever as his work gained gravity with each passing year. Unconcerned by the sheriff's caveat, the stranger leaned against a tree and read aloud the story of Prospero, Miranda, Sebastian, Adrian, Gonzalo, and Antonio, Shakespeare's civilized protagonists who find themselves shipwrecked on an island in a prehistoric wilderness. "Be not afraid, this land is full of noises. Sounds and sweet aires that give delight and hurt not."

Still a howling wilderness, the stonemason insisted.

Argue for your limitations, the stranger replied, and they shall be yours.

The pastor said he personally knew of a family that had sailed on the *Mayflower* in 1620. Those so-called "separatists" will be the spiritual founders of America, he said. One of their leaders, William Bradford, had called them "Pilgrims."

Everybody nodded. They knew of this small Protestant sect, many of them followers of John Calvin who had sought to "purify" the corrupt church of England, and failed, and so invoked the Second Book of Corinthians: "Come out from among them and be ye separate, saith the Lord." They had settled for awhile in the Netherlands, and many found it unsuitable, and so a group returned to England to plot their bold exodus to America.

Not even half the people on the *Mayflower* were Puritans, the stonemason said.

True, the stranger replied. But the Puritans provided the leadership. They wrote the *Mayflower Compact,* by which the settlers agreed "to convent and combine" themselves into a body politic that vested authority in elected leaders.

Elected leaders? This idea sent ripples through the small crowd.

The stonemason said that more than half of the Pilgrims died their first winter in America.

But many survived thanks to the kindness of local Indians, the pastor said. And now they numbered more than 400.

Most of them are prosperous and contented, the stranger added. He looked at the faces around him and asked, Have any of you been to London lately? It's a dismal place, where more and more people work harder and harder for less and less. The urban working class is a seething mass of depression and disease. Charles I is an arbitrary and callous monarch; he is chronically broke and seems determined to anger Parliament just for the sport of it. The Orthodox Anglicans ignore every Puritan protest, and some say civil war is inevitable. If you want religious freedom and profits and free land, go to America.

Free land. It sounded like alchemy, like turning water to wine.

The idea of a national park, a place that belonged to everyone and to no one, where man could repudiate his thirsty dominance over nature, and wildness would be celebrated rather than vanquished, was utterly beyond the scope of thinking of English men and women in 1633. Not for another 199 years, in 1832, would an American artist, George Catlin, first articulate the national park idea, an idea that came to him after watching Sioux Indians slaughter buffalo for whiskey money.

THE STONEMASON'S DAUGHTER SAID THAT IN AMERICA THERE IS A PLACE CALLED New England, is that right?

That's right, the stranger replied. It was a name given by Capt. John Smith, while on a voyage of discovery in 1614.

Does that make this Old England? she asked. Tired England?

Nobody spoke. Yet a few people nodded in silent agreement. England somehow didn't seem the same since Good Queen Bess – Elizabeth I, the last of the Tudor line – died 30 years ago.

Where does America end? The daughter asked. Her big eyes never blinked.

End? The stranger offered a rueful smile. I don't know. Nobody knows. Somewhere far to the west. I think Sir Francis Drake found the other end of America, didn't he?

People shrugged and shook their heads. Nobody knew. America was unfathomable to them, boundless and wild. Somebody asked the stranger where he lived, and he said, In the forest. It suits me. The forest is a poor man's overcoat.

Yet if he was poor, how could he afford spectacles? Perhaps he was a thief. Yet if he was a thief, why would he have books? How is it he could read? He said he would make his way in America in the tobacco fields. Yet his hands were clean and without calluses.

He spoke of America as if it were a garden, not the punishing desert of Moses and Isaiah. He reminded his listeners that America held great promise for any man willing to work hard and take risks. Eden, he reminded the people around him, was the Hebrew word for "delight." He quoted the Old Testament and spoke of "a good land, a land of brooks of water, of fountains and springs."

The pastor nodded; the young man might know his Bible, but he did not know America, not firsthand, and his recitations were inappropriate. The pastor reminded everyone that shortly after his time with John the Baptist, Christ was "led up by the Spirit into the wilderness to be tempted by the devil." There was no shortage of wilderness in America, and no shortage of temptation.

The young stranger chuckled; though he intended no insult, the effect was just that, and no one found it more so than the pastor himself, who after hundreds of sermons was accustomed to his flock behaving like good sheep whenever he recited scripture. He opened his mouth to speak, but the stranger preempted him, asking if he remembered Saint Basil the Great, who established a monastery south of the Black Sea in the fourth century and wrote,

"I am living...in the wilderness wherein the Lord dwealt."

I know it, the pastor said, adding that the monks who lived there saw the wilderness as having virtue only as an escape from a corrupt civilization, as the unbroken ground from which they could level the forests and till the earth and make a paradise.

As Englishmen are now making in America, the stranger said. It is a paradise, an Eden. It's a chance to create instead of inherit. He looked at the cautious faces around him as he packed his books and flute into the burlap bag. The stonemason pulled his children down the road toward the town. His oldest daughter resisted, and in her mother's eyes the stranger saw sympathy for the girl. Perhaps the mother remembered when she, too, years ago, fell in love with a hard-headed man who wished to carve stones in the Old World, rather than a homestead in the new one.

NOBODY SAW HIM AFTER THAT. THE STRANGER DISAPPEARED DOWN THE ROAD toward Plymouth, where ships sailed west beyond the curve of the Earth. For years people of the town spoke of him. And when civil war did come and Oliver Cromwell's men ravaged forests and families alike, and Parliament was dissolved and Charles I was beheaded, and the Great Plague killed nearly 70,000 people in London in three months, the young girl with the willowy arms, who was now an old woman, could still see the face of the stranger with the unruly blond hair. She could still hear his words about free land and open country, about the chance to make something more of yourself than the station of your birth.

She never did learn to read, but her eldest grandson did. And in private moments she asked him to recite from *The Tempest,* the part where the shipwrecked party first assesses the wilderness around them. "The air breathes upon us here most sweetly," says Adrian.

Answers Sebastian, "As if it had lungs, and rotten ones."

"Or as twere perfum'd by a fen," says Antonio.

"Here is everything advantageous to life."

"True, save means to live."

"Of that there's none, or little."

None or little, she thought to herself, but enough. There has to be. It is the promise of America. She closed her eyes and dreamed again of Virginia.

TIME LINE OF WESTERN AWARENESS

1800 | 1810 | 1820 | 1830 | 1840 | 1850

EXPLORATIONS

1804-06
Lewis and Clark Expedition

1819
Maj. Stephen H. Long's expedition to Upper Missouri River; first renditions of the Rocky Mountains by artists Samuel Seymour and Titian Peale

1822-31
Jedediah Smith follows the Missouri River west into the Bighorn Basin and to Great Salt Lake.

1833-34
Swiss artist Karl Bodmer joins expedition to Upper Missouri with Prince Maximilian of Germany.

WILKES EXPEDITION, MOUNT RAINIER, 1842

ARTISTS

THOMAS COLE, 1825

1825
The Hudson River School of Art is founded, with Thomas Cole as its leader.

1831
Artist George Catlin begins portraits of the Upper Missouri Plains Indians.

GEORGE CATLIN, 1831

1843
Artist/ornithologist John James Audubon paints animals along the Missouri River for *Quadrapeds of North America* series.

1854
Henry David Thoreau publishes *Walden.*

1845
George Caleb Bingham paints his most famous work: "Fur Traders Descending the Missouri."

1837
Artist Alfred Miller travels on the Oregon Trail.

1848
Artist Richard Kern sketches Canyon de Chelly and Taos Valley.

NATIONAL PARKS

1807
John Colter explores the geysers and hot springs of the Yellowstone area.

1832
Hot Springs Reservation in Arkansas is created.

1851
Yosemite Valley explored

THOMAS A. AYERS, 1855

U.S. HISTORY

1800
Thomas Jefferson is elected President.

1803
Louisiana Purchase

1812-15
War of 1812 fought between U.S. and Great Britain

1819
Florida recovered from Spain.

1830
Recent immigrants estimated at 150,000; a century of immigration will add more than 30 million.

1848
Mexico gives up claim to Texas; U.S. gets what will become California, Nevada, Utah, and parts of New Mexico, Colorado, Wyoming, and Arizona.

1849
California gold rush begins.

1853
Gadsen Purchase: Mexico sells territory that will become Arizona and New Mexico.

1860 | 1870 | 1880 | 1890 | 1900 | 1910 | 1920

1867
King Surveys of the 40th Parallel with photographer Timothy O'Sullivan

DUTTON EXPEDITION, GRAND CANYON, 1882

1882
Dutton Expedition to the Grand Canyon with artist William Henry Holmes

1869-79
Powell Surveys of the Grand Canyon with artists Thomas Moran and William Henry Holmes, and photographer Jack Hillers

1870
Langford/Doane Expedition into Yellowstone country

1899
Harriman Expedition to Alaska with photographer Edward S. Curtis

1871
Hayden Yellowstone Survey with artist Thomas Moran and photographer William Henry Jackson

1871
Wheeler's Surveys beyond the 100th Meridian with photographer Timothy O'Sullivan

HARRIMAN EXPEDITION, ALASKA, 1899

1859-75
Artist Albert Bierstadt paints the West, including the Oregon Trail and Yosemite.

THOMAS MORAN, 1872

1916
14-year-old Ansel Adams takes his first pictures of Yosemite.

1864
Yosemite Valley granted to California as state park

1872
Congress designates Yellowstone the first national park as a result of Jackson's and Moran's images.

1889
Casa Grande Indian Ruins, second national park

1906
Antiquities Act establishes national monuments designation.

1902
Crater Lake National Park

1919
Grand Canyon National Park

1916
Organic Act establishes National Park Service.

1890
Sequoia, third national park
Kings Canyon, fourth national park
Yosemite, fifth national park

1915
Rocky Mountain National Park

1899
Mount Rainier National Park

1861-65
Civil War

1876
Battle of Little Big Horn occurs.

1867
Alaska purchased from the Russians

1869
First transcontinental railroad is completed.

1891
Forest Reserve Act passes.

1901
Ten miles of paved road in U.S.

Their rype corne
Their greene corne
Corne newly sprong
Their sitting at meate
The place of solemne prayer
The howse wherin the Tombe of their Herounds standeth
SECOTON
A Ceremony in their prayers with strange iestures and songs dansing about posts carued on the topps lyke mens faces
7

CHAPTER ONE

A Land of Rural Virtue

"VACUUM DOMICILIUM," ANNOUNCED JOHN WINTHROP, JR., GOVERNOR OF THE MASSACHUSETTS BAY COMPANY. THOUGH SHORT ON WORDS, HIS EDICT, BACKED BY ROYAL CHARTER, WAS LONG ON RAMIFICATIONS. IT PROCLAIMED THAT THOSE LANDS NOT ALREADY SUBDUED BY EUROPEAN-STYLE CULTIVATION COULD NOW, WITH THE BLESSING OF CHARLES I, BE LEGITIMATELY TAKEN AND "IMPROVED." INDIANS WERE SAVAGES WHO HAD NO GOVERNMENT, AND IN HAVING NO GOVERNMENT THEY HAD NO SOVEREIGNTY. A FLOOD OF WHITE PEOPLE POURED INTO AMERICA IN THE 1630S. THEY SETTLED FROM NEW ENGLAND TO VIRGINIA, AND

This illustration of Secoton, an Indian village on Roanoke Island, depicts living quarters, stages of corn, ceremonial dancing, and trading.

brought with them their own language of exclusivity; their own muskets, plows, smallpox, and theological reasonings; their own political structures that made straight lines and strict rules where the Indians lived amid a quilt of cultures based on storytelling and the vast wildness that nurtured them. The Algonquins and Narragansetts, the Pequots and Mohegans, the Powhatans and dozens of others, all stood on the edge of a great abyss, facing the last vision of who they were and where they came from. The land as they knew it, like a village elder, would soon be gone.

Seventeenth century Englishmen found biblical virtue in the subjugation of the forest. Bowed at their backs and sweat-stained in their fields, they worked hard to make the land bountiful, to feed those they loved. They lived their entire lives within the constructs of their time, far outside the comprehension of a family vacation, a paved highway, a private automobile, a national park, or a designated wilderness – prized for its very wildness, and so established by a United States Congress to remain forever wild and thus peaceful, as a tonic for an agitated, hyper-driven culture. No, that would not happen for another three hundred years, after countless habitats had been fenced, paved, and plowed. America in the 17th and 18th centuries was a daunting ocean of richness and challenge, a place for the taming, and in that taming pioneers would take great pride and define themselves. Many would profess a love of nature, which to them was a tidy and well-manicured garden cut from the wilds; again, like so much else, a reconstruction of the Old World, confirming that despite everything they claimed to be – Calvinists and Catholics, Separatists and Socialists – all would change the American land vastly more than it would change them.

Folklore added to their fear of the wilds. In many tales handed down from medieval times, dark woods harbored supernatural beings – wood sprites, trolls, and goat men – who defiled women and stole children. All too easily the crooked limbs of a tree, seen against the cloud-veiled moon, became the arms of a terrible beast. The Wild Man of European legend was superimposed on the vast American forest and became a frightful, magnified creature.

Francis Higginson, a pioneer in New England in the 1630s, wrote of terrible "discommodities," and elaborated that "this Countey being very full of Woods and Wildernesses, doth also much abound with Snakes and Serpents of strange colours and huge greatnesse." A kernel of truth wrapped in a husk of exaggeration, yet Higginson went on, adding that some snakes had "Rattles in their Tayles that will not fly from a Man...but will flye upon him and sting him so mortally, that he will dye within a quarter of an houre after." Many decades later Cotton Mather would write of "the rabid and howling Wolves of the Wilderness [which]

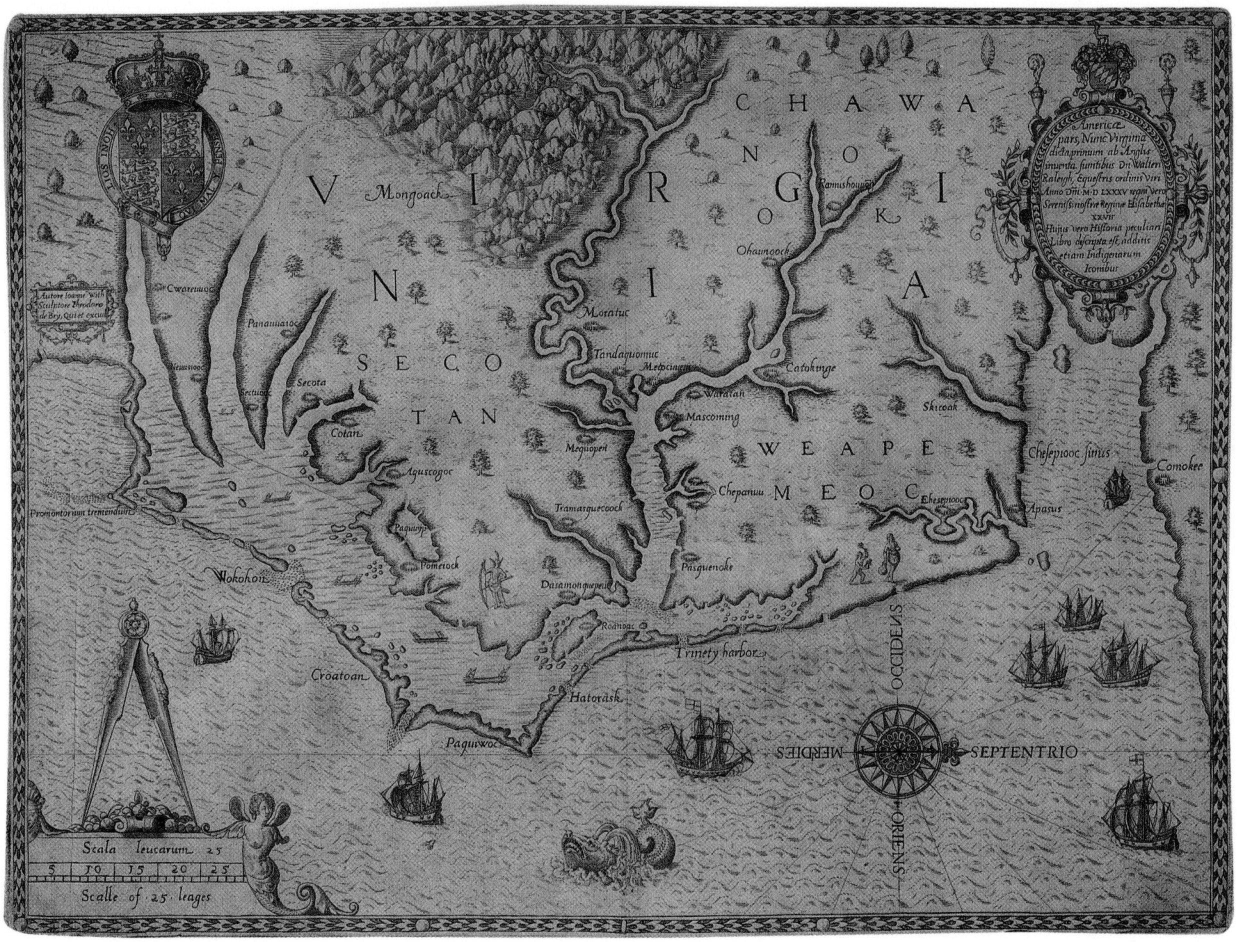

A map drawn by Englishman and cartographer John White in the mid-1590s purports to show the location of the famous lost colony of "Roanoac," established on an island off North Carolina in 1587. All the inhabitants vanished, with little evidence of their fates. Perhaps they were massacred, devastated by disease, or forced to abandon their settlement due to crop failure. Historians speculate that other sites on the map depict Indian villages where the Roanoac inhabitants might have lived after their colony failed.

A map of Virginia by Capt. John Smith shows an American utopia based on his 1608 explorations of the Potomac and Rappahannock Rivers.

would make...Havock among you, and not leave the Bones until morning."

Little wonder that the words wilderness and bewilder became cousins in the American lexicon. Wild lands were the adversary, so confirmed by pioneers who used military metaphors in their westward march, referring to the frontier as an "enemy" to be vanquished and conquered in mortal combat.

"To describe America as a hideous wilderness," wrote historian Leo Marx in *The Machine in the Garden,* "is to envisage it as another field for the exercise of power. This violent image expresses a need to mobilize energy, postpone immediate pleasures, and rehearse the perils and purposes of community. Life in a garden is relaxed, quiet, and sweet, like the life of Virgil's Tityrus, but survival in a howling desert demands action, the unceasing manipulation and mastery of the forces of nature, including, of course, human nature."

Back in England, people saw America through rose-colored glasses. One Londoner gushed about the bountiful Virginia soil and game, adding that "nor is the present wildernesse of it without a particular beauty, being all over a natural Grove of Oaks, Pines, Cedars...all of so a delectable an aspect, that the melanchollyest eye in the World cannot look upon it without contentment, nor content himselfe without admiration."

Hardly. Settlers in Jamestown and elsewhere, at first enamored with the notion of discovering gold, had forsaken that foolish dream to the harsh realities of everyday survival, and now worked the earth with their sleeves rolled to the elbows. How strange the news from England and Europe seemed to them: the speed limit for London hackney coaches reduced to three miles an hour, and in France the sale of tobacco restricted to apothecaries, only on a doctor's prescription. America seemed lawless by comparison, which for some people was a tonic, and others, a temptation.

In 1637 the Dutch tulip trade collapsed, and Americans feared the same could happen to their prized tobacco. So they worked all the harder to clear the forests and plant the land. That same year the Pequot War foreshadowed the many atrocities against American Indians that would follow across the continent for another 250 years. "We must burn them," said one marauding white leader after he and his men murdered old Pequot men, women, and children, catching them in their early morning sleep.

Such behavior appalled some white settlers, as did John Winthrop's edict, and these settlers founded the colony of Providence Plantation, later to be called Rhode Island, and other new communities. Yet, despite their better sensibilities, they too had appetites and dreams, and so went about their genocide more slowly – clearing the forests, building fences, and planting neat rows of crops – displacing the Indians by attrition if not outright attack.

WE IMAGINE THE LAND AS UNTOUCHED PRIOR TO THE ARRIVAL OF Europeans, yet historian Francis Jennings described America as having been altered by the coming and the leaving of the Indians. "The American land was more like a widow than a virgin. Europeans did not find a wilderness here; rather, however involuntary, they made one. Jamestown, Plymouth, Salem, Boston, Providence, New Amsterdam, Philadelphia – all grew upon sites previously occupied by Indian communities.... The so-called settlement of America was a resettlement, a reoccupation of a land made waste by the diseases and demoralization introduced by the newcomers."

An estimated seven to ten million Native Americans lived in North America at that time, and already their lives had begun to unravel. Soon their numbers would be reduced to 250,000, and their homeland would be gone.

Powerful European minds of the middle of the 17th century helped to confirm Western man's separation from, and dominance over, the natural world. In his 1644 treatise, *Principia Philosophicae,* René Descartes exclaimed, "Cogito ergo sum" – I think, therefore I am – which in effect announced that man alone thinks, that everything else does not and is therefore at his disposal. This rationale, a separation of mind and spirit called Cartesian dualism, conveniently exalted man above other earthly beings. It made him the dispassionate scientist. It freed him of any emotional connection to other species. It provided a perfect preamble for utilitarianism, the long and insatiable harvest-minded approach to a seemingly inexhaustible bounty that surrounded him.

Such a vision first came to Descartes 25 years before when, as a young thinker lying on the banks of the Danube River, he beheld himself floating above a world wherein every process and organism moved in a mechanistic, mathematically determined pattern. This notion embraced Plato's concept of a thinker separate from the world he thinks about and came as an affront to the Aristotlean view that said just the opposite, that humankind belonged to nature, that everything we think about comes from our senses. Descartes stood Aristotle on his head and started the modern scientific revolution, a 350-year schism between deductive reason and spiritual oneness with nature.

Sir Francis Bacon, lord chancellor of England and a contemporary of Descartes, confirmed the young Frenchman's ideas in his book, *The New Atlantis,* which argued man's separation from nature allowed for a separation of science and religion. Facts, he said, had no moral significance when derived from the scientific method; good and evil were matters of "moral knowledge," and were the only ones of religious importance. "This facile distinction," an observer noted centuries later, "carried a profound implication: the new power derived from scientific knowledge could be used to dominate nature with moral impunity."

Yet some 20 years after Descartes, John Milton, a former secretary to Oliver Cromwell, and by now completely blind, published his epic poem, *Paradise Lost,* which was called "the last superb embodiment of a prescientific universe." Although the poem portrayed man's fall from grace in the eyes of God, readers found it a steady reminder of a despoiled Eden and wondered how it might play into their own lives and temptations.

In America, reflections on rural life always included "disdain for those unimproved lands" that were still wild and frightful, a stark contrast to the appealing gardens and orchards that every year consumed more and more acreage. The pastoral ideal of America, held dear by early Elizabethans, persisted in Robert Beverley's 1705 book, *The History and Present State of Virginia,* wherein he gushed about potatoes the size of a child's thigh, a frog big enough to feed six Frenchmen, and grapes so abundant that a single vine could fill a London cart.

IN 1719, ONE HUNDRED YEARS AFTER DESCARTES HAD HIS MOMENTous dream, a book appeared that circled the world and fascinated thousands of readers. Written by Daniel Defoe in his late 50s, after he had authored satires against High Church domination and been arrested half a dozen times, it was his first novel – the story of a lone sailor, Robinson Crusoe, shipwrecked on an island. Defoe described Crusoe as a young man with no nautical background but with a thirst for adventure, who sought to go to sea against his father's wishes. He opened the book with the father asking the boy why he would want to abandon a life of "ease and pleasure." According to young Crusoe, the father "pressed me earnestly, and in the most affectionate manner, not to play the young man, not to precipitate myself into miseries which nature and the station of life I was born in seemed to have provided against…."

In his plea for his son to stay home and follow a common path, the father began to cry. Said young Crusoe, "I observed the tears run down his face very plentifully, especially when he spoke of my brother who was killed; and that when he spoke of my having leisure to repent, and none to assist me, he was so moved that he broke off the discourse, and told me his heart was so full he could say no more to me…. I was sincerely affected by his discourse, as indeed who could not be otherwise? And I resolved not to think of going abroad any more, but to settle at home according to my father's desire. But alas! A few days wore it all off; and in short, to prevent my father's further importunities…I resolved to run quite away from him."

Here lay the connection to America as the utopian ideal, the freedom of the

James Peak fashioned this 1761 depiction of an American colonial farm after a romanticized painting of colonial life by English artist Paul Sanby. Surrounded by manicured grounds and gentle waters, the manor house and mill stand in bright relief against the forest darkness from which they were cut, thus confirming man's rightful subjugation of wild nature. In large part this is a pastoral illusion, as it shows not a stitch of the slavery, hard work, or heartbreak that were often required to create and maintain a frontier farm in early America.

In this painting by Frederic E. Church, Pastor Thomas Hooker leads his congregation into a lush Connecticut valley and the founding of Hartford in 1636. While Church's early work showed man's inroads into nature, his later paintings left mankind out and portrayed virgin wildness as something to celebrate.

sea as a prelude to the greatest freedom of all, open land, something more vast than the deck of any ship, with each man his own captain. Self-actualized American pioneers connected deeply with Robinson Crusoe. Having an entire island to oneself had much greater appeal than participating in a born station in life. America was the implied – if not stated – destination of anybody who hungered for a new beginning across big water.

But young Crusoe, after sailing around Cape Horn, found himself the lone survivor of a shipwreck, marooned on an unmapped, unnamed island, barely surviving a "dreadful deliverance" onto shore. "For I was wet, had no clothes to shift me, nor anything either to eat or drink to comfort me, neither did I see any prospect before me but that of perishing with hunger or being devoured by wild beasts; and that which was particular afflicting to me was that I had no weapon either to hunt and kill any creature for my sustenance or to defend myself against any other creature that might desire to kill me for theirs. In a word, I had nothing about me but a knife, a tobacco-pipe, and a little tobacco in a box; this was all my provision, and this threw me into terrible agonies of mind, that for awhile I ran about like a madman. Night coming upon me, I began with a heavy heart to consider what would be my lot if there were any ravenous beasts in that country, seeing at night they always come abroad for their prey."

The situation was obvious. On this island as in any wilderness, north or south, east or west, man who was not a predator became another predator's prey. Yet Crusoe, an innovative and resourceful fellow beyond his own expectations, began to make a comfortable life for himself. He built a "fortress" and resigned himself to his fate. He made a distinction between being lonely and being alone. He drew up a list of those things good and evil about his predicament, each appearing to cancel the other out. The weeks rolled into months, the months into years, and he said, "I began to conclude in my mind that it was possible for me to be more happy in this forsaken, solitary condition than it was probable I should ever have been in any other particular state in the world; and with this thought I was going to give thanks to God for bringing me to this place."

One deliverance begot another. One man with no neighbors, no conflicts, and no laws beyond those imposed by nature, it seemed so horrible and yet so inviting. Robinson Crusoe entered the American conscience a full century before Daniel Boone. As an old man about to die in 1820, Boone would lament the loss of wild Kentucky, the wilderness he so loved and helped to destroy by bringing more and more people through Cumberland Gap, where quickly the trees fell, homesteads became farms, and farms became towns. It was said that Boone himself, unhappy at the sight of another man's chimney fire from his own cabin, kept moving west, and others followed, for he was as much a harbinger of humankind as he was an escapee from it.

The same shock hit Crusoe. While out walking one day he discovered the naked footprint of another man in the sand, and his whole island – his only world for two years – changed. The readers are left to decide for themselves if it changed for the worse or for the better. "I stood like one thunderstruck, or as if I had seen an apparation; I listened, I looked round me. I could hear nothing, nor see anything...." He didn't sleep that night, so filled was he with apprehension, thinking it might be the Devil. In time he befriended the man who made the footprint, a "poor savage" he named Friday.

Elmer Boyd Smith's drawing depicts the fictitious Robinson Crusoe staring out across the sea that stranded him, alone on his island and warmed by a fire. Based on a true story of a sailor who was marooned off the Chilean coast, Crusoe resonated with critics in Europe who disdained the fetid, crowded, industrial cities where human beings became cogs in their own machinery. Crusoe showed the benefits open to any man who offered himself to nature and lived by his wits. In so doing he could see the world anew and make a paradise of his prison.

Crusoe finally got off the island and returned home after an absence of 35 years. But there was nothing for him in England anymore; that busy world had passed him by. So with "my man Friday," his new friend, he sailed south for Lisbon and on to Brazil, a citizen of the far longitudes, searching, we assume, for another place where life was slower and simpler.

DESPITE THE DISTANCES IN GEOGRAPHY AND CULTURE, EUROPEAN ideas continued to influence America. Romanticism flowered from the mid-1700s into the mid-1800s, when literary, artistic, and philosophical minds shunned rigid neoclassical reasoning for imagination, emotion, and the appreciation – often the worship – of "primitive" nature. Emblematic of this was the French humanist and philosopher, Jean-Jacques Rousseau, who challenged aristocracies and described the "Noble Savage" as a man who, given his closeness to nature and his innocence of agriculture and commerce, lived by a higher moral code, like Crusoe and Friday. In 1755 Rousseau wrote: "It is iron and wheat that have civilized men and ruined the human race.... From the cultivation of land, its division necessarily followed.... When inheritances increased in number and extent to the point of covering the entire earth and of bordering one on the other, some of them had to be enlarged at the expense of others.... Nascent society gave way to the most horrible state of war." The rich lorded over the poor, and over the land itself. They made a habit of war, and always on the casualty list was nature, the shrinking forest, and the dying river. The delicate shore, once a home for herons, was now lined with homesteads, farms, and erosion. Bordering on misanthropy, Rousseau added in *Emile* in 1762 that "Everything is perfect coming from the hands of the Creator; everything degenerates in the hands of man."

Rousseau didn't make it to America, but other European romanticists did. His countryman Francois-René de Chateaubriand traveled the forests and empty pathways of upper New York and spoke of a "sort of delirium" he felt in the absence of towns, roads, edicts, monarchs, and all manner of commerce and stilted hierarchy. He traveled with fur traders and befriended Indians. And when he returned home penniless and married a 17-year-old heiress and moved to Paris, he wrote, "in vain does the imagination try to roam the large midst [of Europe's] cultivated plains...but in this deserted region [of America] the soul delights to bury and lose itself amidst boundless forests...to mix and confound...with the wild sublimities of Nature." His voice resonated with younger people, who devoured his two novelettes, *Atala* and *Rene,* with their idyllic, light-on-his-feet hero who thrived in the "magnificent wilds of Kentucky," searching for "something to fill the vast emptiness of my existence."

Among those confounded by the wilds in America, but who found little about it sublime, were British troops who faced a ragtag Colonial Army during the Revolutionary War. One English commander described the Americans outside Boston as nothing more than "rabble in arms," but got his comeuppance when that rabble melted into the woods and used their home terrain as an ally.

In 1784 Abigail Adams, a firm patriot and prolific letter writer, accompanied her

In his painting "Daniel Boone coming through the Cumberland Gap," George Caleb Bingham shows the pioneer carrying a rifle on his shoulder and leading his brave followers on the Wilderness Road through the Allegheny Mountains in 1774. Boone's objective was the fertile valley of the Ohio River.

husband John Adams to Paris, where he served as the U.S. ambassador to France. The next year they moved to London, where, as in France, they enjoyed the finest privileges and most glamorous festivities shoulder-to-shoulder with royalty and aristocracy. "Almost desperately she sought ways to reconfirm her faith in America," wrote historian Roderick Nash in *Wilderness and the American Mind.* "Nature offered a possibility, which she explored in a letter…in 1786 to a friend in Massachusetts. 'I will not dispute,' she remarked, 'what every person must assent to; that [in Europe] the fine arts, manufacturers, and agriculture have arrived at a greater degree of maturity and perfection.' But in some respects she felt the New World had the edge; 'do you know that European birds have not half the melody of ours? Nor is their fruit half so sweet, nor their flowers half so fragrant, nor their manners half so pure, nor their people half so virtuous.' Still Abigail Adams was only half convinced, and she warned her correspondent to 'keep this to yourself, or I shall be thought more than half deficient in understanding and taste.' "

NEARLY A CENTURY LATER HISTORIAN HENRY ADAMS, THE GREAT grandson of Abigail and John Adams, second President of the United States, wrote of life in America in the year 1800: "Even after two centuries of struggle the land was still untamed; forest covered every portion, except here and there a strip of cultivated soil; the minerals lay undisturbed in their rocky beds, and more than two-thirds of the people clung to the seaboard within fifty miles of tidewater, where alone the wants of civilized life could be supplied."

A little more than five million people lived in the young United States then, one-fifth of them black slaves. From the centers of population in Philadelphia, Washington, and Baltimore, two wagon roads reached into western Pennsylvania: one from Philadelphia to Pittsburgh, the other from the Potomac River to the Monongahela. A third reached southwest from Virginia to Knoxville and branched over the Cumberland Gap into Kentucky, the famous route pioneered by Daniel Boone.

The Ohio Territory was the end of the world, home to only 45,000 whites. "The Indians," wrote Adams, "had been pushed back to the Cuyahoga River, and a few cabins were built on the site of Cleveland; but in 1800, as in 1700, this intermediate region was only a portage where emigrants and merchandise were transferred…. Even western New York remained a wilderness: Buffalo was not laid out; Indian titles were not extinguished; Rochester did not exist….

"Nature was rather man's master than servant, and the five million Americans struggling with the untamed continent seemed hardly more competent to their task than the beavers and buffalo which had for countless generations made bridges and roads of their own." Little wonder that the wilderness was feared, as it offered no allowance for mistakes or foolish behavior.

"Here is the manner of their dying," wrote historian and essayist Scott Russell Sanders in *Wilderness Plots* of the early pioneers in Ohio. "Eliakim Goss drank too much tanglefoot whiskey while out surveying, and that dire liquid, plus the heat, finished him off.

The making of a myth: This 1856 engraving renders Daniel Boone's exploits in a knife-and-claw battle with a wild bear. Known as "The First White Man of the West," Boone traveled the Wilderness Road from Virginia into Kentucky. In 1775 he settled there with his wife and daughter. As settlement increased, black bears retreated into what forests they could find; grizzlies became extinct. Boone admitted to killing many bears, but never with a knife. Indians were a more constant danger. The Cherokee tortured and murdered his son, James. The Shawnee captured Boone himself and held him for five months. He escaped in time to help free his home, Fort Boonesborough, from a ten-day siege by the British during the American Revolutionary War.

"Sticking with his gristmill during the April flood, George DePeyster was carried away with it down the Tuscarawas River....

"Robert Wright, owner of a bad reputation, was found on the banks of Silver Creek with his throat cut from ear to ear....

"On Muddy Lake, Zenas Carter was trying out the floating qualities of his new dugout canoe, which capsized, sending him to the bottom with his doeskin leggings....

"Samantha Frazer died from having her tooth extracted by the blacksmith....

"On her way to church, Jemima Palmer was surprised by two calves jumping from the bushes, and she fell down on the spot, dead of wonder.

"Their dying was as various as their living, a compost of souls."

In 1800 the general mail route from Portland, Maine, to Louisville, Georgia, required 20 days on horseback. Henry Adams described "difficulties and perils of travel so great as to form a barrier almost insuperable. Even Virginia was no exception.... At each interval of a few miles the horseman found himself stopped by a river, liable to sudden freshets, and rarely bridged. [Thomas] Jefferson in his frequent journeys between Monticello and Washington was happy to reach the end of the hundred miles without some vexatious delay. 'Of eight rivers between here and Washington,' he wrote to his attorney general in 1801, 'five have neither bridges nor boats.' "

In his long and distinguished life, Jefferson would never venture farther west than Harper's Ferry, West Virginia, yet his vision reached well beyond that horizon, a vision that would earn him the moniker "grand architect of Manifest Destiny."

As early as the 1780s he had shown a keen interest in the trans-Mississippi West. Concerned that English expeditions planned for the region would preempt American interests, he asked the Revolutionary War hero Gen. George Rogers Clark if he would lead an expedition into Missouri River country, but Clark declined. Roughly ten years later, as Alexander Mackenzie was completing the first trek by a white man across Canada, Jefferson mounted another effort "to find the shortest & most convenient route of communication between the U.S. & the Pacific Ocean, within the temperate latitudes." Historian Stephen E. Ambrose painted a broader brush stroke for

Jefferson's ambitions, writing in *Undaunted Courage:* "Beyond the fur trade and other commerce, beyond the acquisition of knowledge, Jefferson and the subscribers wanted to tie the two coasts together, using the Missouri-Columbia waterway to form the knot, in order to create a continent-wide empire for the United States. It was a breathtaking vision."

From the journals and maps of Captains Cook and Vancouver, and an American sea captain, Robert Gray, who had sailed into the mouth of the Columbia River in 1792, Jefferson knew that the continent spanned roughly three thousand miles.

His proposed expedition, under the auspices and financing of the American Philosophical Society of Philadelphia, needed a leader. An 18-year-old Army officer named Meriwether Lewis applied for the job, but Jefferson turned him down as too young and inexperienced. He chose instead a French botanist, Andre Michaux, and instructed him to "take notice of the country you pass through, its general face, soil, river, mountains, its productions animal, vegetable, & mineral so far as they may be new to us & may also be useful; the latitude of places...; the names, numbers, & dwellings of the inhabitants, and such particularities as you can learn from them."

Michaux had barely reached Kentucky when Jefferson learned of his true mission as a secret agent for the French Republic and his true aim to raise an attack force against Spanish holdings southwest of the Mississippi River. Jefferson had him recalled, and for the next ten years, while occupied with politics, he thought little of the American West.

As President, Jefferson set in motion a tide of resolve to acquire lands west of the Mississippi and to explore and inventory them. France had recently obtained the Louisiana Territory from Spain, and Napoleon, hungry for funds to finance his campaigns for an expanding European empire, appeared a willing seller. Jefferson wrote James Monroe before dispatching him to Paris in January 1803, "All eyes, all hopes, are now fixed on you.... On the event of this mission depends the future destinies of

W. Alexander del: from a Sketch taken on the Spot by J. Sykes

Mount Rainier, sentinel of Puget Sound, was named by Capt. George Vancouver in honor of his friend Rear Admiral Rainier of the British Royal Navy. This rendition comes from Vancouver's Voyage of Discovery to the North Pacific Ocean and Round the World, *published in 1798, the year Vancouver died.*

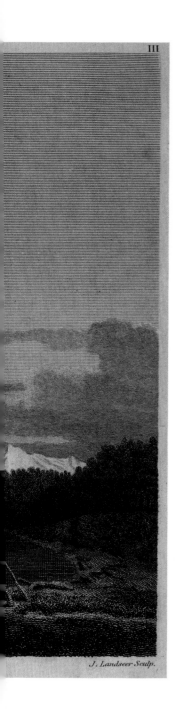

this republic." That same month he asked Congress for $2,500 to advance an expedition and received it, establishing a precedent for military funds and personnel to open the American West for the rest of the century.

He called the expedition the Corps of Discovery.

CAPT. MERIWETHER LEWIS, NOW WELL POSITIONED AS PRESIDENT Jefferson's secretary, would lead the expedition, together with Capt. William Clark, the younger brother of George Rogers Clark. All observations, according to Jefferson, were "to be taken with great pains & accuracy, to be entered distinctly, & intelligibly for others as well as for yourself." In case of loss, all journals and notes would be duplicated and put "into the care of the most trustworthy of your attendants."

The expedition departed St. Louis in May 1804 and returned in September 1806, with all objectives achieved. "By any standard," wrote historian Herman J. Viola, "their enterprise had been as successful as it was monumental. The first white men to cross this vast land, they had not only survived, they had thrived. Though they had encountered every hazard from hostile Indians to aggressive grizzly bears, only one of their number had died (probably from a ruptured appendix). They had walked, ridden horseback, paddled canoes, and poled barges; they had crossed seemingly endless prairies, scaled mountains, and braved torrential waters. Thanks to the even-handed discipline of their two captains, the explorers had overcome every obstacle, met every challenge. No other 19th-century expedition to the Far West would be so free of blunders."

Lewis himself wrote of country that was "beautifull in the extreme...I ascended to the top of the cutt bluff this morning, from which I had a most delightfull view of the country, the whole of which except the vally formed by the Missouri [River] is void of timber or underbrush, exposing to the first glance of the spectator immence herds of Buffaloe, Elk, deer, & Antelopes feeding in one common and boundless pasture...walking on shore this evening I met with a buffaloe calf which attached itself to me and continued to follow close at my heels untill I embarked and left it." At one point Lewis was so fascinated with his discoveries that he spent 500 words to describe a new bird.

Then came the mountains, not one great range but two, the Rockies and the Cascades, where in deepening snow the exploration members fought off hunger and cold and nearly died. Such difficult terrain was beyond comprehension for Jefferson. Comfortable back in the White House, he believed, in the words of one scholar: "That

Terra incognita awaited Meriwether Lewis and William Clark in 1804 as they headed into unknown terrain to assess the breadth and bounty of the new country. Their only guide was a map (opposite, above) by cartographer Aaron Arrowsmith that showed everything west of the upper Missouri Basin as blank. After the expedition, Clark produced a map (opposite, lower), which was called "one of the most important maps ever made in America." Begun in 1810, Clark updated it many times as he gathered information from trappers and other explorers.

the Blue Ridge Mountains of Virginia might be the highest on the continent; that the mammoth, the giant ground sloth, and other prehistoric creatures would be found along the upper Missouri; that a mountain of pure salt a mile long lay somewhere on the Great Plains; that volcanoes might still be erupting in the Badlands of the upper Missouri; that all the great rivers of the West – the Missouri, Columbia, Colorado, and Rio Grande – rose from a single 'height of land' and flowed off in their several directions to the seas of the hemisphere. Most important, he believed there might be a water connection, linked by a low portage across the mountains, that would lead to the Pacific."

Back in St. Louis in 1806, his journey complete, Lewis penned a letter to the President, saying navigation of the Missouri was "safe and good," as was, for the most part, the Clearwater-Snake-Columbia path to the Pacific. But the distance between them was another matter: a 340-mile portage, 200 along a good route, but the other 140 through the Bitterroot Mountains of Montana and Idaho, "the most formidable part of the tract…over tremendous mountains for which 60 mls. are covered with perpetual snows."

"With those words," wrote Stephen Ambrose, "Lewis put an end to the search for the Northwest Passage."

To counterbalance news he knew would disappoint Jefferson, Lewis hatched a bold prediction, saying that the area northwest of the Mississippi could be plundered of furs, and those furs sent down the Columbia River and shipped to Canton markets in China at great speed and profit. The problem of crossing the northern Rockies would be solved by Shoshone and Nez Perce horse herds, which he said crossed the mountains every summer from late June to the end of September. The entire proposal reversed the way things were done at the time in western Canada, where furs were shipped east to Montreal, then down the St. Lawrence River to the Atlantic, to London, and then around the Cape of Good Hope to China. Conservation was the last thing on his mind, for Lewis, like Jefferson, believed the vast American continent inexhaustible. He ended his proposition with a single bold sentence that helped to launch an American fur rush and to blueprint human settlement in the American West. "The Missouri and all its branches from the Cheyenne upwards," he wrote, "abound more in beaver and Common Otter, than any other streams on earth, particularly that proportion of them lying within the Rocky Mountains."

Jefferson predicted it would take Americans one thousand years to settle the continent from sea to sea. He was wrong. Fueled by furs and then gold, it would take them less than fifty. Despite his forward thinking, Jefferson could not fathom the

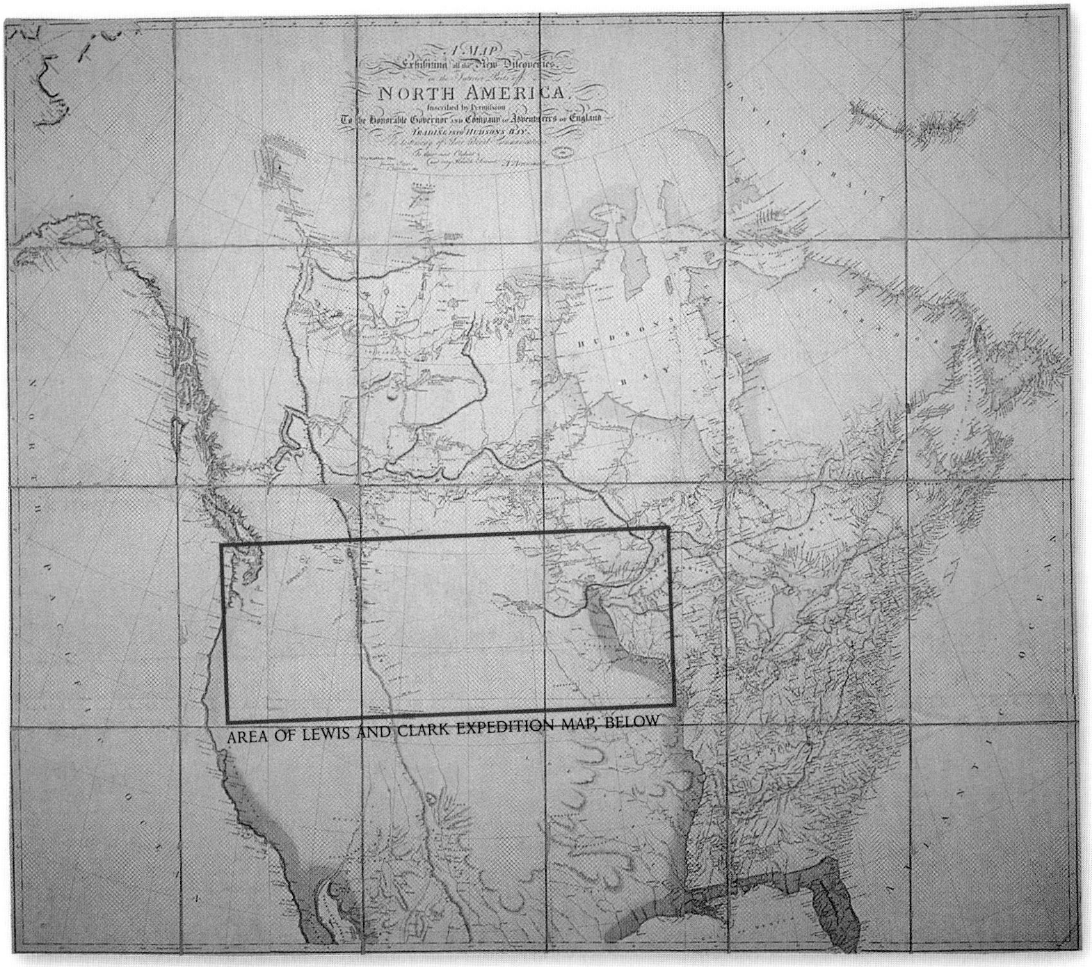
A MAP
Exhibiting all the New Discoveries
NORTH AMERICA,
Inscribed by Permission
To the Honorable Governor and Company of Adventurers of England
TRADING INTO HUDSONS BAY,
HUDSONS
BAY
AREA OF LEWIS AND CLARK EXPEDITION MAP, BELOW

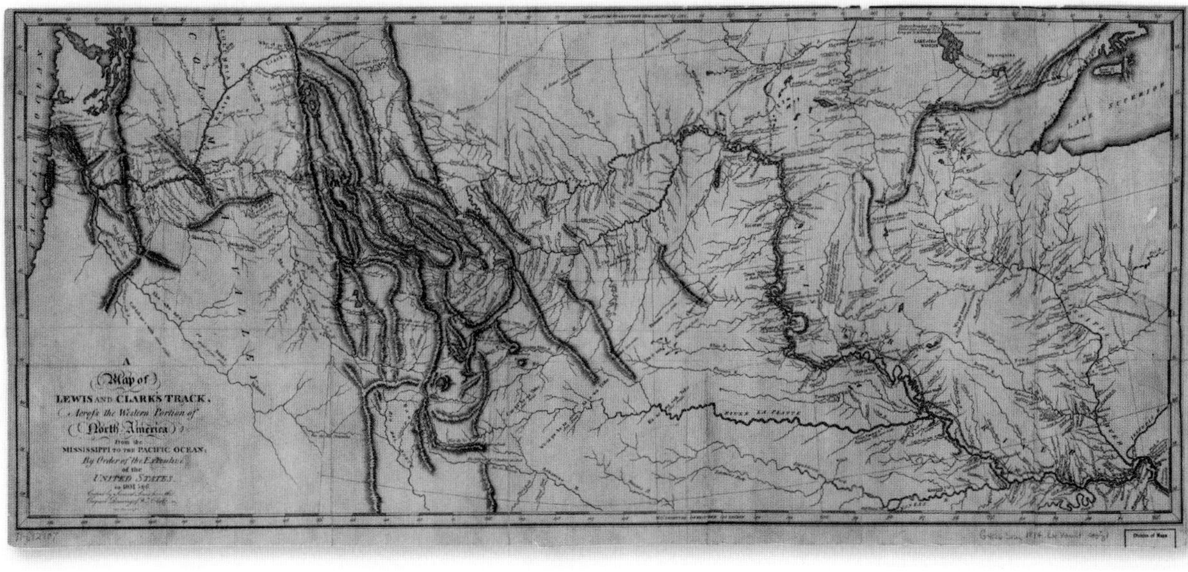
A
Map of
LEWIS AND CLARKS TRACK,
Across the Western Portion of
North America
from the
MISSISSIPPI TO THE PACIFIC OCEAN;
By Order of the Executive
of the
UNITED STATES

Impressions from the Corps of Discovery: William Clark's keelboat (sketched, opposite) was built to his specifications in Pittsburgh: 55 feet long with enough displacement to support 12 tons and 22 men. An engraving entitled "A Canoe Striking a Tree" (above) appeared in the first illustrated expedition journal published. Clark sketched a bighorn ram (below), which "bounded from rock to rock with apparent unconcern...this animal appears to frequent such precipices and cliffs where...they are perfectly secure from...wolf, bear or even man himself."

Defin. of the word Sense

Sense is a faculty of the Soul, whereby it perceives external Objects, by means of the impressions they make on certain organs of the body. These organs are commonly reckoned 5, Viz: the Eye, whereby we see Objects; the ear, which enables us to hear sounds; the nose, by which we receive the ideas of different smells; The Palate, by which we judge of tastes, and the Skin, which enables us to feel the different forms, hardness, or softness of bodies.

2 Men takes up 3 feet — Boat 31 feet in Hol. / do 14 do in Cabn / do 8-4 wide

Inches 32 Long, 22 Wide — a Board

Lockers must be 2-6 wide, do 31 feet Long, do about 1-6 Deep — 156 feet of Planks

Lockers in the Cabin 14-0 long, do Wide 3-0 wide, do 3-6 Deep — 84 feet

Ends & Dubinons do do do 60

900

Calculate 1/4 for waste & wood 75

375

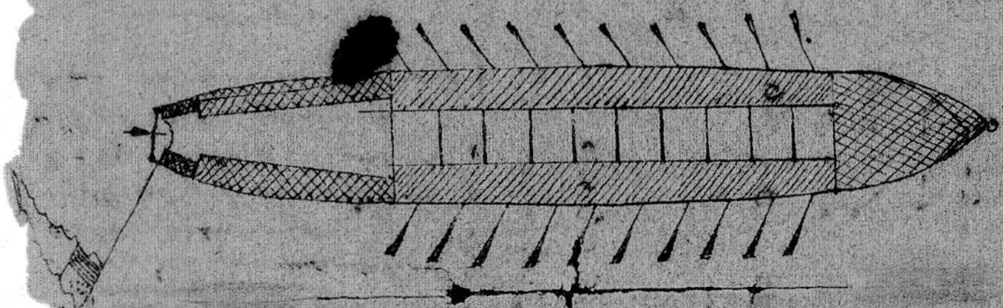

a Timber Stops to be down of 32 feet long ... post for ... the ... of 57 feet ... to ... the ... the ... the Stops & ...

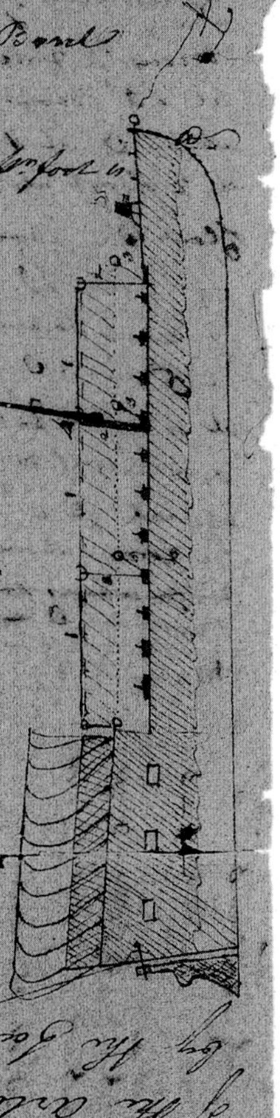

Which Shall be formed in the following manner, Viz. one Judge at least to act as president and at least 1/2 Con. Officers & 3 private members the Court to Consist of not less than 7 members, in Capital offences and at other times when convenient one of the Capt. will preside at the Court in that Case the Court will have an addition to their number of a presid. who will have 2 votes but in all cases Capt. L & C reserve to themselves the right of inflicting such punishment (reducing N.C. Officers at will) as they may think right agreeable to Law at any time when from the nature of the offence & the good of the Service require it) This Court will act agreeable to the rules and regulations of the Articles of War and such others as may be established by the Capt. L & C from time to time.

ingenuity and avarice that would soon spill across America, a driving ambition to produce railroads, interstate highways, faster and faster commerce and communications, urban sprawl, coast-to-coast strip malls, and unprecedented national affluence. As for the Indians, he was aware of the assistance his brave captains had received from a French trapper and his Shoshone wife, Sacajawea. In his book, *Notes on Virginia,* written some 20 years before, he had devoted an entire chapter to America's indigenous peoples, praising tribal chiefs for their wisdom, grace, and impressive oratorical skills. He hoped for future amicable relations as American whites moved westward. But if problems arose, he had little concern for their outcome. In a letter to the territorial governor of Ohio in 1803, Jefferson wrote of Indians that "it is essential to cultivate their love. As to their fear, we presume that our strength and their weakness is now so visible that they must see that we have only to shut our hand to crush them, and that all our liberties to them proceed from motives of pure humanity only."

An American sphinx, Jefferson was both a pastoralist and a President, a slave owner and the author of the Declaration of Independence, the man who opened the American West and envisioned a single great sea-to-sea nation; yet he could not fathom how radically that same western land would change in the next 200 years. Federalists made a sport of irritating him. They pooh-poohed the Lewis and Clark Expedition as little more than an adventure that contributed nothing to the young nation. President John Quincy Adams was such a detractor, and decades later his grandson, Henry Adams, echoed him, saying that the expedition "was a great feat, but was nothing more." The larger accomplishment from that time, he said, was Robert Fulton's early work on the steamship.

Perhaps like some Elizabethan sailor, Jefferson's image of America was a grand pastoral illusion, a fable of sorts, something that could never last in a hyper-consumptive culture where each generation would destroy – or modify – the creations of the generations before, beginning first and most significantly with the men who felled the forests to make from the wilderness a gardenlike scene. "Beginning in Jefferson's time," wrote Leo Marx in *The Machine in the Garden,* "the cardinal image of American aspirations was a rural landscape, a well-ordered green garden magnified to continental size. Although it probably shows a farmhouse or a neat white village, the scene usually is dominated by natural objects: the foreground a pasture, a twisting brook with cattle grazing nearby, then a clump of elms on a rise in the middle distance and beyond that, way off on the western horizon, a line of dark hills. This is the countryside of the old Republic, a chaste, uncomplicated land of rural virtue.... On the whole, Americans were unsentimental about unmodified nature."

That is, they desired wilderness only as the raw material from which other things could be made, things of greater value in their ledger books and bank accounts.

ON THE OTHER SIDE OF THE ATLANTIC, A POET DISAGREED.

While Meriwether Lewis traveled in the Northwest and concluded that it had great commercial potential, the poet lived in the Lake District of England and found a peaceful perfection in every element of nature, from the way sunlight played on a grand scenery of mountain and shore, to the behavior of wildflowers in a breeze, to the aerial dramas of swallows and hawks. He was William Wordsworth, who together with his dear friend, Samuel Taylor Coleridge, had written an anonymous collection of poems that heralded the English Romantic Period. Now, inspired by his surroundings and his young family, and what he called the moral "impulses" that emanated from the woods, Wordsworth produced some of his greatest work, concluding with a radical notion: that the entire Lake District of England, so inspiring and beneficial just as it is – wild and free, unhedged and unfenced – should be saved as a national property for all the people of England. Not private land, but rather a commons, a place for everyone in equal measure. Though he didn't use the term national park, he was the first to frame the idea.

If the English landscape could inspire such notions, then what of America? Alexander Wilson, a Scottish-born ornithologist, lamented in 1804 that America's "wild grandeur" remained largely unsung. True, he said, America in her youth did not have the pageantry of European culture, the monuments and statues and depth of time that could trace a monarchy back a thousand years. But she did have stupendous mountains and forests and rivers, a topographic scope and majesty that England and France could only dream of. Speaking before the American Academy of Art, political leader DeWitt Clinton asked rhetorically, "Can there be a country in the world better calculated than ours to exercise and to exalt the imagination?" In America, he said, "nature has conducted her operations on a magnificent scale.... The wild, romantic, and awful scenery is calculated to produce a correspondent impression in the imagination – to elevate all the faculties of the mind, and to exhalt all the feelings of the heart." As historian Roderick Nash would say a century and a half later, "Anyone [back then] venturing to suggest that 'a man will not necessarily be a great poet because he lives near a great mountain' was shouted down as disloyal to his country."

Washington Irving, James Fenimore Cooper, and an aging Daniel Boone shared the same concerns about Americans who, though clever and hardworking, seemed to

continued on page 54

Artist George Catlin, an early champion of the national park idea, found the Plains Indians and their buffalo hunts a thrilling subject. A native of Pennsylvania who studied law before becoming an artist, he made more than 500 paintings and sketches of the Plains Indians (left) and exhibited many of them in the United States and Europe, from 1837 to 1845.

PRECEDING PAGES

Longs Peak commands the Colorado horizon in this earliest known rendition of the mountain published in Account of an Expedition from Pittsburgh to the Rocky Mountains in the Years 1819-1820, *compiled by Maj. Stephen H. Long.*

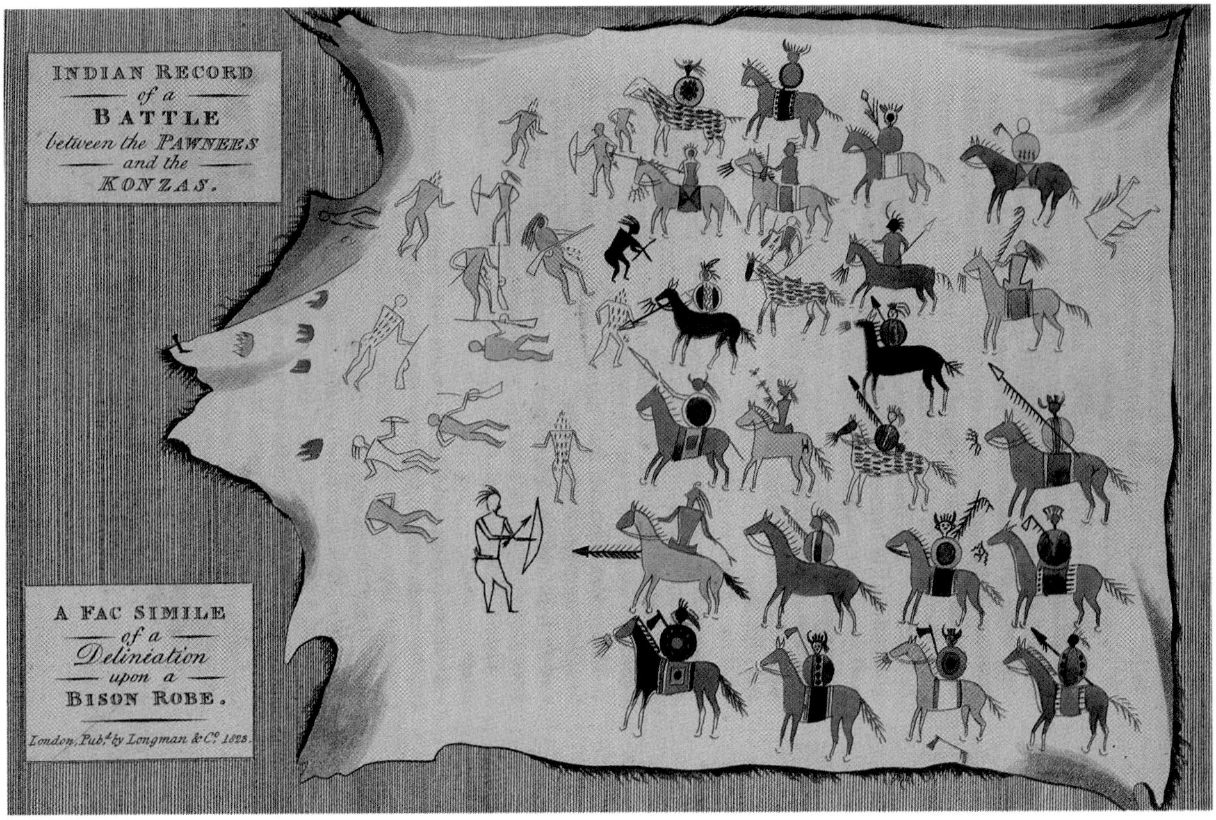

The Mandan chief, Mah-to-toh-pa (opposite), stands immortalized by artist George Catlin. Catlin's book, North American Indian Portfolio: Hunting Scenes and Amusements of the Rocky Mountains and Prairies of America, *was published in 1844. An unknown artist's depiction of an Indian battle appears on a bison robe (above). The painting was published in 1823 in Major Long's report:* Account of an Expedition from Pittsburgh to the Rocky Mountains in the Years 1819-1820.

JAMES FENIMORE COOPER

James Fenimore Cooper was born in New Jersey in 1789. His first novels patterned the work of Jane Austen and Sir Walter Scott. But his third novel, The Pioneers, *was rich with originality. In it he introduced his readers to Natty Bumpo, also known as Leatherstocking, an admirable and aging wilderness scout who opposes the "march of progress" across wild America. In later titles (including* The Last of the Mohicans*), Cooper portrayed Leatherstocking as a younger man whose virtue comes from the wild places that other Americans seem determined to destroy. Cooper died in 1851, the same year that Melville's* Moby Dick *was published.*

continued from page 47

regard nothing sacred beyond God and freedom; so blinded by headlong enterprise, they destroyed the temple at their feet, the wild lands of a virgin continent, a grand panoply of ecosystems in the making for millennia. In 1815 Irving traveled to Europe, where he remained for 17 years, charmed, he said, to "tread...in the footsteps of antiquity – to loiter about the ruined castle – to meditate on the falling tower – to escape, in short, from the commonplace reality of the present, and lose myself among the shadowy grandeurs of the past." Though it was the past, here at last was something the people respected.

Daniel Boone lived long enough – into his mid-80s – to watch America grow tame and insipid compared to what it had been, a tameness he recognized in part as his own creation. "Why, at the time when I was caught by Indians," he told a young John James Audubon, speaking of 30 years before, "you would not have walked out in any direction for more than a mile without shooting a buck or a bear. There were thousands of buffaloes on the hills in Kentucky, the land looked as if it would never become poor; and the hunt in those days was a pleasure indeed. But when I was left to myself on the banks of the Green River, I daresay for the last time in my life, a few signs only of deer were to be seen, and, as to a deer itself, I saw none."

Thus, by 1820, the year Boone died, Thomas Jefferson was at Monticello writing his daily letters and practicing, as best he could in old age, "noble husbandry," tending to his tobacco crops and black slaves. As for Boone, who had once called himself "an instrument ordained to settle the wilderness," he realized before his death, with more than a little regret, that inexhaustibility was a fairy tale. The wilderness could not and would not go on forever. The archetype pioneer, he had destroyed the very thing he loved; but unlike most men of his same conquering spirit, he at least humbled himself enough to recognize it. A pity so few listened.

John James Audubon did. Traveling the Ohio River Valley after his time with Boone, he encountered scene after scene of destruction, and lamented, "The greedy mills told the sad tale, that in a century the noble forests...should exist no more." While Jefferson applied nobility to man, Audubon applied it to forests; two visions of America that in the decades ahead would search for compatibility on a changing curve of values.

THE DICHOTOMY OF MAN AND NATURE CEMENTED BY DESCARTES two hundred years before now stood as an ideological temple made for destruction. Only a deft and artful character could tear it down, somebody who was strong yet sensitive, tough but kind. Somebody who questioned insatiable agriculture and "the march of progress," and who found not just comfort in the wilderness, but also a pure and guiding moral influence. To effectively reach a broad audience that character would need to be a literary hero, a fiction perhaps, and so he was. Created by America's first major novelist, James Fenimore Cooper, the character was a wilderness scout called Natty Bumppo. But Cooper gave him another name, Leatherstocking. The string of novels that told his story – *The Pioneers, The Last of the Mohicans, The Prairie* (all published in the 1820s) – became the *Leatherstocking Tales.* "Identified from the start with the vanishing wilderness and its natives," wrote one reviewer, "Leatherstocking was an unalterably elegiac figure, wifeless and childless, hauntingly loyal to a lost cause." In *The Prairie,* Leatherstocking dies facing west, reaching for the setting sun with supplicating arms as he takes his final breath and calls, "Here! Take me with you."

Another reviewer claimed that "The Leatherstocking novels gave Cooper's countrymen reason to feel both proud and ashamed at conquering wilderness."

The 11th of 12 children of a federalist congressman and a New Jersey Quaker, Cooper had excelled at Latin in Yale, but was tossed out in his junior year for a prank. In 1826, now famous, he traveled to France and befriended the old Revolutionary War hero, Lafayette. During this time, another Frenchman, Alexis de Tocqueville, only 26, crossed the Atlantic going in the other direction, east to west. A fragile, almost diminutive man who was cold to strangers and yet capable of deep friendships, he visited America for nine months and keenly observed every aspect of life, politics, and society. Upon returning to Europe, he wrote *Democracy in America,* a classic that one philosopher said ranked him as "undoubtedly the most illustrious of all political analysts since Aristotle and Machiavelli."

Alexis de Tocqueville remarked again and again on the bright ingenuity of American commerce and how it energized an entire nation. Yet that same commerce seemed to him a sad affront when applied to natural splendor, such as at Niagara Falls, where men built signs and sold scenery and regarded profit as a prophet. "Democratic nations," he summarized, "will habitually prefer the useful to the beautiful, and they will require that the beautiful should be useful."

As literature began to question the insatiable consumption of American resources, art began to celebrate the land itself, the unblemished vista and lyrical woodland. The same year that Cooper introduced the world to Leatherstocking, a young man in Ohio, Thomas Cole, abandoned a career as a portrait painter and focused his talents on a celebration of the American landscape, what he called "the wild and great features of nature: mountain forests that know not man." He moved to New York

Karl Bodmer, trained as an engraver in his native Switzerland, accompanied German Prince Maximilian to America; in 1833 he journeyed more than 2,000 miles up the Missouri River to its headwaters in Blackfoot Indian country. That winter Bodmer created many fine paintings of the Missouri frontier, including "View of the Rocky Mountains" (right). His portraits of the Mandan Indians, filled with ethnological detail, depicted a proud and free people only a few years before they were decimated by a smallpox epidemic.

On his 1833 journey along the Missouri River, Karl Bodmer painted a montage of sedimentary features – spires, cliffs, and cones – that had been formed by thousands of years of erosion. For later pioneers who traveled this same route, Bodmer's depictions became a guidepost and a reassurance that others had passed this way before and returned home safely.

and settled in the Catskill Mountains, where high on rocky flanks he transformed three dimensions into two. Huddled in storms with a coat over his canvas, he found himself torn between the wild exhilaration of wind and rain and the desire to race home to safety. Yet he stayed and captured the land and the weather, a drama, like dialogue, between Earth and sky. His work showed no sign of humans, and thus broke with tradition, portraying elegant scenes of crimson autumns and placid lakes, but also scenes of wildness in its darkest hours, with storm clouds and blackened cliffs. Cooper praised Cole for the brilliance and bravery of his work. And soon other artists – Thomas Doughty and Asher Durand – joined Cole and gave birth to the Hudson River School, a group of artists, nationalistic and proud, who from about 1825 to 1870 would celebrate the American land as a treasure in itself, unimproved by man, distinct from Europe, places of profound and delicate beauty that if destroyed could not be replaced.

George Catlin took it one step further. A relatively unknown artist who also quit portrait work, he sailed up the Missouri River in 1832, in search of what he called, "the grace and beauty of Nature." Determined to live Leatherstocking's dream and chase the sun before it set a final time on everything wild, Catlin, like many Americans, had heard outlandish tales about the sunburned, snow-veiled lands beyond the advance of civilization.

How marvelous and quixotic and wild it sounded. Catlin knew of John Colter, a member of the Lewis and Clark Expedition who had chosen to stay behind when the others returned to St. Louis. Alone and on foot, Colter had walked into the Rocky Mountains, in today's Wyoming, and stumbled into a rumored world of geysers and hot springs and volcanic yellow stones today known as "Colter's Hell." After him came Lt. Zebulon Pike, a military officer of uncommon courage and endurance, yet described by one historian as "a poor explorer with a knack for getting lost, and even a poorer judge of character." Pike traversed Colorado, made one misjudgment after another, and became so disenchanted with the country that in a final mistake he called the Great Plains worthless for agriculture, an "American Sahara." His reports helped to perpetuate the myth of vast lands west of the Mississippi River as the Great American Desert, a myth that would persist until after the Civil War.

Another Army officer, Maj. Stephen H. Long, led five expeditions from Minnesota to Oklahoma and achieved some good science along the way; yet he added to Pike's pessimism by calling the southern plains "almost wholly unfit for cultivation."

Among whites, it was mountain men, not military men, who best understood

JOHN JAMES AUDUBON

The illegitimate son of a French naval officer, John James Audubon (below) was born in Haiti in 1785 and raised in France. At 18 he was sent to the United States to enter business. After several failed ventures he turned to his passions of art and birds. By the mid-1820s he had amassed enough drawings to embark on

a 12-year project: The Birds of America, *a four-volume set of books that contained 435 hand-colored plates. He later produced 150 plates (opposite) for another important work,* Viviparous Quadrupeds of North America. *His art played an important role in awakening Americans to the varied and wondrous wildlife of the New World.*

and appreciated the American West. In 1812, while a pompous Zebulon Pike announced in the war with Britain that "You will hear of my fame or my death," a quiet fur trapper named Robert Stuart skirted the Wind River Range of today's Wyoming, found South Pass – the easiest route over the Continental Divide – and blazed what would one day be called the Oregon Trail. Afterward, beginning in 1825, fur trappers convened from every corner of the Rockies at an agreed-upon place to sell their pelts and drink their fortunes and share truths and lies. This gathering was known as the "summer rendezvous," and as one historian put it, "You were considered dead until you did show up." Emblematic among these men was Jedediah Smith, who had survived grizzly attacks and trapped 668 beaver in a single season. In 1826 he walked from the Rockies to California, making him the first white man to cross the Great Basin and the Sierra Nevada.

Such were the visions of wildness and abundance that filled George Catlin's dreams as he traveled up the Missouri River in 1832. What were these landscapes – and times – that made men so right and so wrong? Six hundred and sixty-eight beavers trapped by one man in one season. How long could it last? In every direction, Catlin found the bluffs and grasslands open like a sea, and the sky overhead a great bowl of blue. The Indians stood before him in ceremonial dress, proud to be painted and immortalized. And Catlin, equally proud to paint them, worked with intensity, knowing, as perhaps they did too, that the curtain was falling on one of the most beautiful sights on Earth.

At Fort Pierre, South Dakota, saddened after watching Sioux braves slaughter bison for whiskey money, Catlin climbed a hill and spread out a map of the United States. How large yet vulnerable it seemed, a continental evanescence, all that space, shrinking each year. He wrote, "Many are the rudenesses and wilds in Nature's works which are destined to fall before the deadly axe and desolating hands of cultivating man." Then, seeking a solution, he added in a stroke of genius: "Why could not the Indian, the buffalo, and their wild homeland be protected in a magnificent park.... What a beautiful and thrilling specimen for America to preserve and hold up to the view of her refined citizens and the world, in future ages! A *nation's Park,* containing man and beast, in all the wild freshness of their nature's beauty."

Why not indeed. Forty years later America – and the world – would have its first national park, Yellowstone. And the human race would never again be quite the same.

Nº 20.
PLATE XCIX.
ORD.

Nº 26.
PLATE CXXVIII.
CAPRA AMERICANA, BLAINVILLE.

Mambrino's Helmet

CHAPTER TWO

Transcendence

IN 1833, ONE YEAR AFTER GEORGE CATLIN FIRST ARTICULATED THE NATIONAL PARK IDEA, 46-YEAR-OLD DAVY CROCKETT WROTE HIS AUTOBIOGRAPHY AND INTRODUCED AMERICAN READERS TO VIVID DESCRIPTIONS OF THE TENNESSEE FRONTIERSMAN, FACE TO FACE WITH GRIZZLY BEARS. HIS STORIES FROM THE MOUNTAINS WERE ALMOST AS FRIGHTENING AS HIS EXPERIENCES ON CAPITOL HILL, WHERE HE SERVED IN THE U.S. HOUSE OF REPRESENTATIVES. NO WONDER THAT FOR MOST AMERICANS THE WILDERNESS PERSISTED AS A DAUNTING AND DANGEROUS PLACE, WHILE IN EUROPE, THE ACKNOWLEDGED CENTER OF WESTERN ART AND SCIENCE,

The frontispiece of the book The American Landscape, *by William Cullen Bryant, beckons readers into a virtuous frontier.*

Originally an American Fur Trading Company post, Fort Laramie, situated on the North Platte River, bustles with activity in this 1837 painting by Alfred Jacob Miller. Oglala Sioux camp outside the fort, while the Stars and Stripes flutter above. Explorer John C. Frémont visited here in 1842 and 1843.

aramie or Sublette's Fort
near the Nebraska
or Platte River

Frederick Chopin composed 12 études in a single year, Johannes Peter Muller began work on *The Handbook of Human Physiology,* and the British Empire abolished slavery.

Amid these pinwheeling times an unheralded mathematician, William Forster Lloyd, sketched a theory that made little if any splash. Through the decades, though, the ripples would grow and expand until they washed ashore on our social conscience and on the way we see ourselves and how we treat land, especially those lands that belong to society as a whole – lands called "the commons," the best among them being national parks.

First and foremost, Lloyd took a different view from economist Adam Smith, whose 1776 benchmark book, *The Wealth of Nations,* popularized the notion that an individual working for his own personal gain is led by an "invisible hand" that benefits the public at large. Many years later, biologist Garrett Hardin would bring Lloyd out of obscurity and write in his important treatise, *The Tragedy of the Commons,* that Smith "contributed to a dominant tendency of thought that has ever since interfered with positive action based on rational analysis, namely, the tendency to assume that decisions reached individually will, in fact, be the best decisions for an entire society."

By speaking of tragedy, Hardin meant not unhappiness, but what one philosopher called "the solemnity of the remorseless workings of things." That is, the human condition, in its attitude toward land and other possessions and toward other fellow humans.

"Picture a pasture open to all," wrote Hardin, explaining in words what Lloyd had sketched in numbers. On this pasture – the so-called commons – "...each herdsman will try to keep as many cattle as possible. Such an arrangement may work reasonably satisfactorily for centuries because tribal wars, poaching, and disease keep the numbers of both man and beasts well below the carrying capacity of the land. Finally, however, comes the day of reckoning, that is, the day when the long-desired goal of social stability becomes a reality. At this point, the inherent logic of the commons remorselessly generates tragedy.

"As a rational being, each herdsman seeks to maximize his gain." So one herdsman a bit more enterprising than the others adds an animal to the herd, from which he alone benefits. This of course creates overgrazing, which must be shared by every herdsman. Lloyd showed this benefit to the enterprising herdsman as a value just shy of +1, while the cost to him and every other herdsman was a fraction of –1. The enterprising herdsman thus gains while every other herdsman loses, which might be tolerable if it stopped there, but it never does. The herdsman adds another animal, and another, and in time, explains Hardin, "this is the conclusion reached by each and every rational herdsman sharing a commons. Therein is the tragedy. Each man is locked into a system that compels him to increase his herd without limit – in a world that is limited. Ruin is the destination toward which all men rush, each pursuing his own best interest in a society that believes in the freedom of the commons. Freedom in a commons brings ruin to all."

FEW HEARTS AND MINDS WERE PREPARED TO HEAR SUCH NONSENSE in America in the early 19th century. The land seemed bountiful and boundless, open as far as the imagination could run; and if a commons fell into ruin, then people would simply move on, leapfrogging west through the generations, drunk on dreams of cutting roads into country where only a few years before a man could barely walk. That was the emblem of progress, achievement, and the making of a better life, not so different from our values today. As Hardin said, "natural selection favors the forces of psychological denial. The individual benefits as an individual from his ability to deny the truth even though society as a whole, of which he is a part, suffers."

Then, as now, the man who steals a sheep off the commons can be tried and convicted, while the man who steals the commons from under the sheep isn't even arrested.

It would take awhile for modern techno-agrarian societies to understand what aboriginal hunter-gatherers had known for a long time: that the lessons of good stewardship lived in stories, song lines, and parables and were not to be toyed with. The message was always the same: It was foolish – even taboo – to take more than you needed. The land deserved deep respect, and furthermore should remain untouched here and there as sacred ground, places that were neither harvested nor hunted, but set aside for other creatures to go freely about their lives.

Clearly, if any pieces of pre-Columbian North America were to be saved before they fell to testosterone and Old Testament virtues of ax and plow, it would require a new way of thinking. It would require an anti-Cartesian realignment to where man saw himself not in nature, but of nature, a transcendence that planted seeds for others to one day have the vision, the hope, the courage to stand against prevailing economic and political orders, and create these miracles called national parks.

That is precisely what happened.

While William Forster Lloyd and his mathematical theory lived in relative obscurity, Ralph Waldo Emerson did not. That same year, 1833, when he was only 30, Emerson returned home to Concord, Massachusetts, after a sojourn to Europe. His young wife had died two years before, and his grief was so great as to make him question his Christian heritage and inherited profession. In Europe he had met William Wordsworth, who told him that poetry was the only truth. He had also met Samuel Taylor Coleridge, Wordsworth's friend, and Thomas Carlyle, the son of poor parents, who at the age of 14 had walked 90 miles to enroll in the University of Edinburgh.

These three men had an immense influence on Emerson, especially Carlyle, who coined the term "industrialism," and would remain Emerson's friend for nearly 50 years. Carlyle's essay, *Signs of the Times,* published in 1829, had described the machine – any machine – as the most telling "sign" of modern life. If asked to name his own age, he would have replied that he would not call it the "Heroical, Devotional, Philosophical or Moral Age, but, above all others, the Mechanical Age. It is the Age of Machinery, in every outward and inward sense of the word." Carlyle meant the machine not just as a prelude to technology or as an emerging economic system, but also as a metaphor, the beginning of "a mighty change in our manner of existence."

Back in America, Emerson embarked on a series of public lectures rich with anecdote, proverb, and wit. Meanwhile, in Great Britain, Carlyle published *Sartor Resartus* in 1834, a book that Emerson devoured, as did other rising literary figures, including Herman Melville. The book focused on a semiautobiographical professor who at middle age finds himself overwhelmed with the meaninglessness of his own paltry life, a depression that can afflict anybody of conscience in a changing environment, but which Carlyle, using the juggernaut of industrialism, made more acute. "To me," the professor reflected with sadness, "the Universe was all void of Life, of Purpose, of Violation, even of Hostility: it was one huge, dead, immeasurable Steam-engine, rolling on, in its dead indifference, to grind me limb from limb." Invented by man and worshiped by man, the machine, in Carlyle's estimation, would one day annihilate the moral force of man.

Two years later, in 1836, inspired and alarmed by Carlyle's "dead indifference," Emerson completed a thin little book that repudiated man's dominion attitude toward the natural world and helped launch the transcendental movement in the United States. He called the book *Nature,* and though only 1,000 copies were published, it had a lot to say. "To go into solitude," he began, "a man needs to retire as much from his chamber as from society. I am not solitary whilst I read and write, though nobody is with me. But if a man would be alone, let him look at the stars. The rays that come from those heavenly worlds will separate between him and what he touches. One might think the atmosphere was made transparent with this design, to give man, in the heavenly bodies, the perpetual presence of the sublime."

He spoke of stars that smile, and an Earth that laughs in flowers. He said that the simple elegance and beauty of nature is essential; that to "the body and mind which have been cramped by noxious work or company, nature is medicinal and restores their tone. The tradesman, the attorney comes out of the din and craft of the street and sees the sky and the woods, and is a man again. In their eternal calm, he finds himself. The health of the eye seems to demand a horizon. We are never tired, so long as we can see far enough." For himself, Emerson admitted that "in the wilderness, I find something more dear and connate than in the streets or villages...in the woods we return to reason and faith."

This book was analytical and yet lyrical, both a confession and a prophecy. It identified nature's ministerial powers and became the framework for subsequent works. "The American Scholar," a lecture Emerson delivered one year later at Harvard, was well received but a thinly veiled challenge to the Harvard intelligentsia, as it warned an agitated student body against pedantry and the imitation of others. It debunked traditionalism and scholarship unrelated to everyday life and heralded the importance of nature in transferring wisdom from the divine to man.

Next came the "Address at Divinity College," one year later, also delivered at Harvard, this time as an invitation not by the officers of the school but by the student body. This speech dismissed religious institutions as failures in man's attempt to encounter the deity directly. "It is time," Emerson said, "that this ill-suppressed murmur of all thoughtful men against the famine of our churches; this moaning of the heart because it is bereaved of consolation, the hope, the grandeur that come alone out of the culture of the moral nature – should be heard over the sleep of indolence, and over the din of routine." Be a nonconformist, Emerson exhorted. Listen to your own heart, not the shouts of others. Read the scriptures of leaves and trees. God didn't live exclusively in a church or a cathedral or some Unitarian construct; God lived in the forests and streams and stars, precisely where he had been all along, visible everywhere until man came along and created the smoke and grime of the city and blinded himself.

AMONG THE REGENTS AND OTHER CONSERVATIVES AT HARVARD, Emerson's message was sacrilege; he would not be invited to speak there again for almost 30 years. Yet he excited many young students into an awakening, one of them a soul-eyed son of a pencil maker who would become his most famous disciple, Henry David Thoreau. Thoreau in fact spoke at his own commencement in 1837, and at 19 had already expressed dismay – some would say revolt – at insectivorous men who droned after dollars and converted flowered fields into factories and farms.

A professed dreamer and admirer of clouds, Thoreau worked for a while as a surveyor, "but he was daily beset with graver questions, which he manually confronted," Emerson would say of him at his funeral address in 1862, when Thoreau, traveling in Minnesota to study Native American customs, contracted tuberculosis and died at 44. "He interrogated every custom, and wished to settle all his practice on an ideal foundation.... He was bred to no profession, he never married; he lived alone; he never went to church; he never voted; he refused to pay a tax to the State; he ate no flesh, he drank no wine, he never knew the use of tobacco; and, though a naturalist, he used neither trap nor gun. He chose, wisely no doubt for himself, to be the bachelor of thought and nature. He had no talent for wealth, and knew how to be poor without the least hint of squalor or inelegance.... A fine house, dress, the manners and talk of highly cultivated people were all thrown away on him. He much preferred a good Indian, and considered these refinements as impediments to conversation, wishing to meet his companion on the simplest terms. He declined invitations to dinner parties, because there each was in every one's way, and he could not meet the individuals to any purpose. 'They make their pride,' he said, 'in making their dinner cost too much; I make my pride in making my dinner cost little.' When asked at table what dish he preferred, he answered, 'The nearest.' He did not like the taste of wine, and never had a vice in his life.... He chose to be rich by making his wants few, and supplying them himself."

At times a strain existed between them, and Emerson would be the first to admit that Thoreau could be difficult. "He wanted a fallacy to expose, a blunder to pillory, I may say required a little sense of victory, a roll of the drum, to call his powers to exercise. It cost him nothing to say No; indeed he found it much easier than to say Yes. It seemed as if his first instinct on hearing a proposition was to controvert it, so impatient was he of the limitations of our daily thought."

In 1846, when Thoreau spent a night in jail to protest slavery, Emerson came to visit and said to him through the metal bars, "Henry, what are you doing in there?"

"Ralph," he replied, "what are you doing out there?"

Thoreau worked for a while as a handyman at Emerson's Concord house and took long walks in the woods. He loved to discover arrowheads on the forest floor, or a single flower amid the moss, or a lynx, the catlike eyes staring back at him through the long reach of ancient memory. Such vestiges of wildness confirmed for him "that all is not a garden and cultivated field crops, that there are square rods in Middlesex

HENRY DAVID THOREAU

"We need the tonic of wildness," wrote Thoreau a century and a half before it was fashionable to spend leisure time in the woods. For little more than $28 he built a cabin on the shore of Walden Pond, near his home in Concord,

Massachusetts, and lived there from July 1845 until September 1847. "My purpose in going to Walden Pond," he wrote, "was not to live cheaply nor to live dearly there, but to transact some private business with the fewest obstacles." His most significant work, Walden, *was published in 1854 and has never been out of print. In 1861 he traveled to Minnesota to study the lives of Sioux Indians. Weakened by tuberculosis, he returned home and died in May 1862. Thoreau's writings have inspired generations of activists to fight for human justice and the preservation of wild nature.*

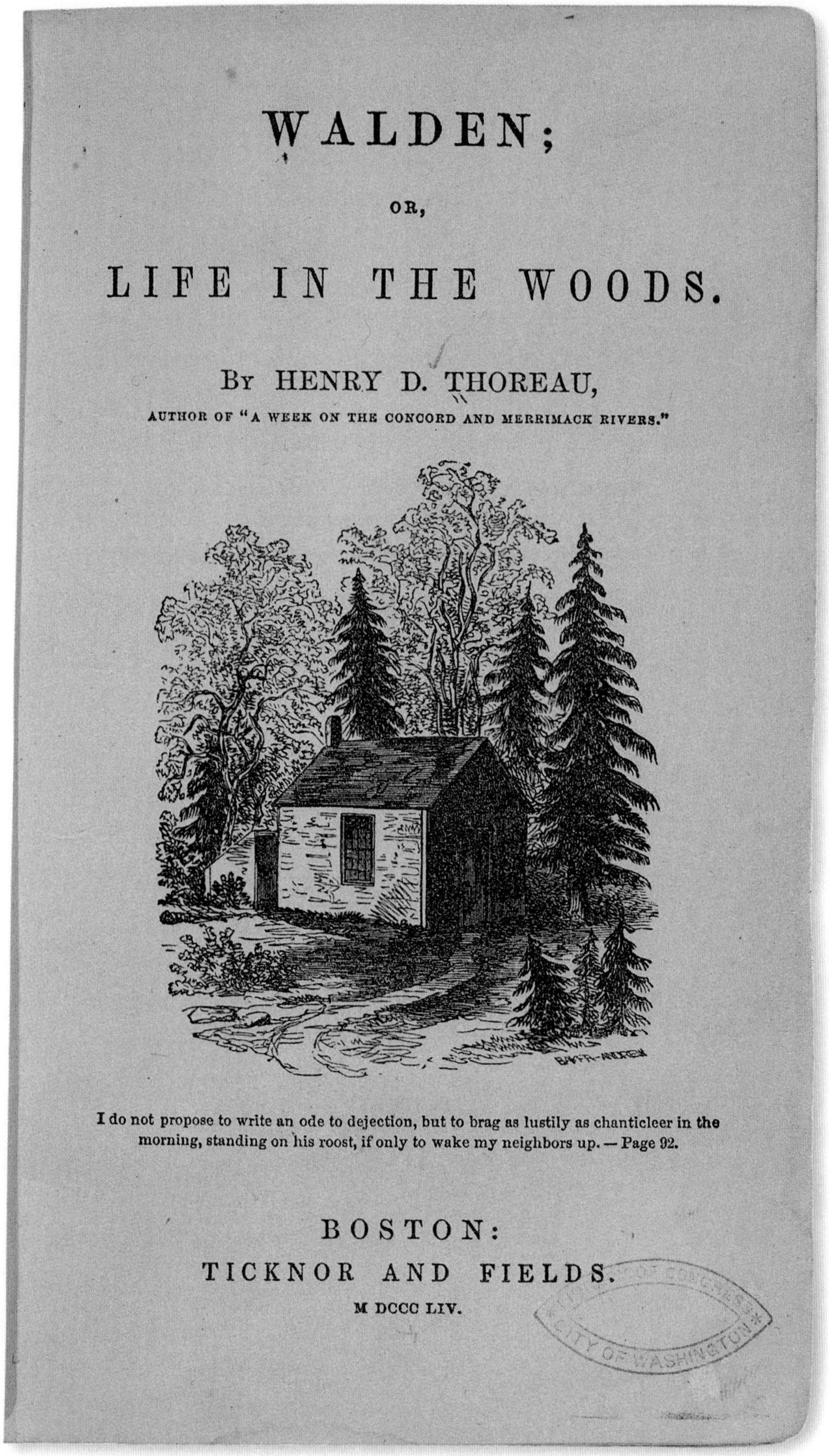

WALDEN;

OR,

LIFE IN THE WOODS.

BY HENRY D. THOREAU,

AUTHOR OF "A WEEK ON THE CONCORD AND MERRIMACK RIVERS."

I do not propose to write an ode to dejection, but to brag as lustily as chanticleer in the morning, standing on his roost, if only to wake my neighbors up. — Page 92.

BOSTON:

TICKNOR AND FIELDS.

M DCCC LIV.

County as purely primitive as they were a thousand years ago...little oases of wildness in the desert of our civilization."

Little oases that would one day be called wildlife preserves and refuges and national parks – those few places that retained their ecological intactness. Though Thoreau didn't use the term "park" as George Catlin did, he framed the idea as an essential need, something required not just to save America, but also Americans. Schooled in history and philosophy, he understood the power of change, especially social change on the cusp of the industrial revolution. He understood it as a mad acceleration, not just a velocity, and knew that without new and radical ways of thinking, his society, so eager to grow new branches, would rot away at its roots. He recognized that the Concord of his day would look, sound, and taste much different in a hundred years. More than a single-sense naturalist, he was a full quintet, an explorer of the fragrant and tactile, of the grand and scenic, but also, and perhaps more important, of the small and unheralded. He never stopped admiring the ground at his feet, and thus learned to be home, rooted and perennial, singing the praises of belonging. It was this rootedness and dedication to place that would be needed, Thoreau said, echoing Emerson, to defend wildness in America.

So it was that Emerson founded the Transcendental Club, and in 1840, with help from Margaret Fuller, he launched *The Dial,* a short-lived magazine wherein many of his most famous essays were born: *History, Self-Reliance, Compensation, Friendship, The Poet and Politics.*

Dare to be different, Emerson said again and again. Nonconformity works. It has virtue. It requires that we look at the world anew – as Thoreau added, that we find heaven underfoot as well as overhead.

But these were headlong times in America. New roads, canals, and cities seemed to rise up from the Earth and remake the land. Steamboats plied rivers and harbors with wondrous paddlewheels working against currents and tides. Commerce was everywhere; nothing seemed impossible. And most revolutionary of all, the Baltimore and Ohio Railroad was laying down tracks, as the great beast called the locomotive was about to whistle a new song of enterprise. Historian Leo Marx noted: "[T]he abundance of land and the scarcity of labor had intensified the demand for machinery. Between 1830 and 1860 the nation was to put down more than 30,000 miles of railroad track, pivot of the transportation revolution which in turn quickened industrialization. By the time Carlyle's book (*Sartor Resartus*) was read in America the economy was expanding at a remarkable rate, the new technology was proving itself indispensable, and the nation was on the verge of the 'take-off' into the era of rapid industrialization."

The 1830s witnessed the births of three powerful industrialists and bankers – Andrew Carnegie, J. P. Morgan, and John D. Rockefeller – who by the end of the century would play an important role in driving the nation's economy, elevating the consumption of natural resources to unprecedented rates. Yet, by the end of his 98 years, J. D. Rockefeller, the world's first billionaire, would recognize a wealth beyond money, and so enlightened would become a major benefactor of national parks, donating vast amounts of acreage in the American West.

He said that as a boy he had read Emerson, and not until the twilight of his life did the words have clarity, as if only then could he see the stars and flowers. What Emerson, Thoreau, and other transcendentalists asked was simple: Did technological civilization and the pursuit of progress represent the best path, or might something older and wiser be lost along the way? Yes, the mechanized, industrialized world had much to offer, but might it also pulverize innocence and simplicity and fair-mindedness? Should not a few places be left inviolate of runaway commerce and men who could hear a dollar bill fall on the forest floor?

"The Transcendental conception of man added indirectly to the attractiveness of wilderness," wrote Roderick Nash in *Wilderness and the American Mind.* "Instead of the residue of evil in every heart, which Calvinism postulated, Emerson, Thoreau, and their colleagues discerned a spark of divinity. Under the prod of Calvin, Puritans feared the innate sinfulness of human nature would run rampant if left to itself in the moral vacuum of the wilderness. Men might degenerate to beasts or worse on stepping into the woods. Transcendentalists, on the contrary, saw no such danger in the wild country because they believed in man's basic goodness. Reversing Puritan assumptions, they argued that one's chances of attaining moral perfection and knowing God were maximized by entering wilderness. The fears which the first New Englanders experienced in contact with the primeval forest gave way to their Concord descendants confidence – in both wilderness and man."

WALKING IN THE WOODS OF NEW ENGLAND WAS A MILD ENDEAVOR compared to climbing storm-raked peaks in the Rocky Mountains; yet each in its own way contributed to how a young nation saw itself and its destiny. As if in a Greek drama, the westward march of explorers showed how Americans could both praise and destroy what attracted them to a place; and in a symbolic manner, it also showed how a prized chalice hidden beyond the horizon, once at their feet, could become a crushed shard in the aftermath of another expansionist conquest.

In 1842, while Emerson and Thoreau used quill pens, church halls, and Aristotlean ambulations to explore man's relationship with nature, John C. Frémont, an ambitious 29-year-old lieutenant with the U.S. Army's elite Corps of Topographical Engineers, entered the Wind River Range of today's Wyoming. Without food or extra provisions he scaled a summit he believed to be the highest in the Rockies. For a thousand miles he had led his expedition over the Great Plains, up the Missouri and Platte Rivers, and through South Pass, which he likened to a stroll up Capitol Hill in Washington, D.C. The analogy came easily to him, as he considered himself well placed in American politics. Three years earlier he had risked his career by falling in love with Jessie Benton, the fetching 16-year-old daughter of Thomas Hart Benton, the powerful Missouri senator who flew into a rage when he discovered that Frémont and his daughter had eloped.

Jessie Benton was headstrong, however, and together with her charming husband she convinced her father of their deep and abiding love. He soon forgave them, and moreover embraced Frémont as his protégé. According to author David Roberts in *A Newer World,* the senator was a "great champion of westward expansion...who had served in the Senate since 1821. A close confidant of Thomas Jefferson, Benton had tirelessly lobbied for expeditions to take up the challenge laid down by Lewis and Clark; in the last meeting he ever had with an ailing Jefferson, in 1824, their talk had been of the need for further exploration of the unknown West." So it was that Senator Benton found in his new son-in-law an ambitious yet somehow fragile instrument of his expansionist campaign.

Throughout his journal Frémont would describe the scenery before him as "magnificent" and "grand" and "romantic." Even bad fortune didn't deter him from his rapture. After he and his men spilled in rapids on the Platte River and lost valuable equipment, including a daguerreotype camera, he wrote of scenery that "was extremely picturesque, and not withstanding our forlorn condition, we were frequently obliged to stop and admire it."

Upon entering the Wind River Range and alpine meadows brilliant with August wildflowers, he wrote: "It seemed as if from the vast expanse of uninteresting prairie we had passed over, nature had collected all her beauties together in one chosen place." He gathered colorful specimens and had them delivered to Harvard and Princeton, where Asa Gray and John Torrey, distinguished professors of botany, would key them into their phylogenetic families. Higher still, the mountains seemed

continued on page 84

The Hudson River School of Art

Thomas Cole, 1801-1848

As 19th-century America went in search of a national identity as lasting as the castles and cathedrals of Europe, the young country needed something to inspire people who were raised on a cultured diet of Shakespeare, Milton, and Michelangelo. The ancient marvels of the West – labeled "earth monuments" – provided just such an antiquity. The California redwoods, wrote Horace Greeley in 1859, "were of very substantial size when David danced before the ark, when Solomon laid the foundation of the Temple...." The search for a national image did not begin in the American West, however, where landscape painters cut their canvas by the yard. Instead it began in the East, where a subdued topography inspired attention to detail. Artists such as Thomas Cole (above) chose not to go west when nature in all her moods could be found in New York's Catskills (right) and the White Mountains of New Hampshire. Thus the Hudson River School of Art was founded, built on the portfolios of Cole, Asher B. Durand, Thomas Doughty, and Frederic E. Church,

Thomas Cole, 1825, LAKE WITH DEAD TREES (CATSKILL), *oil on canvas*

Thomas Cole, 1827, VIEW OF THE WHITE MOUNTAINS, *oil on canvas*

among others. Durand exhorted his young disciples, "Go not abroad then in search of material for the exercise of your pencil while the virgin charms of our native land have claims on your deepest affections." The idea of landscape painting might seem unspectacular today in a modern culture that publishes colorful books and calendars filled with nature, art, and photography. But consider that not until the Renaissance did a European painting show nature unaltered by man. A desirable life back then was one free from the vagaries of nature. To paint a wild forest was unthinkable; to paint a wolf would have been heresy. Artists most often painted deities and messiahs. Monarchs and merchants paid handsomely to see themselves at the center of their worlds. Thomas Cole and fellow artists of the Hudson River School repudiated this and did so with careful attention to color, detail, texture, light, and shadow. Cole's paintings (above and opposite) proclaimed wild places as inspiring, an altogether new concept. Art in America would never again be the same.

Thomas Cole, 1826, FALLS OF KAATERSKILL, *oil on canvas*

Thomas Cole, 1827, THE CLOVE, CATSKILLS, *oil on canvas*

Autumn sunset warms the brooding Catskills in this oil on canvas by Thomas Cole. Cole's big break came in 1825 when Col. John Trumbull and the painter Asher B. Durand purchased his work from a shop window in New York and found him patrons, assuring him future commercial success. The following year Cole made his home in Catskill, New York, on the west bank of the Hudson River, where he founded a school of art dedicated to botanical accuracy and a reverence for nature. Cole would travel about New England on foot to make his pencil sketches, then retreat to his studio to paint in the winter.

When Thomas Cole died prematurely in 1848, his admirer Asher B. Durand (above) painted the tribute, "Kindred Spirits" (opposite). It shows Cole with his good friend, poet William Cullen Bryant, against a backdrop of Catskill Mountain scenery. It was presented to Bryant in appreciation of the eulogy he delivered for Cole. Durand, who also created "A Pine Tree, Lake George" (right), believed that only after the artist had became intimate with nature could he approach it on what he called "more familiar terms, even venturing to choose and reject some portions of her unbounded wealth."

Asher B. Durand, 1894, A PINE TREE, LAKE GEORGE, *lithograph*

Asher B. Durand, 1849, KINDRED SPIRITS, *oil on canvas*

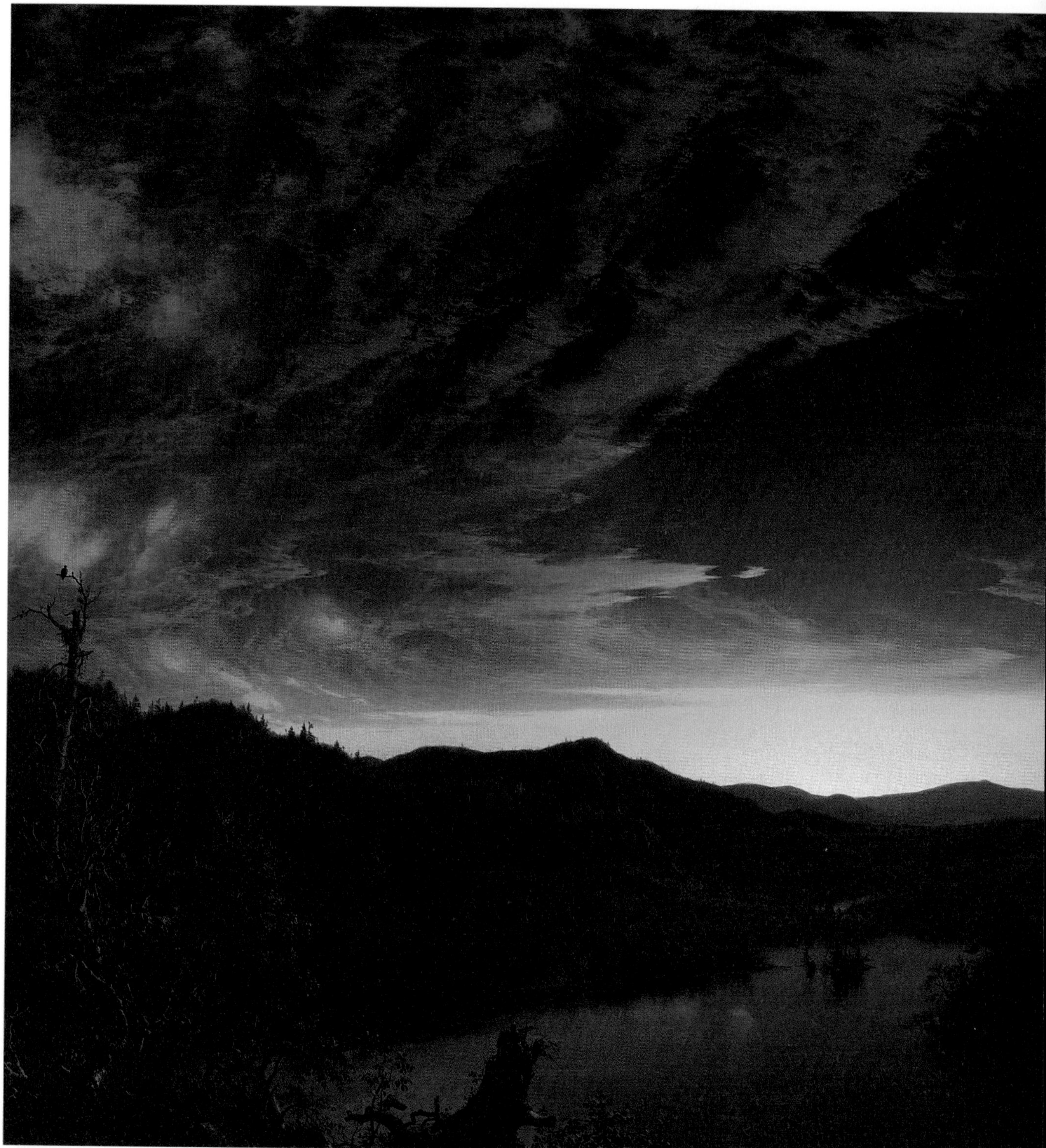

A student of Thomas Cole, Frederic E. Church painted "Twilight in the Wilderness" in 1860, 12 years after his mentor's death. It is in Church's later work, according to historian Roderick Nash, that the American wilderness "received triumphant portrayal." Previous work by Church showed foregrounds with a road or two, and a few domestic sheep. But in this painting, says Nash, "all traces of the pastoral have vanished...." Two years after Church made this painting, Henry David Thoreau died. But not his ideas or the paintings of Cole, Durand, Church, and others. Art and literature henceforth celebrated the beauty and sanctity of wilderness in America and formed a rallying point for its defense.

Frederic E. Church, 1860, TWILIGHT IN THE WILDERNESS, *oil on canvas*

continued from page 73

to lean into him, casting long shadows where Frémont described a "savage sublimity of naked rock" and "a confusion of defiles." Still, he pushed on until the summit "appeared so near" that he left the mules and several men at a base camp and set off on foot with a small group, alpine style, with no food or overcoats, convinced he would reach the summit and return by nightfall.

Like Zebulon Pike some 35 years before, Frémont fell victim to the effects of mountain foreshortening, where high peaks seen from a distance appear closer than they really are. But while Pike never reached the top of his mountain, Frémont did, and America would immortalize him for it. He and his small party fired their guns from the summit and shouted hurrah. Frémont took an elevation reading using a barometer and determined the summit to be 13,570 feet. Cold, tired, and hungry, he and his men then headed down. Upon returning to St. Louis, he found Jessie confined to her bed with their first child, and in a grand gesture he spread an American flag over wife and child and announced, "This flag was raised over the highest peak of the Rocky Mountains; I have brought it to you."

Such theater won Frémont wide acclaim, despite the fact that more than 30 summits in the Rockies were higher. And despite the fact that Charles Preuss, a German cartographer who had accompanied him, noted that he was often "childish" and "foolhardy" in his manner of exploring. Later, Frémont found the tedium of report writing so difficult that it gave him nosebleeds, and it might have made him more ill had not Jessie helped, taking dictation while he told his stories. Already he and his father-in-law were planning his next expedition west, which would add to his sobriquet "Pathfinder." The entire nation talked about him as if he were half myth, and many years later, after he had crisscrossed America more than any other man of the period, Jessie, his ever faithful booster, would write that, "Cities have risen on the ashes of his lonely campfires."

But every hero has his tragedy, and Frémont had his. He became a millionaire off the California goldfields and served for a short time as governor of California, then later as a senator. He would be the first candidate to run for President with the new Republican party; he lost to James Buchanan in 1856. Yet his own flamboyance and bullheadedness got him in trouble, as he faced a military court-martial after a scrap in California with a West Point man, the equally vain and bullheaded Gen. Stephen Watts Kearny. It was a disgrace that shamed Frémont for the rest of his life.

Years later, as he crafted his *Memoirs of My Life,* Frémont would look back over his career and find that solace in nature, not camaraderie among other men, brought him his happiest moments out West. He remembered his youthful days along the Platte River, those magical times amid the alpine wildflowers of Wyoming. He would write, "I close the page because my path of life led out from among the grand and lovely features of nature, and its pure and wholesome air, into the poisoned atmosphere and jarring circumstances of conflict among men, made subtle and malignant by clashing interests."

Though he didn't find paths so much as make them, and his supposedly scientific expeditions often looked militaristic – in one case with armed men pulling a 12-pound Howitzer cannon – Frémont's contributions to the understanding of the American West were enormous, especially in the field of cartography. Historian William H. Goetzmann noted that he "went west for several reasons, but one of the most important of these was to…make a beginning toward the absolute measurement of its surface topography."

Frémont often managed to lose many of his scientific specimens before leaving the wilderness. And during one expedition into Colorado's San Juan Mountains, he ignored advice from mountain men and pushed into the high country to explore a railroad route for his father-in-law. Trapped by winter snow, he and his party suffered frostbite and starvation, what one man called "days of horror desolation despair." They killed and ate their mules, and by the time they staggered back down to the low country, 10 of 33 men had died. The ordeal should have illuminated Frémont as a bungler, yet it served instead to magnify his image as a resourceful leader who could survive any danger.

Historian Herman J. Viola noted in his book *Exploring the West* that Frémont "succeeded beyond any reasonable expectations as a popularizer of the West." And try as they might, no one could ever replace the Pathfinder in the imagination of the American people. The public devoured his romantic adventures much as later generations devoured the dime novels of Ned Buntline and the stories of Zane Grey. Frémont in fact found writing difficult. He would pace about his study and tell his embellished (and sometimes inaccurate) stories while his faithful wife, Jessie, wrote them down. "I wrote more easily by dictation," Frémont said, which of course meant not writing at all. He explained that writing gave him "too much time to think and dwell upon words as well as ideas." Jessie, on the other hand, was a skilled writer who loved the language. She colored her husband's stories with such drama as to make them gifts not only to a vast compendium of U.S. government reports, but to American literature as well. Through her words the American people also learned about Kit Carson: "Mounted on a fine horse, without a saddle, and scouring bareheaded over the prairies, Kit was one

JOHN C. FRÉMONT

John Charles Frémont was born in Savannah, Georgia, in 1813. He was an unknown surveyor and expedition leader until he married Jessie Benton, daughter of Senator Thomas Hart Benton from Missouri. Thereafter, with strong political ties, Frémont led several expeditions out West, quickly embroiling himself in a California power struggle. His popularity undimmed by a court-martial, he became a millionaire during the California gold rush, and later a senator who strongly opposed slavery. In 1856, as the first presidential candidate for the new Republican Party, he lost to James Buchanan. Frémont eventually lost his fortune as well. He died in 1890 in New York City.

of the finest pictures of a horseman I have ever seen." Herman Viola added that "Frémont's reports, printed by the thousands, were consumed by restless Americans eager to follow the paths into the Far West that he had blazed so dramatically and eloquently."

OTHER EXPLORERS HELPED TO FILL IN THE MAPS. IN 1841 LT. CHARLES Wilkes of the U.S. Navy sailed into Puget Sound with keen interest in the Oregon Territory. Having already charted the waters of Antarctica and hundreds of Pacific islands, he now sent an overland party south to the Willamette Valley, then into California and down the Sacramento River to San Francisco Bay. His four-year expedition, always falling behind schedule and now nearing its end, had earned the name "everlasting expedition." It was the first in U.S. maritime history to combine scientific and naval personnel. Among the nine "scientifics" were James Dwight Dana, the eminent geologist/zoologist, and Titian Ramsey Peale, an artist/naturalist of the distinguished Peale family of Philadelphia. Their finished reports added greatly to an understanding of the Northwest. Still, they defined the expedition less than did Wilkes himself, a moody martinet whom Dana admired for his cartographic skills but criticized for "never praising his officers, but always finding fault with them – and often very unjustly."

Of the six ships that began the expedition, only two would return. One foundered off Cape Horn with all hands lost. One was sent home as unseaworthy; one foundered at the mouth of the Columbia River; and another Wilkes sold in Singapore. In Hawaii, Dana and Peale made valuable impressions of a living volcanic landscape – what would one day be part of Hawaii Volcanoes National Park. Also in Hawaii, after two years at sea under strict discipline, 50 men abandoned the expedition and walked away. "Stormy Petrel" became Wilkes's moniker, and he, like Frémont, suffered a court-martial for his misdeeds. Not once, but twice.

While Frémont and Wilkes lived by rigid codes and made many poor decisions, like Lewis and Clark before them, they saw sights of such profound beauty that each admitted the inadequacy of his own words. The same could be said of explorers Stephen H. Long and Benjamin L. E. Bonneville as they traversed the American West. In 1836, the same year that Emerson published *Nature,* a trapper named Osbourne Russell worked his way into the Lamar Valley – which would one day be part of Yellowstone National Park – and wrote breathlessly, "There is something in the romantic scenery of this valley which I cannot...describe but the impression made upon my mind while gazing from a high eminence on the surrounding landscape one evening as the sun was gently gliding behind the western mountain and casting its

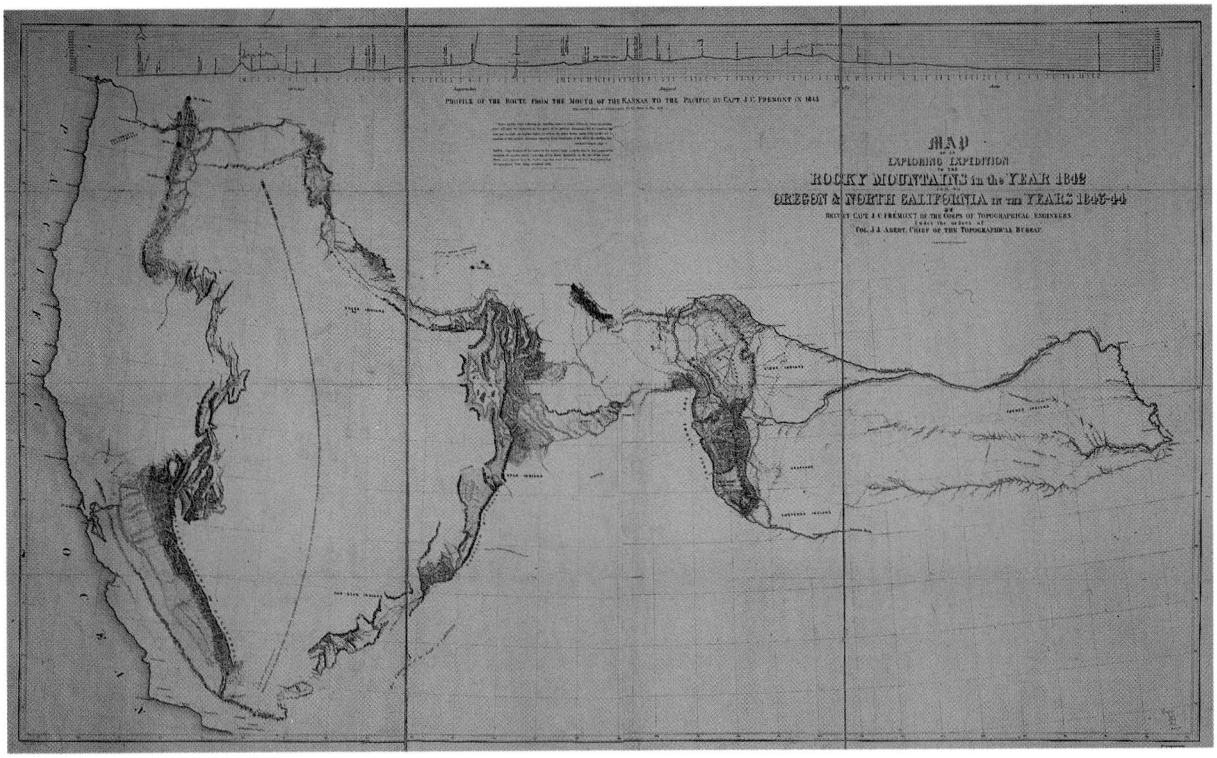

The Frémont-Gibbs-Smith map combined the cartographic knowledge of John C. Frémont with that of mountain man Jedediah Smith. Before Smith died in 1831, he gave his map of the West to George Gibbs, who transcribed the information onto a map by Frémont. For many years this map was the only one to show such knowledge of the American West, due in great part to Smith, the first white man to traverse the Great Basin from the Rockies to California.

gigantic shadows across the vale were such as time can never efface from my memory but as I am neither Poet Painter or Romance writer I must content myself to be what I am a humble journalist and leave this beautiful vale in Obscurity until visited by some more skillful admirer of the beauties of nature."

Journalists added to the breathtaking image of the West when Charles Fenno Hoffman, a New York writer and editor who wanted to see things for himself, traveled to the Mississippi Valley. In letters sent back to the *New York American,* he described a "perfect wilderness" and summarized that if people would only stop to admire what was around them, they too would find a "singular joyousness in a wilderness." So compelling were his descriptions that he collected them into a book, *A Winter in the West.* "I have felt," he said, "among some scenes a kind of selfish pleasure, a wild delight, that the spot so lovely and so lonely...bloomed alone for me." This was a far cry from previous condemnations of wild country, and Hoffman continued his romantic praises when he assumed the helmsmanship at *American Monthly* magazine, in New York City.

At the same time, in the Everglades of southern Florida, a vast, wet region denounced by white settlers as a good-for-nothing "swamp," an Army unit sent in search of Seminole Indians stopped for a rest, and the surgeon among them, able to

Into the Wind River Range of today's Wyoming, German topographer Charles Preuss accompanied John C. Frémont in 1842 and made some sketches. While the peaks of the Wind River Range impressed Frémont, Preuss, who had once toured the Alps, found them less than sensational.

The American Falls on the Snake River, near Fort Hall in the Oregon Territory, is depicted in John C. Frémont's report of his expeditions of 1842-1844. From his field notes, Frémont wrote, "The River here enters between low mural banks, which consist of a fine vesicular trap rock, the intermediate portions being compact and crystalline. Gradually becoming higher in its downward course, these banks of scoriated volcanic rock form, with occasional interruptions, its characteristic feature along the whole line to the Dalles of the Lower Columbia, resembling a chasm which had been rent through the country, and which the river had afterwards taken for its bed."

momentarily deafen himself to the biases of his comrades, described how he "gazed with a mingled emotion of delight and awe" at "the wild romance of nature."

From revulsion to romanticism to expansionism, Americans cycled through a quixotic set of relationships with their land, in some instances with each new generation embracing a new ethos. Yet in most parts of the frontier, attitudes seemed cemented in the past. Historian Roderick Nash noted: "Romantic enthusiasm for wilderness never seriously challenged the aversion in the pioneer mind. Appreciation, rather, resulted from a momentary relaxation of the dominant antipathy. A surprising number of fur traders, for instance, were acquainted with the noble savage convention and occasionally used Indian virtues as a foil for society's shortcomings, but they did not accept the idea as literal truth."

Romanticism was a favorite child of Europeans and Eastern literati, while expansionism became the adopted son of a few persuasive, westward-looking politicians, including Andrew Jackson and Thomas Hart Benton and the flamboyant editor of the *New York Morning News,* John L. O'Sullivan. In 1845 O'Sullivan wrote that it was the "manifest destiny of this nation to overspread the continent allotted by Providence for the free development of our yearly multiplying millions."

Part fantasy and part avarice, Manifest Destiny became a mission to sweep west across North America, if not the entire hemisphere, and repudiate the Old World by remaking it into a new one. Earlier versions of this same sentiment had expressed themselves in other ways – first by the Puritans as a search for religious liberties; then by the Founding Fathers as a principle of government based on the consent of the governed, free of a bothersome and sophomoric aristocracy; then as states' rights against federal encroachment; and finally in the persisting dream of a single nation continent.

Another champion of such thinking was the editor of the *United States Journal,* Theophilus Fisk, who one historian described as a "left-wing Jacksonian, a hard-money man, an anti-clerical...defender of slavery" and an "ultra-expansionist." Any man unburdened by the subjugation of one race by another apparently had little reservations about the conquest of land. Thus, in the spring of 1845, Fisk wrote, "There is a new spirit abroad in the land, young, restless, vigorous and omnipotent.... It sprang from the warm sympathies and high hopes of youthful life, and will dare to take antiquity by the beard, and tear the cloak from hoary-headed hypocrisy. Too young to be corrupt...it is Young America, awakened to a sense of her own intellectual greatness by her soaring spirit. It stands in strength, the voice of the majority.... It demands the immediate annexation of Texas at any and every hazard. It will plant its right foot on the northern verge of Oregon, and its left upon the Atlantic crag, and waving the stars and stripes in the once proud Mistress of the Ocean, bid her, if she dare, 'Cry havoc, and let slip the dogs of war.' "

That same year, 1845, Texas and Florida did indeed gain statehood. Andrew Jackson died, James Polk was inaugurated as the 11th President of the United States – a young flexing nation with roughly 20 million people – and Henry David Thoreau, just shy of his 28th birthday, began to consider a different kind of expansion, one of ideas rather than geography, a discovery of simplicity and staying put, of learning to be home and grounded. On the shore of Walden Pond, not far from his hometown, he borrowed an ax, cleared a piece of forest, built a small cabin, turned his back on the commercialism of Concord, and announced in his journal, "I would rather sit on a pumpkin and have it all to myself, than be crowded on a velvet cushion."

A sketch of Nevada's Pyramid Lake made by Frémont's topographer George Preuss in 1844 shows tufa mounds that 24 years later, in 1867, were captured on film by Timothy O'Sullivan. A former Civil War photographer who worked for Matthew Brady, O'Sullivan later accompanied Clarence King on his Geological Exploration of the 40th Parallel.

Expansion was more than just a westward affair then. The radius of every small town increased yearly, with its perimeter marching toward those of every other town. Like ripples from pebbles dropped in a pool, the reflection was not what it used to be.

"I hear the whistle of the locomotive in the woods," Emerson had written in 1842, the same time Frémont stood atop his mountain in today's Wyoming. "Wherever that music comes it has a sequel. It is the voice of the civility of the Nineteenth Century saying, 'Here I am,' It is the interrogative: it is prophetic: and this Cassandra is believed: "Whew! Whew! Whew!...I will plant a dozen houses on this pasture next noon, and a village anon...."

Also near Concord at this time, Nathaniel Hawthorne settled himself in the woods one July day and performed an experiment. He listened, and recorded what he heard. At first came the musical sounds of birds in the branches, and squirrels, and a wind in the leaves. Then, as his ears sensitized, he heard a distant village clock, and a cowbell, and men cutting grass with their scythes. "But, hark!" he then noted, "There is the whistle of the locomotive – the long shriek, harsh, above all other harshness, for the space of a mile cannot mollify it into harmony. It tells the story of busy men, citizens, from the hot street, who have come to spend a day in a country village, men of business; in short of all unquietness; and no wonder that it gives such a startling shriek, since it brings the noisy world into the midst of our slumbrous peace."

Thoreau also conducted an experiment. Unlike Hawthorne, who listened for an afternoon, Thoreau listened for two years and two months, from July of 1845 until September 1847, while he lived at Walden Pond. "We must learn to reawaken and keep ourselves awake," he wrote, "not by mechanical aids, but by an infinite

KIT CARSON

Born in 1809, the same year as Abraham Lincoln, Kit Carson won his reputation as a trapper, soldier, scout, and Indian agent, surviving many wild adventures to become an American folk hero (opposite). A chance

encounter with John C. Frémont in 1842 tied him inextricably to that man and his grand ambitions. Carson guided Frémont out West three times, and in 1846 found himself pressed into service in the war with Mexico. The Mexicans, who wanted desperately to capture the fearless Carson, called him "the wolf." He later served as a colonel with the Union Army in the Civil War and as superintendent of Indian Affairs for the Colorado Territory, a post he held until he died in 1868.

expectation of the dawn, which does not forsake us in our soundest sleep. I know of no more encouraging fact than the unquestionable ability of man to elevate his life by a conscious endeavor. It is something to be able to paint a particular picture, or to carve a statute, and so to make a few objects beautiful; but it is far more glorious to carve and paint the very atmosphere and medium through which we look, which morally we can do. To affect the quality of the day, that is the highest of arts. Every man is tasked to make his life, even in its details, worthy of the contemplation of his most elevated and critical hour. If we refused, or rather used up, such paltry information as we get, the oracles would distinctly inform us on how this might be done.

"I went to the woods because I wished to live deliberately, to front only the essential facts of life, and see if I could not learn what it had to teach, and not, when I came to die, discover that I had not lived."

He reveled in every detail of his time at Walden. He noted when buds opened and when leaves fell. He apprenticed himself to patterns and cycles. He measured the depth of the pond and spent many hours out there in a small boat, drinking the silence. He kept three chairs in his small cabin, he said, "one for solitude, two for friendship, three for society."

Thoreau questioned the relentless marching of mankind over everything that could be converted or controlled and bought and sold, yet he offered no practical or political solution to escape this way of life. As Emerson had said, he believed that "the whole of nature is a metaphor for the human mind." Wilderness, then, represented every capacity undiscovered in every individual. But how to apply those alternatives to the men who made the machines?

On occasion Thoreau would walk from Walden into Concord to have dinner at Emerson's house, and he walked on railroad tracks. Midway through his two-year experiment, he went to jail for one night to protest slavery. Soon after, he journeyed north to Maine – the first of three trips there – to taste truly primeval America. Rather than feeling exuberant, he found himself daunted by the severe scope and degree of hostile country. It shocked him. Climbing Mount Katahdin, he described woods "even more grim and wild than... anticipated, a deep and intricate wilderness...savage and dreary."

Back in Massachusetts, Thoreau began to rethink how mankind could live with one foot in wilderness and one in civilization, simultaneously benefiting from the vitality of open air and the intellectual stimulation of good company. "The natural remedy," he decided, "is to be found in the proportion which the night bears to the day, the winter to the summer, thought to experience."

After his night in jail, Thoreau wrote his well-known essay, *Civil Disobedience,* which

began: "I heartily accept the motto, – 'That government is best which governs least;' and I should like to see it acted up to more rapidly and systematically. Carried out, it finally amounts to this, which also I believe, – 'That government is best which governs not at all;' and when men are prepared for it, that will be the kind of government which they will have. Government is at best but an expedient; but most governments are usually, and all governments are sometimes, inexpedient."

No. 230
No. 230
Munro's Ten Cent Novels
KIT CARSON, THE SGOUT.
GEORGE MUNRO, PUBLISHER, 84 Beekman Street N. Y.
THE AMERICAN NEWS CO., New York.

His words slid into the American consciousness as a little voice in the back of our heads saying, "Is bigger better?" "Must we plow and pave it all?" He lived to see none of his sweeping influence, and no doubt would have been alarmed, or at least surprised, when the federal government became the instrument of conservation that established national parks, saving those places that would one day be the largest islands of wilderness and biodiversity remaining in a sea of spreading monoculture and capitalism. Furthermore, that railroads would play a significant role in the establishment of those parks would have surprised him as well.

Historians today refer to the "Crusoe fantasy" and "Walden instinct" as examples of iconoclastic yet untenable sentiments. They are, as one historian added, "an appeal buried in every member of the high civilization, buried in every human being: the impulse to knock down the building blocks so painfully erected.... Strictly speaking, these feelings are delusive. Crusoe had a shipful of civilized products or he would have perished, just as Thoreau brought with him an ax, a bag of nails, some beans, and other forms of capital. But feelings are stronger than facts when it is a question of bringing a civilization to its close; for the particular feelings that demand renewal at any cost have behind them the tremendous force of unreasoning hate against what must seem to a passionate man an endless series of cages. 'I feel something within me,' said the Chieftain from the North, 'that compels me to burn Rome.' "

In truth, Crusoe and Thoreau didn't harbor hate, and they didn't wish to burn Rome or sack Concord; they were simply disillusioned, and at times disheartened. Thoreau walked into his jail cell freely, spent a night, and later wrote that while the

After traveling with Charles Wilkes's United States Exploring Expedition in 1840, Titian R. Peale painted a fiery Kilauea volcano on the flank of Hawaii's Mauna Loa, site of today's Hawaii Volcanoes National Park. Of the six ships that embarked on Wilkes's expedition, only two returned home. The son of the famous artist and naturalist Charles Willson Peale, Titian had earlier accompanied Maj. Stephen H. Long on his expedition to the Rocky Mountains in 1819-20. While in Hawaii Titian and the others found excellent scientific collecting; they returned home with specimens of several bird species that later became extinct.

authorities could lock up his body, they could never imprison his mind. His experiences in Maine – not his night in jail – are what moderated him. He knew that the juggernaut of commerce would not gear down in his lifetime. The trick, as he saw it, was to find a balance between the extremes of wilderness and civilization and to live in that balance without remorse. The national park movement, indeed the entire American political conservation movement, at least in a political sense, would postdate him. But his fluid ideas helped to birth it and water it from infancy to its adolescence of today, giving others the inspiration and language required to create something that had never been created before. Not a King's Forest, but a people's forest, an unprecedented commons that belonged to everyone and to no one, if they could keep it. And not so much something created, but rather something left as it was – nature unaltered and untrammeled. "A man is rich in proportion to the number of things that he can afford to let alone," Thoreau said. And people began to listen.

Soon after his stay at Walden, gold was discovered in California, and locusts of dreamers headed west, some overland by wagon and foot, some around Cape Horn by ship and sail – the choice for many determined by how they least wished to die: scalping or shipwreck. The exodus made manifest destiny a fait accompli, fulfilling Jefferson's dream of a sea-to-sea nation within a quarter century of his death.

What a rich and breathtaking and sometimes unforgiving land these pioneers found: the tallgrass prairie, the Rocky Mountains, the Cascades volcanoes, the Colorado Plateau, the California coast, the Sonoran Desert, the Dakota badlands, the Great Basin, the Sierra Nevada; they also came across aspen groves, salt flats, gypsum dunes, basalt colonnade, granite domes, red slickrock, stairstep waterfalls, riparian cottonwoods, bobcats, grizzly bears, coyotes, condors, antelope, clouds of geese, and bison in such vast numbers that they filled the plains – and the dreams of those who saw them.

The stolid accounts of some pioneers provided unembellished authenticity to the padded reports of official military expeditions that had passed that way before. Added to these were specimens of plants, birds, mammals, and fossils collected by naturalists who sometimes risked their lives to inventory the American ark: John Kirk Townsend, Thomas Nuttall, Spencer Fullerton Baird, and John James Audubon, to name a few. In 1850 Baird arrived at the Smithsonian Institution in Washington, D.C., with two boxcars of specimens, including a bird skin of the colorful Carolina parakeet, a species that would be extinct by the early 1900s.

The following year, in 1851, a military patrol in pursuit of Indians stumbled into California's Yosemite Valley and stared awestruck at the wondrous granite walls and

After stopping in the Hawaiian Islands, the Exploring Expedition arrived in the Pacific Northwest in 1841. Lt. Charles Wilkes commissioned an overland party to be "satisfied [that Oregon]...was to be full part and parcel of our country." Artist Joseph Drayton's rendering depicts a member of that party and an Indian guide standing before the forests and a volcano of the Cascade Range.

In this 1844 engraving by William E. Tucker, Charles Wilkes's expedition members find impressive trees in Oregon. Though entitled "Pine Forest," the engraving was likely inspired by Douglas fir, western hemlock, or Sitka spruce. Such artistry made its way from government documents into popular books and helped to fuel a rush for tall timber. A century and a half later 90 percent of the old-growth forest of the Pacific Northwest would be logged out, and in some cases entire watersheds were stripped of every tree.

domes, the ribbonlike waterfalls that streaked down naked rock and seemed to fall from heaven itself. Nearly 20 years earlier, in 1833, a mountain man named Joseph Walker had crossed the Sierra Nevada and witnessed the valley from above and said little of it. But this patrol, as far as anybody knew, was the first time white men had entered the valley and grasped its full majesty. Stories of the discovery rippled though California, and the first tourists began trekking into the high country not to cross the mountains, but to see them.

In Wisconsin, a young lad of 13 worked sunup to sundown on his family farm, toiling under the strict demands of his Calvinist father. His family had immigrated from Scotland, and upon first seeing his new home the boy remembered, "Nature streaming into us...every wild lesson a love lesson, not whipped but charmed into us. Oh, that glorious Wisconsin wilderness." His name was John Muir, and he would someday have a lot to say about Yosemite, and national parks.

So would Frederick Law Olmsted. Sixteen years older than Muir and five younger than Thoreau, he was a landscape architect before the profession existed, and an outspoken critic of slavery. His greatest influence would be in American cities; yet like Muir he would also shape national parks and illuminate ways in which people could live in nature, not apart from nature.

Only two days after John Muir's 13th birthday, on April 23, 1851, Thoreau stepped to the lectern before the Concord Lyceum and said in his soft voice, "I wish to speak a word for Nature, for absolute freedom and wildness." The crowd fell silent as the stoop-shouldered man went on. "Let me live where I will...on this side is the city, on that the wilderness, and ever I am leaving the city more and more." He ended with a powerful summation, "In wildness is the preservation of the world."

He did not say wilderness, but wildness, an important distinction.

Whereas wilderness is a state of land, wildness is the human relationship with that land – the implication being that without wildness we could retain no understanding of where we came from, and thus would have an incomplete picture of where we were going; in time the world that nurtured us would perish. Wild America was slipping away, and with it a valuable part of our history and memory. The idea that we could consume habitat to the point of eliminating another species from the face of the Earth was incomprehensible for most people in the mid-19th century. Yet entire landscapes were already disappearing, and with them entire cultures and ways of life.

It would take a tremendous struggle to turn the tide toward conservation and preservation. Henry David Thoreau raised the banner. John Muir would raise the sword.

CHAPTER THREE

A Grand, Good Thing

A DECADE BEFORE THOREAU ISSUED HIS DICTUM, "IN WILDNESS IS THE PRESERVATION OF THE WORLD," A LARGELY UNKNOWN WRITER, HERMAN MELVILLE, FINISHED HIS NOVEL, *MOBY DICK,* AS A PAEAN TO THE SEA AND THE FOLLY OF THOSE WHO TRIED TO TAME IT. THE BOOK OPENS WITH A YOUNG MAN NAMED ISHMAEL WHO WALKS DOWN TO THE DOCKS TO JOIN A WHALING SHIP UNDER THE COMMAND OF A PEG-LEGGED CAPTAIN AHAB –TWO FICTIONAL CHARACTERS WHO WOULD SOON SAIL INTO AMERICAN LITERARY LEGEND. "IS THERE NO GREEN THING TO BE SEEN?" ASKS ISHMAEL EARLY ON. TIRED OF INDUSTRIAL AMERICA, HE SPEAKS OF SATURDAY

A scheme "to annihilate magnificent distances," a railroad runs west to the future, across arid America.

May 10, 1869, a momentous day in America: Locomotives of the Central Pacific and the Union Pacific touch cowcatchers at Promontory, Utah, bridging a nation sea to sea by transcontinental railroad. In the center two men hoist bottles of champagne, while Samuel S. Montagne of the C. P. shakes hands with Grenville M. Dodge of the U. P. By 1870, the first full year of operation, 150,000 passengers would ride the line from Omaha, Nebraska, to Sacramento, California, reducing a six-month journey to less than one week.

afternoons when men like himself would stand about the Manhattan waterfront and stare at the sea, imprisoned by "days pent up in lath and plaster – tied to counters, nailed to benches, clinched to desks. How then is this? Are the green fields gone?"

The sea, of course, was the ultimate commons. Global and seemingly inexhaustible, it became what Melville called the "watery pastures," where restless men go to sing their shanties, but also their requiems, each to himself. At the end of the book a great disaster befalls Ahab and his crew, with every man lost save Ishmael, who floats on a life-buoy coffin, a carefully crafted contradiction.

Historian Leo Marx has observed: "In accomplishing Ishmael's 'salvation,' Melville in effect puts his blessing upon the Ishmaelian view of life: a complex pastoralism in which the ideal is inseparably yoked to its opposite. It is a doctrine that arises at the 'vital centre' of experience. At the same time Melville acknowledges the political ineffectuality of the symbol-maker's truth. Ishmael survives, to be sure, but as an 'orphan' floating helplessly on the margins of the scene as society flounders. Of the qualities necessary for survival, Melville endows Ahab with the power and Ishmael with the wisdom. Ishmael is saved as Job's messengers had been saved, in order that he may deliver to us a warning of disasters to come."

In that year of 1851, two decades had passed since the artist George Catlin first spoke of the national park idea. Another two would pass before a group of visionary men, camping amid Yellowstone's geysers and thermal pools, would suggest a political campaign for the establishment of a national park. A sense of urgency pervaded their words and exists to this day in the writings of Melville and Thoreau. Each was influenced by Emerson and Hawthorne. Each harbored deep concerns about how America expressed her patriotism and the direction industry was taking her, and what she might lose along the way. The national park idea would indeed become yoked to its opposite, as conservation is to development and parks are to railroads. And as commerce spread across the land, each park would become an orphan of sorts, surrounded by a vast sea of more intense development, like Ishmael alone and barely afloat, a survivor.

A suspension bridge was already under construction over Niagara Falls, which would not have surprised Alexis de Tocqueville, who found little in America that was not for sale. Isaac Singer had devised the first continuous-stitch sewing machine. And James Fenimore Cooper, as if he were Leatherstocking himself, the last of a dying breed, died.

Novelist Mary Shelley also died that year. The author of *Frankenstein,* she had raised a question not lost on the moralists of her day: Beyond experimentation and the sanctity of science, did technology render nothing sacred? Would mortal men someday feel compelled – perhaps obligated – to play God and create an immortal man? Would they consummate their love affair with a machine so perfect as to become one and the same: man and machine, a half thing/half man with no beginning and no end? In Mary Shelley's story the monster is imperfect and dies. But had he – had it – been made properly, he would have lived forever. Was this then the end point of technology, to make things faster, bigger, and stronger until human beings removed themselves so far from nature that they would never grow ill and never die?

About this time William Thomson, later Lord Kelvin, began his papers on the conservation of energy. Yet few voices beyond New England's transcendentalists and Europe's primitivists and others such as Melville, with his clever nuance and metaphor, spoke of the conservation of nature itself. Thoreau's dictum left no room for false interpretation, as he intended. What Melville implied, Thoreau stated. If we cannot recognize the value of those wild places that have nurtured us through the ages, he said, and save a few along the way, then we will lose forever any understanding of where we came from and who we truly are and what we should – and should not – become. Somewhere between Leatherstocking and Frankenstein, trees and timber, wilderness and bewilderment, Americans needed a moral compass to understand where they should go and what they could become without losing every vestige of who they once had been. The implications of a we-can-build-anything culture were not so obvious to the common man bent over his daily chores and ledgers, but to anti-industrialists and others who listened to nature rather than to themselves, they were frightening. Where would it end? Was everything in nature expendable, not just the inhabitants but the processes as well? If so, would people someday stop birthing their children and manufacture them instead?

NO MACHINE SO EPITOMIZED AMERICAN OPTIMISM AND ENGENDERED more debate in the 1850s than the railroad, especially the idea of a railroad running west to the Pacific, a scheme "to annihilate magnificent distances." The idea that a Bostonian could someday buy a railroad ticket to California and be there within a week seemed, to one source, "as remote as the fantasies of Jules Verne." Ahead lay deserts, mountains, canyons, Indians. "A railroad to the Pacific," a prominent government official scoffed, "I would not buy a ticket on it for my grandchildren."

Author Keith Wheeler observed: "What the skeptics overlooked – and a handful of visionaries and vigorous entrepreneurs did not – was that with the help of federal loans and land grants the job could be done in short order. Settlement, like water flowing into an irrigation ditch, would surely follow."

For many, the railroad was the essence of growth and goodness running with force and character to the future. In 1853, amid what one observer called "intense factionalism and rivalry and skirmishes over proposed route proposals," Congress appropriated $150,000 to the Pacific Railroad Survey bill, to determine the "most practical and economical" routes across the trans-Mississippi West to the golden shores of the Pacific. Three routes were explored that summer, with Isaac I. Stevens, the young governor of Washington Territory, exploring a northern route championed by Senator Stephen A. Douglas. Capt. John Gunnison followed the 38th parallel (a route proposed years before by Senator Thomas Hart Benton and John C. Frémont). And Lt. Amiel Weeks Whipple followed the 35th parallel. A southernmost fourth route along the 32nd parallel favored by Secretary of War Jefferson Davis was not explored until the following year.

Tensions ran high where white settlers had encroached upon Indian homelands. "The surveyors appreciated the risks and did their best both to protect themselves and to allay the fears of the Indians with whom they came in contact," said one observer, "but...nerves were always on edge. On one occasion four men with Governor Stevens were so convinced an Indian was stalking them through the tall grass that they followed the old western maxim, 'Shoot first and ask questions later.' Approaching their supposedly well-riddled target they discovered only an irate skunk, which promptly made them unfit for polite society."

Gunnison's party should have been more watchful. While camped in Utah's Sevier River valley one October morning, they were attacked by revengeful Paiutes who killed Gunnison and seven other men. His body pierced by 15 arrows, Gunnison became a symbol of Indian atrocity. As word of the "massacre" spread, few industrialists and expansionists sympathized with the Paiute sentiment – that the leader of the attacking party had lost his father to murderous settlers only days before he attacked Gunnison. And again few listened when Chief Seattle appealed to President Franklin Pierce, saying "tell your children that the earth is rich with the lives of our kin. Teach your children what we have taught our children, that the earth is our mother. Whatever befalls the earth befalls the sons of the earth." About this same time, the Committee on Indian Affairs, aware that the United States would quickly run out of land to relocate Indians, proposed that the "only alternative to extinction" was to settle "colonized tribes on government-run reservations" administered by the federal government.

George Catlin's dream of a national park, what he called "some great protecting policy," applied not just to landscapes but to people as well. He sought to protect both

Leipzig.

Felsformation in der Nähe der Mündung von Bill Willia

A topographer, artist, and naturalist, Heinrich Baldwin Mollhausen traveled with Lt. Amiel Weeks Whipple in 1853 to reconnoiter a railroad route along the 35th parallel. Four years later he steamed up the Colorado River with Lt. Joseph Christmas Ives and entered the lower reaches of the Grand Canyon, a region "whose strange sublimity," wrote Ives, "is perhaps unparalleled in any part of the world." Having gained an acute appreciation of the desert, Mollhausen in 1860 painted "Felsformation in der Nahe der Mündung von Bill Williams fork" as a tribute to the wondrous plant and wildlife of the American Southwest. The chromolithograph at left is based on Mollhausen's painting.

the Great Plains and the Plains Indians. To him, each was an essential part of the other. Years later as an old man, after he was relocated to a reservation, the great chief Red Cloud would lament, "You see this barren waste.... Think of it! I, who used to own rich soil in a well-watered country so extensive that I could not ride through it in a week on my fastest pony, am put down here! Why, I have to go five miles for wood for my fire. Washington took our lands and promised to feed and support us. Now I, who used to control 5,000 warriors, must tell Washington when I am hungry. I must beg for that which I own. If I beg hard, they put me in the guard house.... Coughing sickness every winter carries away our best people. My heart is heavy. I am old, I cannot do much more."

And so the railroads came. And with them arrived a flood of white people who, whether they intended to or not, acted as a huge force of ecological and cultural erosion and deposition. Each Pacific Railroad Survey commander announced that his route was the best for a transcontinental railroad. Jefferson Davis endorsed the southern route, which surprised no one, despite the fact that part of it crossed Mexican territory. Davis solved the problem by arranging for a colleague, James Gadsen, the U.S. Minister of Mexico, to negotiate a purchase of the area for ten million dollars. Infuriated, Senator Benton said the southern route was "so utterly desolate, desert, and God-forsaken that Kit Carson says a wolf could not make his living on it." Only military men, he said, could be so stupid. "It takes a grand national school like West Point to put national roads outside of a country and leave the interior without one."

Not until 1869, after a devastating Civil War, would a single rail line span the continent. It followed closely the 38th parallel, the route advocated by Benton and Frémont and surveyed by Gunnison. The other routes would win their railroads too, all in the 1880s, as tendrils of steel sewed America into a single industrial quilt. "Perhaps the most immediate beneficiary of the Pacific Railroad Surveys was the nation's scientific community," wrote historian Herman J. Viola in *Exploring the West,* "for the work of the Topographical Engineers and their civilian associates was memorialized in 13 often lavishly illustrated volumes issued between 1855 and 1860. A veritable encyclopedia of the West, these volumes offered narrative accounts of the individual expeditions as well as detailed reports on geology, botany, animals, and fishes, and ethnographic reports on Indian tribes. In scientific terms, the Pacific Railroad Reports marked the advent of specialization and teamwork in the study of the natural sciences. They also represented a cartographic milestone, as each expedition produced a detailed map of the country it surveyed."

With exploration of the American West came its careful cousin, inventory: the collection, examination, and storage of thousands of specimens of native flora and fauna. A sense of urgency pervaded this work, as the men who directed it – Spencer Fullerton Baird, Joseph Henry, Joseph Leidy, Asa Gray, George Engelmann, and others – grasped the potential irreversible impacts of human settlement on habitats and natural landscapes. In 1850, the year that Spencer Fullerton Baird arrived in Washington, the Smithsonian had about 6,000 plant and animal specimens inside its walls. Eight years later that number would exceed 70,000. As many as one thousand professional and amateur collectors sent materials to Baird over the years. He often worked on Christmas and New Year's when the offices were quiet and he could get more done. An indefatigable correspondent, he wrote more than three thousand letters in one year. He personally advised, trained, and outfitted many collectors, and in 1855 alone received nearly 500 packages of specimens. His daughter once commented on his attention to detail, noting that "No bride ever devoted more thought and attention to her trousseau than did my father to the fitting out of each of these explorers, and he watched the progress of each with anxious personal interest."

In 1856 Baird recommended a young naturalist named Ferdinand V. Hayden to the Army's Corps of Topographical Engineers. It might have seemed an odd sponsorship, as Hayden, unlike most Corps officers, was not a West Point man, let alone a military man. A dedicated naturalist and graduate of the Albany Medical School, he had presented himself to Baird three years before, writing: "I feel as though I could endure cheerfully any amount of toil, hardship, and self denial provided I could gratify my strong desire to labor in the field as a naturalist." In particular, he wanted to pursue paleontology, the study of geological history written with fossils in stone. "But I am poor," he added, "dependent entirely on my own exertions for my support, and every longing desire to engage in that most delightful of pursuits to me must be smothered by poverty.... I am willing to go anywhere, for any length of time and labor with the utmost diligence.... I have taken considerable pains to prepare myself for a collector."

Regrettably, Baird at that time could offer him no position. He suggested that the young man enlist in the Army. Hayden accepted instead an offer from the Upper Missouri Indian agent to work in the Dakotas. In less than two months he collected more than 500 plant specimens and "many rare fossils," all while trespassing in Sioux country. He must have appeared absurd to some. "I...wander off alone for miles...," he wrote, "with a Bag in one hand, Pick in the other, a bottle of Alcohol in my vest pocket, and with a gun to defend myself from Indians and Grizzly Bears." One day while engrossed in his digging, Hayden failed to see a band of Sioux warriors

continued on page 116

ALBERT BIERSTADT

Artist Albert Bierstadt was a creator of grand panoramas who filled his canvases with lush green vegetation, cobalt-blue water, and heavenly mountains. Born in Prussia in 1830, Bierstadt immigrated to the U.S. and was among the last

generation of the Hudson River School of artists. His restlessness quickly took him West where he paid more attention to formula than to accuracy. He freely and unapologetically altered details to create awe and grandeur in his work. His dramatic scenes of Yosemite and the Rocky Mountains (right) helped to win national sentiment for their protection as parks. Bierstadt died in New York City in 1902.

The high hopes and expectations of westering Americans reached their fullest romantic expression in Albert Bierstadt's 1867 oil on canvas, "Emigrants Crossing the Plains," created nearly 20 years after the California gold rush. Bierstadt probably captured a piece of his own nostalgia in this painting. While his first trip out West in 1859 had taken five months by wagon and horseback, his third, by train in 1871, required only six days. Something had been gained but also lost. An era had come and gone, taking many forgotten names and stories with it.

1867, EMIGRANTS CROSSING THE PLAINS, *oil on canvas*

continued from page 111
surround him. Suddenly at a disadvantage, he stood his ground as the Sioux took his bag and emptied it. When a pile of rocks fell at their feet, the Sioux laughed at the obviously addle-brained scientist and named him, "man who picks up stones running." It humored them more than it did Hayden. They let him go.

That winter at Fort Pierre, Hayden sorted his specimens and compiled his field notes, with his geology manuscript running to more than a hundred pages. Although many of his specimens were lost or damaged during shipment back East, his work nonetheless impressed Baird, who arranged for him to travel west with Lt. Gouverneur K. Warren. Warren was an able cartographer, and Hayden an adept collector. They got along famously during the trip, but their relationship soured upon their return when Warren felt that Hayden was trying to garner all of the credit. Hayden then traveled west under the command of Capt. William F. Raynolds, in the last expedition of the Corps of Topographical Engineers, and again he proved to be contentious. "Such expeditions as these," he noted, "are great things to bring out the weaknesses of human nature." One of the expedition's objectives was "Colter's Hell," the headwaters of the Yellowstone River, where the Earth was said to boil with geothermal activity. But early autumn snows turned the expedition back, a great disappointment to the ambitious Hayden.

"Raynolds may not have found a wagon-route across the Dakotas during his two year reconnaissance," wrote Herman Viola, "but he did bring government scientists into the last major unexplored region of the Far West. His expedition, in fact, marked a transition between two eras of western exploration, the one dominated by soldier explorers like Frémont, Gunnison, and Warren, the other by scientists and civilians. Hayden...remained an important force in western scientific explorations, but he had to share the limelight with a new generation of scientists that emerged after the Civil War and included scholars such as John Wesley Powell and Clarence King as well as their young and enthusiastic assistants."

WHILE AUTUMN SNOWS REBUFFED RAYNOLDS AND HAYDEN FROM Yellowstone, tourists trickled into California's Yosemite Valley. Only 180 miles east of the muddy, bustling streets of San Francisco, the valley had kept its secret until the Mariposa Battalion entered it in 1851 and 1852 in pursuit of Miwok-Paiute Indians. Hearing the stories of the Mariposa men, entrepreneurs soon arrived in their tweed suits and derby hats, saddle sore from long miles through rough country. Waterfalls and bird songs filled the valley with sweet music and no doubt astounded the most prosaic of them. Yet amid such glorious scenery they imagined a new music to come

– the ringing of cash registers. They said Yosemite Valley would become the finest tourist destination in all of California, a gold mine in itself. "They saw it not merely as sublime scenery, as the early visitors to the White Mountains or Niagara Falls had done, but imagined its future development," wrote historian John F. Sears in *Sacred Places.* "They had a clear sense of what kind of places made successful tourist attractions, how they were made known, and how they were likely to develop."

An early Yosemite booster was James Hutchings, a writer and publisher whose descriptions of Yosemite's "wild and sublime grandeur" appeared in the *Mariposa Gazette.* He invited an artist into the valley, Thomas A. Ayers. In 1859 the first photographer, Charles Leander Weed, arrived, who took about 20 11-by-14-inch glass plate photographs and 40 stereographs, which appeared in three dimensions when viewed through an optical instrument. The images became a sensation in San Francisco. By 1856 a wagon and carriage trail ran from Mariposa to Yosemite, and the valley had its first hotel. Hutchings often quoted visitors who gazed at the granite walls and idyllic valley floor and saw the Earth transformed as predicted in Revelations. Said one: " 'What, have we come to the end of all things?' Said another: 'Can this be the opening of the Seventh Seal?' "

"Yosemite's rapid ascent to the status of a national monument depended not so much on Hutchings's direct efforts to promote it," wrote Sears, "as on the attention it received from other writers, painters, and photographers partly as a result of his campaign." Horace Greeley, the famous editor, visited the valley in 1859 and published his accounts in the *New York Tribune,* exclaiming to a readership of nearly 300,000 that Yosemite was the "most unique and majestic of nature's marvels." Next came Thomas Starr King, a Boston churchman, Lyceum lecturer, and established travel writer whose prose received praise from critics and the public alike. He moved to San Francisco, visited Yosemite, and exclaimed upon seeing the sweeping face of El Capitan, sentinel of the valley, "Great is granite, and the Yo-Semite is its prophet."

King enjoyed immediate authority with his readership. Perhaps more than any other single writer, he placed Yosemite in a pantheon of national scenic treasures and found his descriptions quoted in America and Europe. Readers praised him, as did sightseers whose numbers swelled into a pilgrimage. Few if any were disappointed. When the photographer Carleton Watkins visited in 1861, his well-composed images won favor back East among a gentry in the midst of a brutal war between the states, a conflict they thought would last months, not years. Yosemite offered something positive and hopeful; if God could create such a heaven on Earth, could He also end the bloodshed? During the middle of the war, Albert Bierstadt, a student of the Hudson River School, arrived to paint the valley. "We are going into the vale," wrote companion Fitz-Hugh Ludlow, "whose giant domes and battlements had months before thrown their photographic shadow through Watkins's camera across the mysterious wide continent, causing exclamations of awe at Goupil's window, and ecstasy in Dr. Holmes's study." Bierstadt's paintings were said by one reviewer to have "lent literal and as well as fanciful elegance" to the waterfalls and granite cliffs of Yosemite.

The first published view of Yosemite Valley came from an October 1855 lithograph, "Yo-Hamite Falls" (above), based on a drawing by Thomas A. Ayers. Publisher James Mason Hutchings used Ayers's work to help attract sightseers into the valley. Nine years later Albert Bierstadt painted the same scene (opposite). A newspaper reported: "Bierstadt...is one of the most indefatigable workers among the artists – for even in mid-June the days are not sufficiently long for his purpose."

On the heels of exploitation came preservation, the fight to save Yosemite Valley from the very men who sought to sell it. "The decision not only to admire nature but to preserve it required stronger incentives," wrote historian Alfred Runte in his acclaimed book, *National Parks: the American Experience.* "Specifically, the impulse to bridge the gap between appreciation and protection needed catalysts of unquestionable drama and visibility." In September of 1863, not long after Bierstadt first arrived, one of those catalysts departed New York City on a steamship bound for California, a journey of one month around Cape Horn, fair winds provided. He was Frederick Law Olmsted, 41 years of age, co-creator with Calvert Vaux of New York City's Central Park.

The son of a prosperous Connecticut family, Olmsted had schooled at Yale and was on a career track that would one day make him America's premier designer and advocate of urban parks. As a young man he had traveled to China and Europe, and before that, as a boy with his family, he had visited Niagara Falls. Only 28 when he first saw Europe, it astounded him. In Paris and London he found parks that were once the exclusive property of royalty and now belonged to the public. "Another impressive milestone on the road to landscape democracy in Great Britain," wrote Alfred Runte of Olmsted's experience, "was Victoria Park, carved from London's crowded East End...it was the first reserve not only managed, but expressly purchased for public instead of private use." In Liverpool, a delighted Olmsted found the same at Birkenhead Park, a place he said was "entirely, unreservedly, and forever the people's own. The poorest British peasant is as free to enjoy it in all its parts as the British queen.... Is it not," he asked, "a grand, good thing?"

From the heart of Manhattan Island the New York legislature had set aside a rectangle of land on the outskirts of the metropolis, and with it Olmsted created Central Park. From rundown farms, pig sties, and garbage dumps emerged a harmony of walkways, gardens, fields, bridges, ponds, rambles, and meadows to afford refuge from the noise and crowding of a growing city. Yosemite would be different, however.

Eadweard Muybridge photographed Albert Bierstadt (below) while he sketched Indians in council in Mariposa, near Yosemite, in 1872 (left). In the spirit of George Catlin, Bierstadt's paintings often countered the idea of Manifest Destiny by showing no scenes with a human element, or if any, only Indians in the dark twilight of their ways of life.

FREDERICK LAW OLMSTED

A landscape architect before the profession existed, Frederick Law Olmsted created many of America's famous urban open spaces: New York City's Central Park, the Stanford University campus, Asheville's Biltmore Estate, and others. Born in Connecticut in 1822, he suffered from sumac poisoning at age 14 and nearly lost his eyesight. In his early 30s he toured the American South for the New York Times. *An outspoken opponent of slavery, he co-founded* The Nation *magazine and earned a strong reputation for his humanitarian views. From 1864 until 1890 he chaired the first Yosemite Park Commission and helped to steer Yosemite Valley away from crass commercialism. He died in 1903 at age 81.*

In a national park one needed to work with what was already there, to complement rather than create. Visitors from Europe and the East Coast found the mountains of the West – the Rockies, Cascades, and Sierra Nevada – utterly fantastic, especially in the eastern Sierra and the Colorado front range where the peaks rose without preamble or foothills. Otherwise verbose men found themselves speechless before waterfalls more than a thousand feet high, canyons more than a mile deep, and deep cathedral-like forests pillared by trees that had been saplings at the time of Christ. The urge to make such places national parks was to sanctify them in whatever manner a man could achieve, to offer some form of protection, not recreation, as was the aim in urban parks.

Olmsted did not go west to work on Yosemite, but rather to manage the Mariposa Estate, a huge enterprise that included a gold mine and was once owned by John C. Frémont. Like many easterners, he expected life in California to be less than civilized, even barbarous. Diagnosed in San Francisco with an enlarged heart due to a sedentary life and irregular eating, he was told that he would be an invalid the rest of his life unless he reduced his writing and other stressful "brain-work" as much as possible. After his wife, Mary, and their children arrived, he decided to take a vacation. By horseback they traveled to the South Fork of the Merced River, then camped at what is today called Wawona Meadow – at a ranch that belonged to Galen Clark, a friendly frontiersman, the first white man to discover the nearby Mariposa Big Tree Grove of giant sequoias. Upon seeing the trees, Mary exclaimed, "I know of no simile to convey to you an idea of the effect these trees produce on one.... They are like cathedral columns or gigantic organ pipes." That night in camp, she said the campfire "Lighted up the giant tree, the effect was sublime and kept one awake in spite of the fatigue of the day." From there the party proceeded into Yosemite Valley. They camped opposite the base of Yosemite Falls, at 2,245 feet, the highest waterfall in North America. "Of course," wrote Olmsted, "it is awfully grand, but it is not frightful or fearful." He found the valley "sweet & peaceful as the meadows of the Avon."

"The unique and affecting charm of Yosemite," wrote Witold Rybczynski, an Olmsted biographer, "...is that it is both wilderness and landscape. The craggy vastness of the chasm is older than any human presence, yet the valley floor appears comfortably domesticated. Olmsted appreciated this curious contrast; he and Vaux had created precisely this effect in Central Park, where the wilderness of the Ramble was side by side with pastoral meadows."

Olmsted's health gradually improved, and he soon found himself heading the Yosemite Commission. At the same time, Senator John Conness from California introduced legislation to grant Yosemite Valley and the Mariposa Big Tree Grove to the State of California "for public use, resort and recreation…inalienable for all time." Amid the distractions of the Civil War, Congress quietly passed, and President Lincoln signed, the Yosemite Park Act of 1864. "It is the will of the nation," wrote Olmsted in his advisory report completed the next year, "that this scenery shall never be private property, but that like certain defensive points upon our coast it shall be held solely for public purposes." He predicted with tremendous foresight that "before many years" the hundreds of visitors who visit the valley annually "will become thousands, and in a century the whole number of visitors will be counted in the millions."

The same month Olmsted joined the Yosemite Commission, he accepted a job to design a public cemetery in Oakland. The money interested him, but more than that he liked the challenge. Many cities back East had found cemeteries a solace for the human spirit, where urban dwellers could open their hearts free from the congestion of daily commerce. It was a special commons, a place to say good-bye, and Olmsted recognized their relationship to natural cathedrals like Yosemite. As one observer noted, "If the nation could provide parklands for the dead, parklands for the living might also be realized."

The trick in Yosemite would be to avoid another Niagara Falls, with its hucksters and curio shops and cleared forests at the most scenic spots. Olmsted did not oppose development on purist sentiment, he merely sought to control and channel it. He supported the idea of an approach road to Yosemite, but maintained the importance of "preservation and maintenance…of the natural scenery." His advisory report concluded that "The enjoyment of scenery employs the mind without fatigue and yet exercises it; tranquilizes it and yet enlivens it; and thus, through the influence of the mind over the body, gives the effect of refreshing rest and reinvigoration of the whole system."

Olmsted resigned his position with the Yosemite Commission in 1865 and returned East to his beloved Central Park. Yosemite lost a champion of preservation, but three years later another arrived to replace him. More of an eccentric than a professional landscape architect, John Muir had intense blue eyes, like Olmsted, and was deeply passionate about nature's healing influences. A few weeks shy of 30 that memorable spring of 1868, he landed by steamer in San Francisco on what he called the "wild side of the continent." He walked across the Central Valley into the Sierra Nevada, "the Range of Light," and Yosemite Valley, "that most holy mansion of the mountains." Muir stayed in the valley only ten days that first year. Little is written of his impressions, but they must have been profound as he would soon marry himself

The famous geologist Josiah Whitney said it was created by catastrophic down faulting; John Muir said glaciers did it. Regardless of its creation, Yosemite Valley became an icon of the American sublime, a New World Notre Dame with its granite domes and waterfall naves, high on the wish lists of tourists in California. In this view, photographed in 1864, Charles Leander Weed captured the valley from the Mariposa Trail, one of the most dramatic entrances.

Photographer Carleton Watkins, one of the first artists to work in Yosemite, took this 1861 image of a man seated beneath a rock formation at the upper Yosemite Fall. Like Albert Bierstadt, who arrived in the fabled valley a couple of years later, Watkins placed his work in galleries back East and generated public fascination for the "curiosities" of the region, all of which contributed to passage of the Yosemite Act of 1864.

to the high granite country of Yosemite, hiking into the clouds and speaking so rapturously of nature that pastors and Presidents would grow to admire him. He climbed mountains, found the signatures of glaciers, and embraced nature as a nurturing, living organism. He exclaimed that "when we try to pick out anything by itself, we find it hitched to everything else in the universe.... The whole wilderness in unity and interrelation is alive and familiar...the very stones seem talkative, sympathetic, brotherly.... No particle is ever wasted or worn out but eternally flowing from use to use."

A LITTLE MORE THAN ONE YEAR AFTER JOHN MUIR FIRST WALKED INTO Yosemite Valley, a polyglot crowd of frontiersmen, saloon keepers, soldiers, journalists, Irish and Chinese workmen, and pompous celebrities of starched heritage gathered in the dust at Utah's Promontory Summit on May 10, 1869. They watched Leland Stanford, president of the Central Pacific Railroad, pound a final spike into America's transcontinental railway. He stood between two cowcatchers of two facing locomotives – one that burned coal, the other, wood – and swung the mighty hammer of history. The spike was wired, so the instant Stanford hit it the nation would learn by telegraph of the portentous deed. He missed. But the telegraph operator sent the message anyway. San Franciscans danced in the streets. Mormons prayed in Salt Lake City. And nobody fooled himself that this was an end of a grand enterprise. It was just a beginning.

The next day, a few hundred miles to the east in Green River, Wyoming, a firecracker of a man named John Wesley Powell disembarked the Union Pacific line with four clumsy wooden boats and a half-crazy ambition. Together with nine other men – an equally outrageous assemblage of four trappers in buckskin pants, a ruddy-faced Englishman, an 18-year-old bullwhacker and vagabond, a hypochondriac sergeant who enjoyed fossil hunting, another ex-officer, and his brother – Powell intended to follow the swollen Green River to where it joined the Colorado River. From there, he would descend down through the sedimentary layers of the Colorado Plateau, geologic epoch by geologic epoch, traveling deep into a time and geography where no white man had ever gone. The leader of the Rocky Mountain Exploring Expedition, Powell was fiercely interested in all fields of science but formally trained in none. He burned with incandescence. Curiosity grabbed him like a child. The fact that he had lost his right arm in the Civil War seemed not to slow him down at all.

"Losing one's right arm is a misfortune," wrote historian Wallace Stegner, a Powell biographer, in *Beyond the Hundredth Meridian*, "to some it would be a disaster, to others an excuse. It affected Wes Powell's life about as much as a stone fallen into a swift stream affects the course of the river. With a velocity like his, he simply foamed over it." Undaunted by his wound, he refused to resign from the Union Army. After a short leave he returned to do recruiting duty, then served as an artillery officer under Generals Grant and Sherman. After the war, Powell taught geology at Illinois Wesleyan University. He spearheaded the opening of a museum so that he could become a curator. He called on General Grant, who was then Secretary of War, to help with appropriations for an exploring expedition into the Dakota Badlands and Rocky Mountains. Powell thus made his way west along the Union Pacific Line and south into Utah's Uinta Mountains. One thing led to another until he found himself, at age 35, a makeshift riverman and desert rat whom historian Bernard DeVoto said "embraced the cult of action."

Down through the Canyon of Desolation, Cataract Canyon, and Dirty Devil, the rapids roared in the men's ears. Uncertainty played on their nerves. They pulled on the oars and no doubt prayed at night, before falling asleep on the sand, with the river nearby, whispering, always with something to say. They lost a boat and one-third of their supplies, and ended up sifting mosquitoes from their flour, eating rancid bacon, and rationing the food that remained. Glen Canyon broke their hearts with its serene beauty and monolithic Navajo sandstone and Moqui ruins. But still, they worried.

"We are now ready to start on our way down the Great Unknown," Powell wrote in camp where the Little Colorado River joins the Colorado, three thousand feet below the rim of the Grand Canyon. Each mile would take them deeper under burnished cliffs and sandstone spires. Bearded, sunburned, apprehensive, overworked, and underfed, his men rumbled of rebellion. "Our boats, tied to a common stake, are chafing each other, as they are tossed by the fretful river. They ride high and buoyant, for their loads are lighter than we could desire. We have but a month's rations remaining. The flour has been resifted through the mosquito-net sieve; the spoiled bacon has been dried, and the worst of it boiled; the few pounds of dried apples have been spread in the sun, and reshrunken to their normal bulk; the sugar has all melted, and gone on its way down the river; but we have a large sack of coffee. The lighting of the boats has this advantage: they will ride the waves better, and we shall have but little to carry when we make a portage.

An early photograph by George Fiske shows Yosemite's Vernal Falls in winter splendor. Images such as this helped to combat campaigns by businessmen and politicians to dam the rivers that fed the waterfalls and to use the water for irrigation and hydroelectric power.

"We are three quarters of a mile in the depths of the earth, and the great river shrinks into insignificance, as it dashes its angry waves against the walls and cliffs, that rise to the world above; they are but puny ripples, and we but pigmies, running up and down the sands, lost among the boulders.

"We have an unknown distance yet to run; an unknown river yet to explore. What falls there are, we know not; what rocks beset the channel, we know not; what walls rise over the river, we know not. Ah, well! we may conjecture many things. The men talk as cheerfully as ever; jests are bandied about freely this morning; but to me the cheer is somber and jests ghastly."

Powell had no guidebooks, cell phones, global positioning systems, or detailed maps. The geography Powell faced was in itself a wild creature, cut over the eons by the river he traveled. The unknown distance he spoke of was 217 miles. Everywhere side canyons narrowed into beautiful fern grottos filled with moss and maidenhair. But in the relentless sun the men dealt with rattlesnakes and mosquitoes, and every morning they emptied their boots, for fear of scorpions.

A few reports of the canyon preceded Powell and his hardscrabble men, all of them incomplete if not inaccurate. Francis Vasquez de Coronado, a disciple of Hernán Cortes, had discovered the Grand Canyon in 1540. From the rim Coronado's men apparently stared at the river far below and saw it not as a river but a little stream, deceived by distance and the depth of everything around them. Father Silvestre Velez de Escalante crossed the Green River in the Unita Valley in 1776, and forded the

continued on page 134

Flushed with nationalism, William H. Brewer, a member of the California Geological Survey, said of Yosemite's Bridalveil Fall that it is "vastly finer than any waterfall in Switzerland," and furthermore "is in fact finer than any in Europe." Photographer Carleton Watkins made this image of the fall in either 1865 or 1866, just a couple of years before John Muir arrived in Yosemite.

Once the transcontinental rails were joined in Utah in 1869, railroads, hotels, and other businesses used brochures and posters (bottom) to advertise the wonders of California's Yosemite Valley. Donaldson & Elmes lithography in Ohio created an 1872 fine-cut tobacco label (top) for John T. Hancock, a company in Dubuque, Iowa. The advertisement shows an artist's conjured image of the waterfalls and mountains of Yosemite Valley. In 1880 Gustav Fagersteen, an enterprising photographer, took tourist portraits of ladies and gentlemen visiting Yosemite in their finest San Francisco fashions (opposite). As national parks entered the public domain, capitalism would find a thousand different ways to market and misrepresent them.

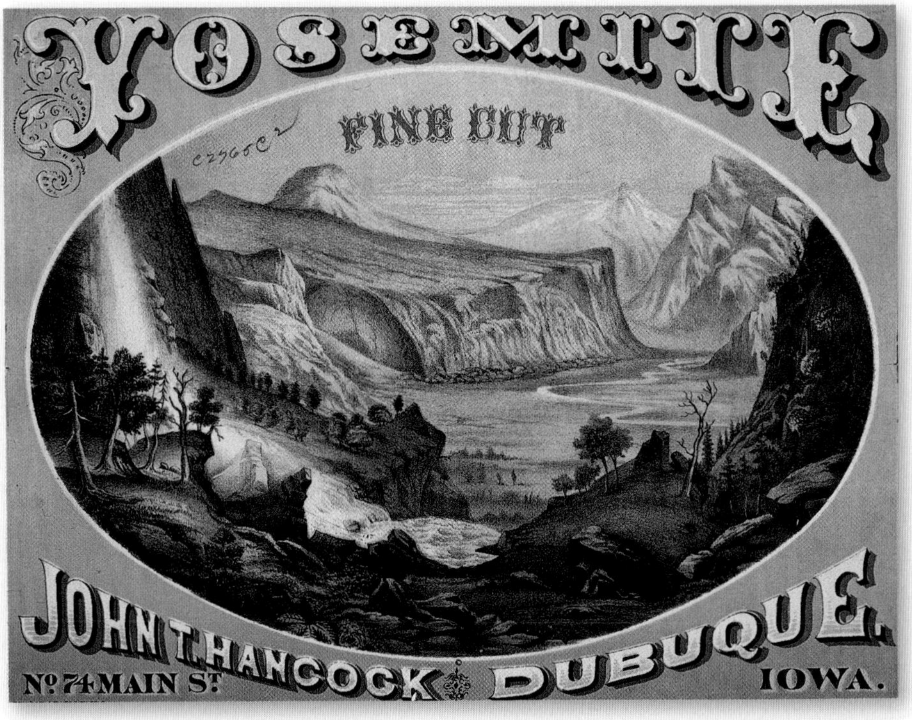

continued from page 128
Colorado River at the lower end of what Powell named Glen Canyon. A few taciturn trappers had worked the surrounding mountains. Frémont and Gunnison skirted the area, with Gunnison losing his life to Indian attack and Frémont coming close.

Detailed descriptions of the canyon did not exist until 1858, 11 years before Powell's big adventure. That year Lt. Joseph Christmas Ives led an expedition up the Colorado River from Fort Yuma in a 54-foot paddlewheeler that was dismantled in Philadelphia, shipped out West to the mouth of the Colorado River, and, according to one source, "reassembled amid a gathering of curious Indians." The expedition naturalist, John Strong Newberry, marveled at the layer-cake stratigraphy of the canyon walls, and produced the first geologic cross section of the region. The illustrations of the expedition artist and topographer, Baron F. W. von Egloffstein, proved to be disappointing. He painted the canyon with such dour exaggeration as to make it a stygian vault. One historian said his work "is essentially a picture of the artist's dismay. Nothing here is realistic: stratification is ignored, forms are falsely seen, narrowness and depth are wildly exaggerated, the rocks might as well be the texture of clouds." Wallace Stegner added that Egloffstein's interpretations "look like the landscapes of nightmare."

This image by early Yosemite photographer Carleton Watkins shows Galen Clark, the first guardian of Yosemite, standing before a massive sequoia in the Mariposa Big Tree Grove. Watkins labeled the photograph "The Grizzly Giant, 1861." Some sources said that Clark was a sequoia himself, one of the only people who could hike the Sierra Nevada stride for stride with John Muir.

Powell suffered no deceptions. While the Grand Canyon of the Colorado would be run, he could not boast of an entirely successful expedition. Near the end of their journey, facing yet another set of daunting rapids, three men elected to leave the party and climb out of the canyon on their own. They would travel on foot and try to reach the nearest Mormon settlements through the withering August heat, a formidable task. Breakfast that morning was, according to Powell, "solemn as a funeral." He later named the site Separation Rapid.

He and his remaining party survived the rapids and returned safely from the lower Colorado. Powell and his brother lingered in St. George, Utah, postponing a hero's welcome home as they awaited word of the three men who had climbed out on foot. Nothing but silence. "Perhaps then more than any time," wrote Stegner, "they felt the implacable emptiness through which they had labored for a hundred days. Other western expeditions had met Indians, buffalo and antelope and elk, grizzlies; they had passed alertly through a wilderness that teemed with life. Their own passed through a wasteland naked even of game, sometimes even of vegetation, and its trademark was the ancient and terrible stillness which was all they heard now, waiting in St. George…."

Two days out on the Mormon Trail and headed home, the news caught up to them. The three men had indeed reached the rim of the Grand Canyon, a remarkable

feat, and made it to the "forested top of the plateau," according to Stegner. "They had made it no farther. They lay out there now, somewhere beside a waterpocket, stripped and filled with Shivwits arrows, victims of an Indian misunderstanding and of their own miscalculation of the algebra of chance."

THAT SAME YEAR, FAR NORTH IN MONTANA, AN EXPEDITION EMBARKED for the fabled Yellowstone country. Until then, 1869, the only white men to visit the area had been isolated trappers and prospectors whose credibility seemed to sink under the weight of tall tales about spouting columns of hot water and steaming rivers and mudholes, stories that sounded more like whiskey talking. The famous trapper, Jim Bridger, had explored the region in 1832, as had other mountain men in the heyday trapping years. Their accounts were said to be "astonishing" by Warren Angus Ferris, a clerk with the American Fur Company, who entered the region in 1834 but could not sleep, he said, as the distant sounds of geysers "filled my slumbers with visions of water spouts, cataracts, fountains, jets d'eau of immense dimension....

"When I arose in the morning, clouds of vapor seemed like a dense fog to overhang the springs, from which frequent reports or explosions of different loudness, constantly assailed our ears. I immediately proceeded to inspect them, and might have exclaimed with the Queen of Sheba, when their full reality of dimensions and novelty burst upon my view, 'The half was not told me.'

"From the surface of a rocky plain or table, burst forth columns of water of various dimensions, projected high in the air, accompanied by loud explosions, and sulphurous vapors, which were highly disagreeable to the smell...."

According to Yellowstone historian Aubrey L. Haines, Ferris "has the triple distinction of being the first tourist to visit the Yellowstone wonders, for he went there out of curiosity rather than for commercial reasons as his contemporaries had." He was also "the first to provide an adequate description of a geyser, and the first to apply the word 'geyser' to Yellowstone thermal features. By virtue of his earlier training as a surveyor, he was the best-educated white man of his period to enter the area, and it is regrettable that he had only a few hours to explore and observe. His is the first factual report; it has neither the inadequacies nor the exaggerations of earlier accounts."

Thus, in 1869, 35 years after Ferris made his observations, two Quakers and a former deep-water sailor ventured into the geothermic netherworld to see if nature could indeed perform such miracles. The Quakers, both literate and well educated, were David E. Folsom and Charles W. Cook; the sailor, who had reinvented himself as a packer and a part-time miner, was William Peterson. All three worked for the Boulder Ditch Company, which supplied water for hydraulic mining in Confederate Gulch. Montana had given birth to many new towns and enterprises since Ferris's time, and cattlemen would soon flood into valleys ripe for ranching. Yet the headwaters of the Yellowstone River remained a fabled place, shrouded in myth and rumor of Indian strongholds. An expedition had been organized with a full military escort and was scheduled to accompany the Folsom party, but last minute unrest elsewhere diverted the troops. So the three men decided to go alone, taking five horses (three for riding, two for packing), a repeating rifle, a Colt revolver, a double-barrel shotgun, ammunition, three sheath knives, and two large buffalo robes. "Good-bye, boys," a friend said to them in Helena, "look out for your hair." Said another: "If you get into a scrap, remember I warned you." And another: "If you get back at all, you will come on foot."

In Bozeman they purchased 175 pounds of flour, 25 pounds of bacon, 30 pounds of sugar, 15 pounds of ground coffee, 10 of salt, 10 of dried fruit, and 50 of potatoes, plus a dozen boxes of yeast powder. Aside from the necessary cooking utensils and some prospecting tools – a pick, shovel, and pan – Folsom brought a compass and a thermometer, and Cook, a pair of French field glasses.

They headed south, and for some 40 miles found scant sign of white men. Once they passed the Bottler Ranch, according to historian Aubrey L. Haines, they saw only "the occasional hoofprints of unshod Indian ponies and drag-marks of travois poles to mark the original trailway up the Yellowstone." A military patrol had come this way the year before, but the country offered no proof of their passing.

Onward into the unknown, they found Calcite Springs, a labyrinth of hot springs and vents that John Colter had stumbled into more than 60 years before. Charles Cook nearly fell into a steam vent himself, and responded with surprising sangfroid, considering the temperature of the vent was measured at 194 degrees Fahrenheit. They crossed the Yellowstone River, camped in a forest glade, and attempted to sleep amid the voices of the chill September night. "The wolf scents us afar and the mournful cadence of his howl adds to our sense of solitude," wrote Folsom. "The roar of the mountain lion awakens the sleeping echoes of the adjacent cliffs and we hear the elk whistling in every direction.... Even the horses seem filled with a feeling of dread, they stop grazing and raise their heads to listen, and then hover around our campfire as if their safety lay in our companionship."

A century later the wolves and mountain lions would be gone, shot out by white

continued on page 148

John Wesley Powell

Powell applied himself diligently to learn the ways and words of Native Americans. In this John K. Hillers photograph (above), he speaks with Tau-Gu, chief of the Paiutes. Geology was an open book for Powell in the Grand Canyon (opposite), where each sedimentary layer appeared as a page pressed between those above and those below.

John Wesley Powell was one of those few explorers who managed to transcend his greatness from one arena to another, and did so many times.

First, he served with distinction in the Union Army in the Civil War, where in the 1862 Battle of Shiloh he lost his lower right arm. Next, he became a popular university professor in Illinois. After that, he led several expeditions into the Rocky Mountains and down the unmapped canyons of the Green and Colorado Rivers, going where no man had gone before.

Once, while climbing cliffs in the Grand Canyon to reconnoiter rapids up ahead, he slipped and found himself hanging off a rock by his one hand, four hundred feet above the river. He called for help and his men climbed up to rescue him, but only after he had hung there for a long time.

He directed a nine-year federal survey of public lands in the American West, and from this published three major works: *Exploration of the Colorado River of the West and Its Tributaries* (1875; revised to *Canyons of the Colorado* in 1895), *Introduction to the Study of Indian Languages* (1877), and

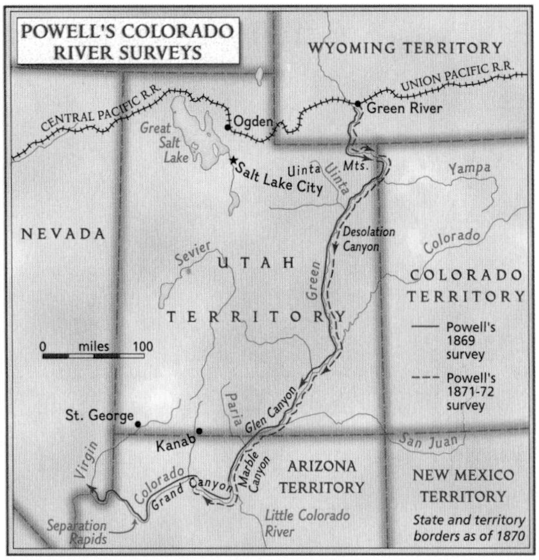

Report on the Lands of the Arid Regions of the United States (1878). All three won acclaim, but the last is regarded as a benchmark in conservation literature.

Still, Powell wasn't finished. In 1879 the Smithsonian Institution established the U.S. Bureau of Ethnology in Washington, D.C., and he became its first director, a position he held for the rest of his life.

He studied Indian linguistics with tremendous passion and produced a distribution map that showed 58 language stocks of the United States and Canada. From 1881 to 1892 he served as director of the U.S. Geological Survey, during which time he helped found the National Geographic Society in 1888.

Powell's importance, noted historian Bernard DeVoto, was that "he tried to conserve the West's natural wealth so that it could play to the full its potential part in the future of the United States. He tried to dissipate illusions about the West, to sweep mirage away. He was a great man and a prophet."

He died in 1902 at age 68.

Camped amid riverside willows in Wyoming (above), the Powell party prepares to launch itself down the Green River. Powell's surveys (opposite, top) and scientific findings were among the most accurate and least embellished to come out of the American West. His theories about the uplift of the Colorado Plateau and attendant erosion were, according to one source, "a major step in understanding the geological forces that shaped the land not only in the trans-Mississippi West but throughout the world." John K. Hillers photographed Temple Creek in stereo (opposite, bottom) so people in the 1870s could experience the canyon topography.

Powell's 1871 Grand Canyon Expedition departs Green River, Wyoming, in three boats. Powell stands highest in the middle boat. While this journey gathered important scientific data, it had neither the thrill nor the mystery of the pioneering 1869 journey. Historian Wallace Stegner wrote in Beyond the Hundredth Meridian *that it "was not an exploration, but a survey; what rendered it scientifically important rendered it dramatically second-hand." Powell was "already looking beyond it to the unmapped hinterland, the great problems of physical geology...." Most of all he wanted to make contact with the Indians, as Wallace Stegner described, "the tribes both extinct and extant that awaited study."*

237

Hours of tranquility punctuated by moments of terror defined Powell's expeditions down the Colorado River, as the men navigated one set of large rapids after another. An engraving from a Powell report (left) depicts a boat in a vortex of powerful water, nearly dashed against the rocks. In 1872 photographers James Fennemore and John K. Hillers took a time exposure of Lava Falls Rapids (opposite), one of the most dreaded rapids on the Colorado. While Powell and his men suffered from beriberi, scurvy, and aches from old Civil War wounds, today's tourists glide down the river in commercially operated rubber rafts and have gourmet meals prepared by expert river guides.

Inner gorge of the Grand Canyon of the Colorado River, photographed by John K. Hillers, shows the canyon free of artistic embellishment, the millions of years of rock strata descending into the river that exposed them. With his powers of observation and a ready grasp of the obvious, John Wesley Powell was among the first to accurately explain the geology of the Grand Canyon. Like Hillers's photographs, he concerned himself with realism and facts and left his detractors with little to stand on.

continued from page 137

hunters and ranchers. The elk, their numbers unregulated by natural predators, would instead be regulated by park managers and rangers who, according to one critic, were "Playing God in Yellowstone." Folsom's fear was more than visceral. It exemplified man-overwhelmed-by-nature and forecasted an attitude of conquest and control that would imbue hundreds of management decisions into the future.

Two days later the three men were riding through a forest. Cook was in the lead, pulling the packhorses, when his saddle horse abruptly stopped on the edge of the Grand Canyon of the Yellowstone River, between what are called today Artist and Sublime Points. Before him stretched a vast and colorful chasm, the likes of which he had never seen, or ever imagined he would see. "I sat there in amazement," he wrote, "while my companions came up, and after that, it seemed to me it was five minutes before anyone spoke."

They found a pleasant place to camp, and the next night Folsom wrote that "language is inadequate to convey a just conception of the awful grandeur and sublimity of this masterpiece of nature's handiwork."

By now, the three men must have felt as if they were floating through the country, a landscape they described as "beautiful, picturesque, magnificent, grand, sublime, awful, terrible." The next day they explored Crater Hills and Mud Volcano, then recrossed the Yellowstone River and followed the east bank to a great blue lake. There they camped on a grassy bench west of Mary Bay and augmented their dwindling larder with geese, ducks, and trout. Back at the outlet of the lake, they forded the river at a riffle near present-day Fishing Bridge. "About noon," according to historian Aubrey Haines in *The Yellowstone Story,* "they came to Bridge Bay, the present site of a crowded campground and bustling marina. Folsom's description of that little Paradise Lost is nostalgic now: 'We came to a small grassy opening upon the opposite side of which was a beautiful little lake, separated from the main lake only by a sandbar, which the surf had thrown up across the narrow neck which formerly connected them.... This was about one thousand yards across and was nearly reefed. Large flocks of geese and ducks were feeding near the shore or floating gracefully on its smooth surface. Beyond the lake the timber was tall and straight and to appearances as thick as cane in a southern swamp. This was one of the beautiful places we had found fashioned by the practised hand of nature, that man had not desecrated.' "

Later, as they ascended a ridge, Folsom looked back and reflected on the lake, "...this inland sea, its crystal waves dancing and sparkling in the sunlight as if laughing with joy for their wild freedom. It is a scene of transcendent beauty which has been viewed by few white men, and we felt glad to have looked upon it before its primeval solitude should be broken by the crowds of pleasure seekers which at no distant day will throng its shores."

They crossed the Continental Divide and descended into Lower Geyser Basin. On the first day of October they passed Great Fountain Geyser and watched the setting sun play on the steam to create a fairyland of ocher light. Enthralled, the three men removed their hats and screamed with delight.

Ten days later they arrived back in Helena amid some consternation and concern, as they were overdue. Folsom and his companions spoke of what they had seen and received guarded looks of skepticism. Folsom declined to speak in detail for risk of ruining his reputation among men he did not know and could not trust. Among the Helena listeners was Nathaniel Pitt Langford, a local businessman, who noted that Folsom "did not wish to be regarded as a liar by those who were unacquainted with his reputation. But the accounts which he gave to [Samuel Thomas] Hauser, [Warren C.] Gillette and myself renewed in us our determination to visit that region during the following year." Langford had arrived in Montana six years earlier after leaving behind a failed family bank in Minnesota. Hauser, a former civil engineer and now president of the First National Bank of Helena, had survived an Indian attack years before when a rifle ball struck him in the chest, hit a thick memo pad in his breast pocket, and lodged over a rib.

After some gentle persuasion, Folsom and Cook collaborated on an article about their experiences, but the manuscript was rejected by the *New York Tribune* and *Scribner's,* as one source said, because "they had a reputation that they could not risk with such unreliable material."

Regardless, stories spread of the Folsom-Cook expedition, and many locals believed every word. No need to embellish in Montana, they said. Folsom found employment that winter with the territorial surveyor-general, Henry D. Washburn, and is credited with suggesting to him that the Yellowstone area should be reserved as a public park. *Western Monthly Magazine* of Chicago finally published the article coauthored by Folsom and Cook in July 1870.

The next month General Washburn departed with 18 other men for the heart of Yellowstone country. Included under his command was Second Lt. Gustavus C. Doane, a veteran of the Civil War who was now a frontier officer "par excellence," plus an Army sergeant and four privates. Also along were Langford and Hauser and Gillette and a young lawyer and correspondent for the *Helena Herald,* the philosophical Cornelius Hedges. Langford had recently been appointed territorial governor of Montana, an office he would never fill due to the conflict back East between President Andrew Johnson and the U.S. Senate.

They followed roughly the same approach route used by Folsom. But while the Folsom party skirted the northwest shore of Lake Yellowstone, the Washburn-Doane party would move along the eastern and southern shores. In the beginning things went well, although Nathaniel Langford nearly lost his life when a frightened horse charged through camp, hooked him in a trailing rope, and dragged him into a rotten log that fortunately proved to be softer than his head. At Tower Falls the party found an idyllic spot they called Camp Comfort – today paved with a parking lot – where they enjoyed a good meal and smoke and a game of cards. One of the military privates, Charles Moore, sketched the falls, perhaps unaware that it was the first pictorial representation of a Yellowstone feature. The party then followed an ancient Indian trail to the summit of Mount Washburn, a view that was "beyond all adequate description," wrote Doane. The others must have agreed; as loquacious as they could be, they wrote nothing. They descended Sulphur Creek into the Grand Canyon of the Yellowstone River, where they scattered to make measurements and record their impressions. Of the upper and lower falls of the Yellowstone River, Langford gushed, "A grander scene...was never witnessed by mortal eyes."

They soon found their first geysers and progressed south toward Lake Yellowstone. In the Crater Hills, Langford had another close call when the crusty margin of an alum spring collapsed beneath his weight; he rolled to safety without being burned to death. Langford's salvation turned out to be Doane's good fortune, for the lieutenant had suffered from an infected hand the entire trip and was unable to sleep. That evening, after Langford sharpened his knife on the pommel of his saddle, he operated on Doane's hand. It took two men to hold his arm steady on a table improvised from a box of Army cartridges. Langford refused to administer chloroform; he had never used it before and was uncertain of the proper dosage. Doane screamed when Langford made the incision. But once the infection was drained, he exclaimed, "That was elegant." For the next 36 hours he did little but sleep.

Rounding the southern end of Lake Yellowstone was not easy. Tangled forests and a marshy labyrinth taxed the men. Several were temporarily lost, but always managed to turn up before nightfall. When a mother grizzly and her two cubs were sighted, six men chased them with rifles into the woods and lost them in thick cover. Moving west, the party crossed the Continental Divide and camped that night, September 9, at the head of Surprise Creek. Only after everyone had settled in did they notice one of their party, Truman Everts, was missing. First they fired signal guns, with no response. They soon moved northwest to Thumb Bay on Lake Yellowstone, a prearranged meeting place, but found no sign of Everts. A storm blew in, and when the weather cleared a search began. They blazed trees and left food caches, which they could ill afford as their own provisions were running low. Still, they found no sign of him. On September 17 they decided to head home, while Gillette and two soldiers would backtrack around Lake Yellowstone and keep searching for Everts.

The main party rode over timbered ridges to the headwaters of the Firehole River. They were a dispirited group. But the minute the Upper Geyser Basin came into view, all sadness was forgotten. As if on cue, Old Faithful saluted them with a blast a hundred feet high. They made camp and eagerly hunted for other geysers all that day and the next morning, giddy as schoolboys. "We gave names to those geysers which we saw in action," recorded Langford, "as we think will best illustrate their peculiarities." Old Faithful, named by General Washburn for its impeccable timing, the Castle, Beehive, the Grotto, the Giant, and the Giantess, with her grand sunset eruption that left every man speechless. Aubrey Haines wrote more than a century later that the "fortunate procedure unquestionably resulted in a nomenclature of the highest priority. Every name is as fitting today as when first given."

The next day they discovered Grand Prismatic Spring and the Lower Geyser Basin and camped that night, September 19, where the Firehole and Gibbon Rivers merge to form the Madison River. Around a campfire, they discussed the future of Yellowstone in tones of real estate. Said one man: Each of us should get a quarter section of land at a prominent point of interest, to make a strong profit when the tourists come. Another mentioned a preemptive land title along the Grand Canyon of the Yellowstone River. No, said another, a quarter section at the Upper Geyser Basin would be more profitable, the location was more accessible. How about if each of us gets a claim, said another, and we throw the lot into a pool for the benefit of the entire party, a sort of corporation.

Then Cornelius Hedges quietly said that he approved of none of the plans. There should be no private ownership of this region, he said; it should be a great national park, a place for all people in equal measure. And each man around the campfire should work to make it so.

Hardly a new idea, but a bold statement nonetheless. Little is written about how the men responded that chill September night as firelight played on their faces. They no doubt retired to their sleeping bags to weigh the balances of opportunity and responsibility, to sleep on the ground and dream of the future.

CHAPTER FOUR

A Breathing Place for the National Lungs

ALL THAT NIGHT NATHANIEL LANGFORD COULD NOT SLEEP. THE NATIONAL PARK IDEA RATTLED IN HIS HEAD, AND HE STIRRED WITH EXCITEMENT. HE WONDERED HOW CONGRESS MIGHT BE CONVINCED OF THE AREA'S TOURISM POTENTIAL AND OF THE IMPORTANCE OF PRESERVING EVERY REMARKABLE THING HE HAD SEEN: GEYSERS, WATERFALLS, THERMAL POOLS. CORNELIUS HEDGES TOSSED AND TURNED AS WELL, AND THE NEXT DAY HE WROTE IN HIS JOURNAL, "DIDN'T SLEEP WELL LAST NIGHT. GOT TO THINKING OF HOME AND BUSINESS." HE DID NOT ELABORATE. UNLIKE OTHER MEMBERS OF THE PARTY, HEDGES WAS LESS OF AN OUTDOORSMAN AND MORE OF AN

In 1871 artist Thomas Moran poses for photographer William Henry Jackson at Yellowstone's Mammoth Hot Springs.

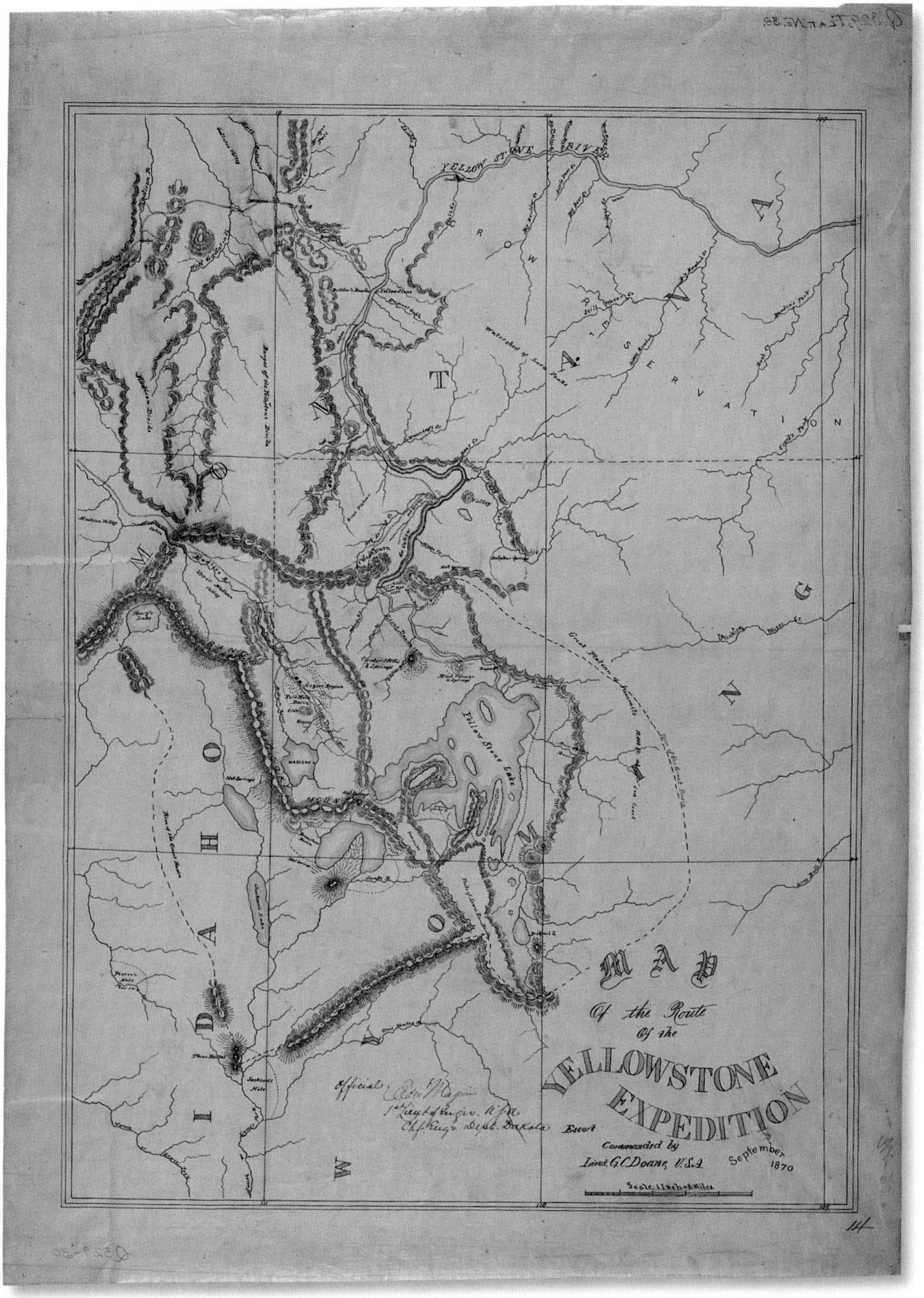
MAP
Of the Route
Of the
YELLOWSTONE
EXPEDITION
Escort
Commanded by
Lieut. G.C.Doane, U.S.A.
September
1870
YELLOW STONE RIVER
Yellow Stone Lake
M O N T A N A
I D A H O
W Y O M
C R O W
R E S E R V A T I O N

armchair philosopher. Langford apparently enjoyed his depth of thinking and sense of humor. A week earlier, while on guard duty in the middle of the night, the two men had quietly broiled and eaten two partridges intended for breakfast; the next morning they allowed the camp dog to take the blame.

Entering Yellowstone in 1870, Lt. Gustavus C. Doane used a rough map (opposite) as he and five soldiers provided a military escort for Nathaniel Langford and other prominent Montana citizens. Four years later William Henry Jackson photographed surveyors (above) during one of many expeditions under the command of Ferdinand V. Hayden.

The park they envisioned was neither the two-million-acre gem of today, nor was it a greater Yellowstone ecosystem designed to encompass the home ranges of large predators and herds of prey. Such vernacular and ecological ways of thinking did not exist then. Instead, the two men dreamed of limited protected acreage around each geyser and along the rims of the canyons. They foresaw a resort with swinging bridges and viewing platforms. According to Alfred Runte in *National Parks: The American Experience,* "wilderness preservation was the least of their aims. Nathaniel P. Langford's visions for Yellowstone Lake...might well have been inspired by Lake Como or the French Riviera. 'How can I sum up its wonderful attraction,' he exclaimed. 'It is dotted with islands of great beauty, as yet unvisited by man, but which at no remote period will be adorned with villas and the ornaments of civilized life.' Even at the moment, he confided to his diary, Yellowstone Lake 'possesses adaptabilities for the highest display of artificial culture, amid the greatest wonders of Nature that the world affords....' Not many years would elapse, he predicted, 'before the march of civil improvements will reclaim this delightful solitude, and garnish it with all the attractions of cultivated taste and refinement.' "

The explorers sought to lend cultural and historical significance to their discoveries and often referred to European icons that paled when compared to Yellowstone's "majestic display of natural architecture." Lieutenant Doane, whose infected thumb had healed thanks to the delicate knifework by Langford, remarked of Yellowstone, "Those who have seen stage representations of Aladdin's Cave and the home of the Dragon Fly, as produced in a first class theatre, can form an idea of the wonderful coloring but not of the intricate frost work of the fairy like yet solid mound of rock growing up amid clouds of steam and showers of boiling water. One instinctively touches the hot ledges with his hands and sounds with a stick the depths of the cavities in the slope in utter doubt in the evidence of his own eyes. The beauty of the scene takes away one's breath. It is overpowering, transcending the visions of Masoleum's Paradise, the earth affords not its equal, it is the most lovely inanimate object in existence."

A page from the journal of Lt. Gustavus Doane (opposite) tells of the memorable day, August 29, 1870, when he and others in the Washburn party observed in the Yellowstone region a "great column of steam, puffing away on the lofty mountain-side." Doane later participated in the Sioux war of 1876, the Nez Perce war of 1877, and the Howgate polar expedition to Greenland in 1880.

Hedges no doubt reasoned that any place that worked such magic on the human heart deserved protection. Yellowstone might not make a poet of a Philistine or a transcendentalist of a fur trader, yet its transforming properties were without question. They needed to be saved from privatization. Furthermore, his idea might not have received unanimous approval around the campfire that night, but clearly it contained something intoxicating. Years before, inspired perhaps by Catlin's national park proposal, Thoreau had written, "The Kings of England formerly had their forests 'to hold the King's game,' for sport or food, sometimes destroying villages to create or extend them; and I think that they were impelled by a true instinct. Why should not we, who have renounced the King's authority, have our national preserves, where no villages need be destroyed, in which the bear and the panther, and some even of the hunter race, may still exist and not be 'civilized off the face of the earth,' – our forest, not to hold the King's game merely, but to hold and preserve the King himself also, the lord of creation, – not for idle sport or food, but for inspiration and our own true recreation."

While the national park idea was an American original, it found little or no acceptance in the Puritan mind-set of the day, and so emerged slowly. The Puritan attitude toward work and nature had always found wickedness in idleness. It spawned no leisure class to champion the idea of parks. It found no sympathy in the writings of Rousseau or Goethe or Emerson or Thoreau. But in time Romanticism and its New World offspring, Transcendentalism, did reframe man's relationship with nature, and none too soon as a conquering culture spread across the American West. Certainly Hedges, a learned man, knew of the creation of Yosemite as a state park in California. He might have envisioned Yellowstone as the same for Montana. His campfire idea banked on the creation of Frederick Law Olmsted and William Cullen Bryant, who had proposed a city park for New York as early as 1836 and pitched it in the *New York Evening Post* in 1844. Long before then, William Penn's original plan for Philadelphia, according to one source, "allocated a number of squares to public use, with the intention of leaving them as tree-shaded islands within the city." Since then, the growing popularity of city parks and Yosemite proved Olmsted's point that mankind, ever more assaulted by his own remaking of the world, needed places to go and breathe.

The national park concept would become a child of democracy and its more aggressive cousin, capitalism. Elements of emancipation also salted the idea. It required a dramatic shift in consciousness. It birthed an understanding that all men, not just royalty, had achieved a station in life where certain lands could be – and should be – reserved for nonutilitarian purposes. The cultivation and therefore enslavement of the

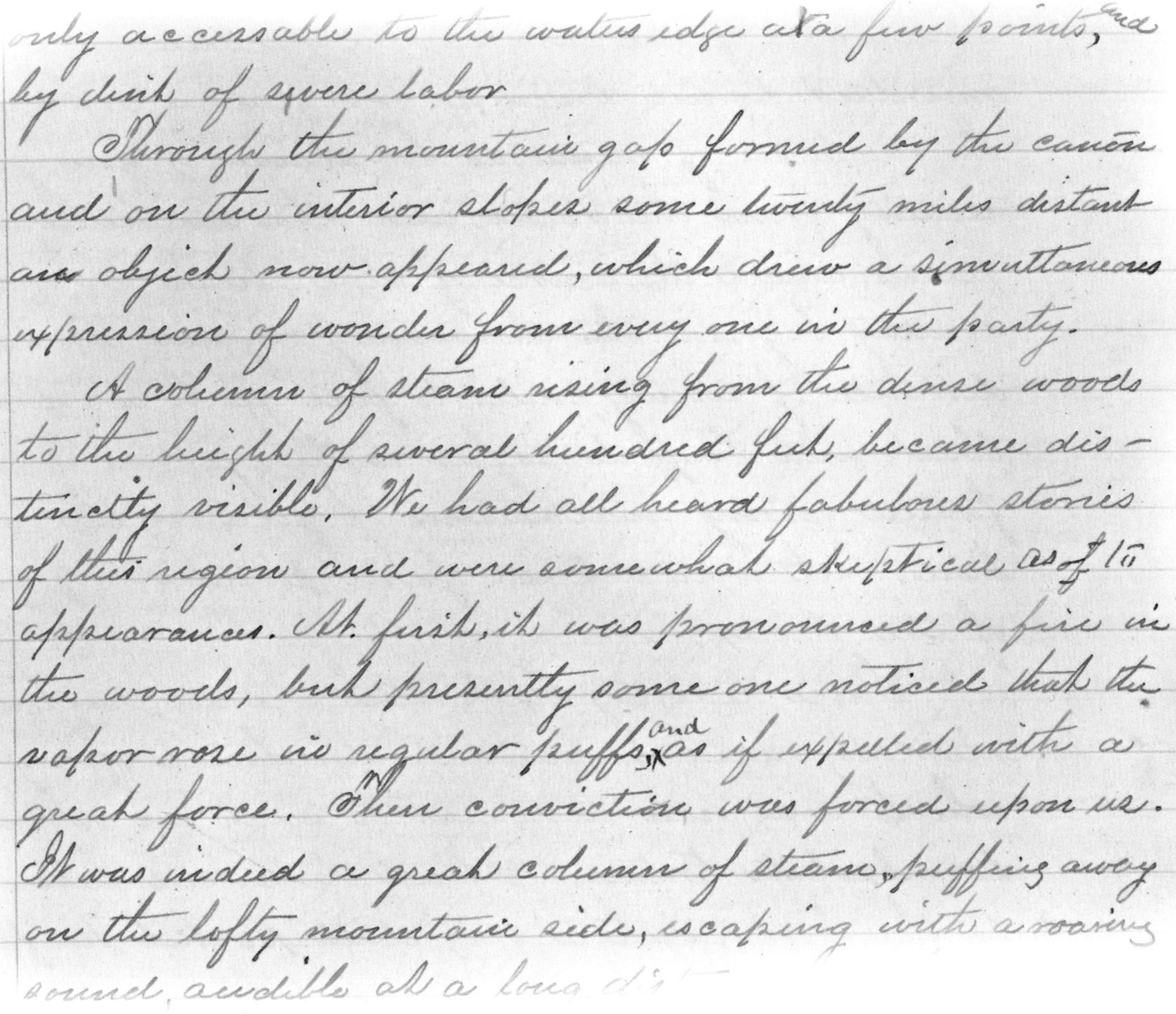
only accessable to the waters edge at a few points, and
by dint of severe labor
Through the mountain gap formed by the canon
and on the interior slopes some twenty miles distant
an object now appeared, which drew a simultaneous
expression of wonder from every one in the party.
A column of steam rising from the dense woods
to the height of several hundred feet, became distinctly visible. We had all heard fabulous stories
of this region and were somewhat skeptical as of to
appearances. At first, it was pronounced a fire in
the woods, but presently some one noticed that the
vapor rose in regular puffs, and as if expelled with a
great force. Then conviction was forced upon us.
It was indeed a great column of steam, puffing away
on the lofty mountain side, escaping with a roaring
sound, audible at a long dis

land itself, even the Jeffersonian attitude of responsible husbandry, seemed different through the passage of time. Landscapes like Yosemite and Yellowstone reframed man's relationship with nature. He could make no improvements here. In places such as this, if left alone, America could hold up her canyons and mountains as something superior to Europe's cathedrals and museums.

Let the land be, said George Perkins Marsh, a lawyer, linguist, legislator, and writer who in 1864, the same year as the Yosemite Park Act, wrote a book that some historians say heralded the beginnings of the ecological movement. Whether or not Hedges or Langford were aware of Marsh is uncertain. A recent exhaustive biography of Olmsted doesn't even mention him. Yet Marsh's book, *Man and Nature,* was an instant commercial success, and it is hard to imagine that the learned men involved in the

PRECEDING PAGES

En route to Yellowstone, William Henry Jackson photographed members of the 1871 Hayden Survey as they looked west from the rocky escarpment of Devil's Gate over the Sweetwater River, near South Pass, on the Oregon Trail. This rugged and sometimes heartbreaking country inspired other similar names, such as Hell's Half Acre, Lizard Head Peak, Crazy Woman Creek, and Poison Spider Creek. Jackson took so many photographs over his years of surveying in the West that in order to organize and catalog them he filed them by number rather than by name.

preservation of Yosemite and Yellowstone knew nothing of him. He indirectly offered an important ecological argument for the creation of national parks, something deeper than gee-whiz monumentalism. "The earth is fast becoming an unfit home for its noblest inhabitant," he said, "and another era of equal human crime and human improvidence...would reduce it to such a condition of impoverished productiveness, of shattered surface, of climatic excess, as to threaten the depravation, barbarism, and perhaps even extinction of the species." Bold, brave words, to which he added, "Man everywhere is a disturbing agent. Wherever he plants his foot, the harmonies of nature are turned to discords.... Our inability to assign definite values to [the] causes of the disturbance of natural arrangements is not a reason for ignoring the existence of such causes in any general view of the relations between man and nature, and we are never justified in assuming a force to be insignificant because its measure is unknown, or even because no physical effect can now be traced to as its origins."

Marsh put the burden of proof on man, not on nature. In contrast to railroad barons and their bought-and-paid-for representatives in Congress, men whose land ethic was as thin as a dollar bill, Marsh said that the assumption that nature could heal herself in the wake of aggressive human enterprises was false. Biographer Peter Borrelli wrote that Marsh "theorized, after years of scholarly research in parts of Asia Minor, northern Africa, Greece, Italy, and Alpine Europe, that deforestation, erosion, and land abandonment were contributory factors in the decline of past civilizations. And he concluded that 'desolation, like that which has overwhelmed many once beautiful and fertile regions of Europe, awaits an important part of the territory of the United States...unless prompt measures are taken to check the action of destructive causes already in operation.' "

So far ahead of his time was Marsh that his apocalyptic message today sounds like something from the 1960s rather than the 1860s. He served in the Vermont State legislature, then as a U.S. congressman from Vermont. He helped to found the Smithsonian Institution and to design the Washington Monument. He then became the U.S. minister to Turkey and the first minister to the new Kingdom of Italy, a post he held for 21 years. He died in Europe and was buried in Rome. "No national environmental organization bears his name or honors his memory," added Borrelli, "And few of today's most prominent activists are familiar with his life or work. Yet George Perkins Marsh deserves to be regarded as this country's original environmentalist." Among his many remarkable accomplishments, none outrank in importance the publication of *Man and Nature.* With his words began a radical shift in thinking and awareness, one that would move like a prairie fire all the way to Montana.

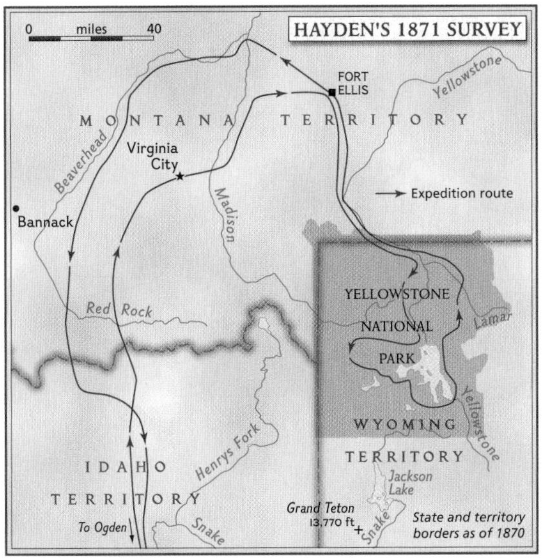

In this photograph by William Henry Jackson, members of the 1870 Hayden Survey pose during lunch in southern Wyoming. Ferdinand V. Hayden is seated at the far end of the table, facing the camera. This was the first of nine surveys on which Jackson served as Hayden's official expedition photographer. The following year, he traveled with Hayden and artist Thomas Moran into Yellowstone country (left).

WILLIAM HENRY JACKSON

Few people watched the American West change more than William Henry Jackson. Born in New York in 1843, he lived until age 99. As a young boy he painted landscapes on screens. After the Civil War he set up a studio in Omaha, Nebraska, where he photographed Indian tribes and the Union Pacific Rail Line. At age 27 Jackson joined a series of government expeditions out West, including the 1871 expedition to Yellowstone. At times only his camera documented scenes and events without embellishment. Displayed prominently in the halls of Congress, Jackson's black-and-white images rendered the mysteries of Yellowstone into an austere beauty and truth.

AS ONE HISTORIAN HAS CAREFULLY POINTED OUT, THE MONTANA frontier of the 1870s was "no intellectual vacuum." Men carried books in their saddlebags. They wrote long letters and made detailed descriptions. They rode the country long and hard, and with intense curiosity. When they set out to explore Yellowstone, as did the Folsom-Cook party and the Washburn-Doane party, they put aside many of their commercial preoccupations and came home exhausted from the intensity of the experience. Upon their arrival back in Helena, Washburn and his men looked like scarecrows. Tattered clothes hung on their frightful, lanky frames. One account said that only one of the 13 men "was fit to be seen on the street." Langford's weight had dropped from 190 pounds to 155. Washburn, fighting consumption, had developed a cold that further debilitated him. The exciting news of Yellowstone's wonders was of course tempered with the sad loss of Truman Everts, and the party's unsuccessful attempts to find him.

A $600 reward for his recovery was established. Within a couple of weeks Everts was found crawling on his hands and knees, weighing next to nothing, shoeless, his feet frostbitten and chafed to the bone, one leg scalded, his eyes vacant. His fingers, according to Aubrey L. Haines, "resembled bird's claws. He was both inarticulate and irrational when found, and doubtless would soon have died of exposure to the cold sleet that was then coating the ground." For a while he could not eat. He had intestinal congestion from a forced diet of thistle roots. A hunter happened upon Everts and his rescuers in a cabin, and gave him a gulp of oil from the fat of a freshly killed bear. The hunter said it would cure him if he drank it straight down, which Everts did. He soon felt much better, and began to eat.

In early November, one month after he had been found, Everts returned to a grand reception in Helena. Said one source, "No shadow now rests over their expedition." During that same time, Cornelius Hedges wrote a series of articles on Yellowstone for the *Helena Herald*. General Washburn's report, subtitled "Explorations in a New and Wonderful Country," was the first account of his party to reach beyond Montana. "Standing and looking down into the steam and vapor of the crater of the Giantess," it read, "with the sun upon your back, the shadow is surrounded by a beautiful rainbow, and getting the proper angle, the rainbow, surrounding only the head, gives that halo so many painters have vainly tried to give in painting of the Savior. Standing near the fountain when in motion, and the sun shining, the scene is grandly magnificent; each of the broken atoms of water shining like so many brilliants, while myriads of rainbows are dancing attendance. No wonder then that our usually staid and sober companions threw up their hats and shouted with ecstasy at the sight."

The report elicited skepticism from more than one source. *The Rocky Mountain News* out of Denver said that Washburn's account, "which while it may interest and astonish the reader, will also draw somewhat on his powers of credulity."

A Montana editor replied: "We assure our contemporaries outside of Montana, that the expedition was composed of intelligent and reliable men, and that their published reports are entitled to and receive the fullest credence in Montana."

The *New York Times* added: "Accounts of travel are often rather disappointing, partly because of the lack of interest in the places visited, and partly through the defective way in which they are described. A poetic imagination may, however, invest the dreariest spots with attraction, and the loveliest nooks of earth, may seem poor and arid if sketched with a dullard's pencil. But, perhaps, the most graphic and effective descriptions of actual scenery come from these 'plain people,' as Mr. Lincoln would have called them, who, aiming at no graces of rhetoric, are unconsciously eloquent by the force of simplicity.

"A record of the Yellowstone Exploring Expedition, which has just happened to reach us, is distinguished by this graphic directness and unpretending eloquence. It is partial and fragmentary, but it reads like the realization of a child's fairy tale. We mean no disparagement, but the reverse, of the Notes of the Surveyor-General of Montana. No unstudied description that we have read of the internal scenery of the American Continent surpasses his notes in any particular. The country he had to describe certainly offers great advantages. But it is much to his credit that he has performed the task in so unpretending a manner. Where temptation to fall into the besetting sins of tourists is great, the merit of avoiding them is equally great."

Langford produced a 13,000-word manuscript of the expedition. He lectured in Helena and Virginia City, then traveled back East. In January 1871 he delivered his talk at the Lincoln Center in Washington, D.C., and in New York City's Cooper Union Hall, reading from the manuscript. This might have put most people to sleep, but Langford spoke with inflection and wit, and his tales of Yellowstone were billed in Washington as "entertainment equal in thrilling interest to any of the season." In the audience listening to every word was Ferdinand V. Hayden, head of the U.S. Geological Survey of the Territories, the fossil hunter whom years before the Sioux had named the "man who picks up stones running."

After serving as a Union surgeon during the Civil War and achieving the rank of brevet lieutenant colonel, Hayden had taught mineralogy and geology at the University of Pennsylvania before resuming what he loved best: surveying the West. By clever networking and sheer force of ambition he secured the command of an impressive chain of geological expeditions to Nebraska, searching for high-quality coal and other resources. During the last of these expeditions he met a young photographer, William Henry Jackson, who was composing images along the Union Pacific Rail Line. Always alert to new tools and methods of self-promotion and persuasion, Hayden saw photography as a tool to publicize the work of his surveys. The following summer he stopped in Omaha en route west with yet another survey party, his largest and best funded to date, 20 men total. Off a dusty street he found Jackson Brothers Photographers and young William, then only 27, whom he invited along. William accepted; it would be the first of nine surveys he made with Hayden. With his own wagon, Jackson carried 300 pounds of equipment that first year, including jars of chemicals, hundreds of sensitive 6.5-by-8.5-inch glass plates, and a portable darkroom.

Upon his return from Nebraska, Hayden heard Langford's descriptions of Yellowstone and hastily organized another expedition made up of 21 men and seven wagons to see the country for himself and determine by his own authority its true potential. Joining him again was Jackson, this time with a larger camera that held 11-by-14-inch glass plates, as well as an artist named Thomas Moran, who begged to come along though he had never ridden a horse in his life.

While most national parks would come into existence already impacted by American Indians, Yellowstone was an exception. Being so high and remote, it offered scant hunting opportunities and no winter shelter, and was occupied only by nomadic Indians such as this Bannock family (above). The greatest Yellowstone attraction came from geothermal features (such as Old Faithful geyser, opposite) that dazzled early explorers and won the area lasting protection.

In some respects Moran would prove to be the most important member of the party. Tall, thin, and 34 that watershed year of 1871, he was the son of textile weavers who had emigrated from industrial England. Bleak working conditions no doubt forced his father to make such a move. But according to his mother it might have been fate as well. While in London two years before, his father had heard the American artist George Catlin deliver a lecture that made a strong impression and certainly contributed to his decision to move. The Moran family settled in a working-class district of Philadelphia, where the elder Moran resumed millwork, albeit under less daunting conditions. Thomas's older brother, Edward, first parted from the weaver tradition to paint, and young Thomas followed. Though he traveled abroad on shoestring study tours, the American landscape would become his first love. In 1870 the editor of *Scribner's Monthly* magazine hired him to rework some crude field sketches that would

continued on page 170

Among the many geysers that inspired the Washburn-Doane party in Yellowstone in 1870, one stood guard northwest of their camp in the Upper Geyser Basin. It sputtered in "a patronizing way," wrote historian Aubrey L. Haines, and reminded the men of a medieval fortress. They named it Castle Geyser (left).

PRECEDING PAGES

The tranquility of Yellowstone Lake lends itself to William Henry Jackson's photographic talents. He used a wet-plate, large-format camera that together with the tripod weighed approximately 70 pounds. The logistics of managing and transporting his photographic gear was in itself a great challenge that required an assistant, a pack mule (his favorite was a reject from the Army mule corps named Hypo), and sometimes an entire wagon to carry his dark-room equipment.

accompany an article written on an exotic land called Yellowstone, written by a man Moran had never heard of – Nathaniel Langford.

"Rarely is the turning point of an artist's career as easy to identify as in the case of Thomas Moran," wrote one art historian. "Commissioned...to amend illustrations of a landscape he had not yet seen, Moran was astute enough to recognize an opportunity not to be missed and resourceful enough to find a way to journey to Yellowstone himself just a few months later." An office manager of the Northern Pacific Railroad, a friend of Moran's, had written to Hayden, asking if the young artist might join the upcoming expedition: "He, of course, expects to pay for his own expenses, and simply wishes to take advantage of your cavalry escort for protection." A second letter noted that Moran "desires to take sketches in the upper Yellowstone region from which to paint some fine pictures upon his return." Referring to the most famous landscape artist in America at the time, Albert Bierstadt, who had painted the Rockies and Yosemite but had not visited Yellowstone, the letter added, "That he will surpass Bierstadt's Yosemite we who know him best fully believe." Hayden said yes, and Moran boarded a train west.

WHAT A TIME THEY HAD. EVERYTHING THEY WITNESSED – FIREHOLE Basin, Old Faithful, Tower Falls – corroborated the accounts of Langford. Moran had to ride his horse with a pillow under his bony body to avoid bruises. But he never complained. In fact, he proved a most congenial and popular member of the party. He showed the others how to bake trout by wrapping it in wet paper and placing it under the fire. He and Jackson became fast friends and often worked side by side to capture the artistic challenges before them. Jackson showed Moran how to operate his camera and expose for shades of gray; Moran showed Jackson how to frame compositions. The "pictorial climax" for Moran was the Grand Canyon of the Yellowstone. He studied it from every possible angle, scurrying from place to place. Jackson noted that his "enthusiasm was greater here than anywhere else." Finally Moran decided on a place known today as Artist's Point, where he worked on several elaborate sketches that he would complete as watercolors. Afterward in Virginia City, he told a *Helena Herald* reporter that Langford's descriptions of Yellowstone, though excellent, were only a prelude. "Mr. Moran pronounced the country the most wonderful region on the Continent," the reporter said. "All the phenomena which elsewhere is found scattered and distributed over widely separated portions of the globe, is here crowded into a region which does not exceed eighty miles in length. What [Alexander von] Humboldt traveled twenty thousand miles to see, may have been seen at a glance. Mr. M. has photographic views of the falls, cascades and canyons of the Yellowstone, and of many points of interest in that vicinity. He is a landscape painter of very fine powers, and we may expect some result of his visit to this country within the next year."

The Hayden party and another in the region at the time, the Barlow-Heap party, each returned with what one source called "incontrovertible evidence of the existence and nature of those thermal features that had been so long rumored to exist upon the Yellowstone Plateau." Yet while Hayden was employed by the government and bound to the scientific mission of the survey, Moran was not. He could produce whatever he wished, and his creative genius soared. Back in his studio in Newark, New Jersey, he transformed his sketches and watercolors into the "Grand Canyon of the Yellowstone," a seven-by-twelve-foot panoramic masterpiece that would require six months to complete. Before finishing it, he invited Hayden to proof the painting for geological accuracy. Pronounced magnificent by the explorer, Moran added two Lilliputian figures at the bottom of the scene—one, Hayden, the other, his assistant, James Stevenson. They appeared like angels at the gates of heaven. "The picture," Moran told Hayden, "is all that I ever expected to make of it, and the indications are that it will make a sensation wherever it is exhibited."

Indeed it did. It opened in a private showing in New York City, then went on public display at the Smithsonian. A shrewd self-promoter, Moran lobbied for exhibition space on Capitol Hill, and within two weeks his huge canvas adorned the old Hall of Representatives where, he said, "every member of Congress will see it."

Before his impressive painting was completed, his watercolors, together with Jackson's photographs and Hayden's direct appeals, put Yellowstone on the lips of everybody on Capitol Hill. Hayden and his associates met in person with many members of Congress. A park bill was introduced and debate ensued. The House Committee on Public Lands requested from Hayden a summary of Yellowstone's qualifications as a national park. So detailed and complete were the geologist's efforts that when he submitted his work, not a word was changed when the committee read its approval of the bill.

Hayden's reputation, though strong, was not beyond criticism. Always hungry for another expedition, he had produced his previous reports at "railroad speed" and laced them with optimism. "He usually managed to find something positive to say about each region he surveyed," wrote historian Herman J. Viola, "assuring him popularity among westerners, who willingly supported his annual requests for additional

continued on page 182

Thomas Moran's West

Thomas Moran on the trail to Yellowstone country, 1871

Every artist dreams of shaping the way people think, perhaps even of changing the course of events and making the world a better place. For Thomas Moran all this came true. He was talented, lucky, hard-working, and clever. His paintings of the American West adorned the walls of Congress and spoke to lawmakers in ways more profound than any poetry or prose.

Born in 1837 in the factory town of Bolton, in Lancashire, England, he was the fifth of ten children of Thomas and Mary Moran. His father emigrated to America when Thomas Jr. was only five, having been inspired by a George Catlin exhibit and speech in London. In 1843 his mother took Thomas and his older brother, Edward, to see another Catlin traveling exhibition and Indian troop in Manchester. The next year Thomas, his mother, brothers, and sisters boarded a ship for America and joined Thomas Sr. The family settled in working-class Kensington, an

1871, TOWER CREEK, YELLOWSTONE, *watercolor*

SCRIBNER'S MONTHLY.

VOL. II. MAY, 1871. No. 1.

THE WONDERS OF THE YELLOWSTONE

I HAD indulged, for several years, a great curiosity to see the wonders of the upper valley of the Yellowstone. The stories told by trappers and mountaineers of the natural phenomena of that region were so strange and marvelous that, as long ago as 1866, I first contemplated the possibility of organizing an expedition for the express purpose of exploring it. During the past year, meeting with several gentlemen who expressed like curiosity, we determined to make the journey in the months of August and September.

The Yellowstone and Columbia, the first flowing into the Missouri and the last into the Pacific, divided from each other by the Rocky Mountains, have their sources within a few miles of each other. Both rise in the mountains which separate Idaho from the new Territory of Wyoming, but the headwaters of the Yellowstone are only accessible from Montana. The mountains surrounding the basin from which they flow are very lofty, covered with pines, and on the southeastern side present to the traveler a precipitous wall of rock, several thousand feet in height. This barrier prevented Captain Reynolds from visiting the headwaters of the Yellowstone while prosecuting an expedition planned by the Government and placed under his command, for the purpose of exploring that river, in 1859.

The source of the Yellowstone is in a

VOL. II.—1

The May 1871 issue of Scribner's Monthly *carried Nathaniel Langford's article on his 1870 expedition into Yellowstone. A member of that expedition (one of the military escorts) made a crude drawing of Tower Falls (A) that Thomas Moran later conjured into an illustration for the* Scribner's *article (B). After Moran saw the falls himself in 1871, he painted a watercolor sketch (C).*

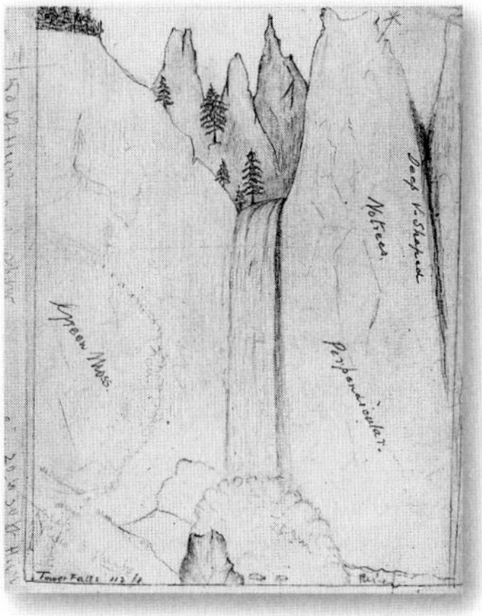

A

B

C

outlying district of Philadelphia, Pennsylvania.

In time, both Thomas and his brother Edward became painters. (Their brother John became a photographer.) Before he was 20, Thomas joined Edward in his studio in Philadelphia to paint full-time. The brothers traveled together to England to sketch and paint, and found castles and sea cliffs among their favorite subjects. Thomas, a voracious reader, spent several weeks immersed in the National Gallery in London, "ferreted away with original works," said one source, "teaching himself to paint by copying pictures by the artist he esteemed above all others," that artist being J. M. W. Turner, an accomplished marine painter. The brothers also heeded the advice of John Ruskin to study the facts of nature. "Mountains are the beginning and the end of all natural scenery," Ruskin wrote in *Modern Painters.* Little wonder that Thomas Moran would find himself in the American West, painting scenery that most people in the East could hardly imagine.

Shortly after his return home, he

married his sweetheart and confidant, Mary Nimmo, in February 1863. His big break came in 1871 when he illustrated Nathaniel Langford's article "Wonders of the Yellowstone" in *Scribner's Monthly* magazine. Although based on the field sketches of Washburn-Doane Expedition members Charles Moore and Walter Trumbull, Moran's illustrations attracted attention and secured him a place on the Hayden Yellowstone Expedition that same year.

Henceforth, he enjoyed a life of adventure, acclaim, and accomplishment, painting the grandest of American landscapes with a mixture of fact and fiction. From 1892 to 1920 he traveled to Arizona's Grand Canyon each year to paint in a studio provided for him in the El Tovar Hotel.

The so-called "dean of American painters," he would sign his paintings TYM, for Thomas "Yellowstone" Moran, a name he had given to himself, believing that Yellowstone had shaped him as much as he, in the minds of Americans, had shaped Yellowstone. He died in 1926 in Santa Barbara, California; he was 89.

1871, THE DEVIL'S SLIDE, YELLOWSTONE, *watercolor*

1872, THE GRAND CANYON OF THE YELLOWSTONE, *oil on canvas*

As Thomas Moran worked feverishly to complete his soon-to-be famous panoramic oil on canvas, "The Grand Canyon of the Yellowstone," invited guests came calling at his Newark, New Jersey, studio. One visitor noted that the remarkable picture was a great effort to "depict for us the culminating wonder of a region new and strange...as different in all its pictorial elements from form and color, as if it were a sudden revelation of another world, governed by other laws than those of the nation which we know." Upon the painting's release Scribner's Monthly *called it "the most remarkable work of art which has been exhibited in this country in a long time." In June 1872 it became the first landscape painting to be installed in the nation's Capitol Building.*

1877, HOT SPRINGS OF GARDENER'S RIVER, YELLOWSTONE, *chromolithograph*

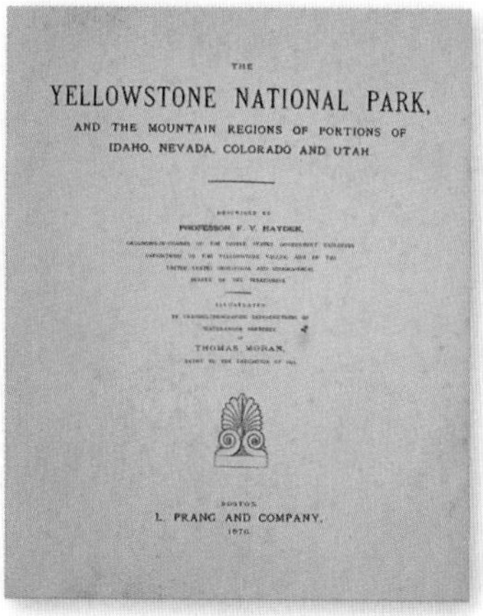

THE
YELLOWSTONE NATIONAL PARK,
AND THE MOUNTAIN REGIONS OF PORTIONS OF
IDAHO, NEVADA, COLORADO AND UTAH

PROFESSOR F. V. HAYDEN.

THOMAS MORAN,

BOSTON.
L. PRANG AND COMPANY.
1876.

Ferdinand Hayden's official government report on the Yellowstone Region (left) was illustrated by chromolithographic reproductions of watercolor sketches by Moran (above and opposite). "All representations of landscape scenery must necessarily lose the greater part of their charm when deprived of color," wrote Hayden in the preface, "...for the wealth of color in which nature has clothed the mountains and the springs of that region constitutes one of the most wonderful elements of their beauty." He heaped praise on Moran's work as

1876, YELLOWSTONE LAKE, YELLOWSTONE, *chromolithograph*

a "perfect success." Hayden added that Moran not only understood "the methods of art but the processes and work of nature, as far as the faithful interpreter of natural scenery must know them." Such praise was calculated to benefit Hayden himself, who asked Moran to join him on subsequent explorations. But Moran declined. Every major scientific exploration of the 1870s — Powell, Wheeler, King — wanted a piece of him after Yellowstone made him famous. His gift was his balance. According to curator Nancy K. Anderson, Moran was a genius at combining "the often opposing mandates of art and science.... [He] had already declared himself unfettered by any slavish adherence to facts. His was an art inspired as much by the imaginative nature of poetry as by the literal lay of the land."

1873-74, CHASM OF THE COLORADO, *oil on canvas*

In the summer of 1873 Thomas Moran joined John Wesley Powell in southern Utah and northern Arizona, a land of cactuses and snakes. In Utah they were photographed by John K. Hillers (above) — Powell, second from left; Moran, fourth from left. Moran sketched the Grand Canyon from various angles and later rendered his vision into a 7-by-12-foot panorama, "Chasm of the Colorado" (left). Over the next five decades he would make hundreds of paintings of the Grand Canyon, but none so famous as this.

continued from page 171

survey funds." But such "blatant boosterism," as Viola called it, sometimes carried absurd and serious inaccuracies. Only a few years before, one of Hayden's appointees, according to Viola, "noted more water and more abundant harvest than normal during a survey of Colorado and New Mexico, prompting him to develop his 'rain-follows-the-plow' theory. The explanation for the unusually plentiful moisture," the report said, was "in some way connected with the settlement of the country; and that, as the population increases, the amount of moisture will increase.... This is the plan which nature herself has pointed out.' Hayden, who should have known better, allowed this untenable theory to be published with his report, thereby exposing his survey to well-warranted scientific criticism."

His detractors said that he drafted his reports too fast; that he was more of a tourist than a surveyor. Hayden ignored them. Momentum was on his side. He urged quick passage of the Yellowstone Park Act that winter, warning : "Persons are now waiting for the spring to open to enter in and take possession of these remarkable curiosities, to make merchandise of these beautiful specimens, to fence in these rare wonders so as to charge visitors a fee, as is now done at Niagara Falls, for the sight of that which ought to be as free as the air and water." He stated that if Congress failed to intervene, "decorations more beautiful than human art" would, "in a single season," be despoiled "beyond recovery."

Once testimony on Yellowstone confirmed its scenic uniqueness, the Senate and House dealt with the more serious matter of whether or not a park, once created, would hamstring economic growth and future extractions of natural resources in the region. Here, a perceived worthlessness played an important role. Putting his reputation on the line, Hayden argued that Yellowstone, at 6,000 feet average elevation, suffered "frost every month of the year." It was too high and cold for agriculture, stock raising, and human settlement; too remote for ranching and lumbering; and too volcanic for minerals and mining. This same argument had worked in favor of the creation of Yosemite State Park in 1864, when Congress set aside only Yosemite Valley and four square miles of the giant sequoia forest, hardly enough acreage to threaten the growing economy of the region or the nation. Rugged and scenic land seemed abundant in America then. If a place like Yellowstone offered no obvious value to other industries, then tourism provided a perfect alternative on both economic and patriotic grounds.

Behind the political rhetoric and reports, the young Northern Pacific Railroad Company pushed quietly yet forcefully for passage of the Yellowstone Park Act. The firm of Jay Cooke & Company, a financier for the railroad, had helped to instigate the Washburn-Doane Expedition with full knowledge of the area's tourism potential. It financed Nathaniel Langford as a nominal employee during his speaking tour. At Moran's request, the Northern Pacific had suggested that the young painter join Hayden. According to the *Helena Herald,* the railroad may have financed William Henry Jackson as well. "The railroad interests hoped that Yellowstone would become a popular national vacation mecca like Niagara Falls or Saratoga Springs with the resulting profit to the only transportation line serving it," wrote Roderick Nash. Once the bill gained momentum in Congress and passage seemed imminent, the railroad kept a low profile.

"From the first, then," wrote park historian Richard West Sellars in *Preserving Nature in the National Parks,* "the national parks served corporate profit motives, the Northern Pacific having imposed continuous influence on the Yellowstone park proposal, beginning even before the 1870 expedition that gave birth to the campfire tradition. With their land grants stretching across the continent, American railroads were already seeking to establish monopolistic trade corridors. By preventing private land claims and limiting competition for tourism in Yellowstone, the federal reservation of the area served, in effect, as a huge appendage to the Northern Pacific's anticipated monopoly across the southern Montana Territory."

The Yellowstone Park Act, introduced in December 1871, passed Congress just a few months later and was signed into law by President Grant on March 1, 1872. It specified the creation of "a public park or pleasuring ground" wherein all "timber, mineral deposits, natural curiosities, or wonders" within the boundaries be preserved "in their natural condition." Congress did not appropriate any money to manage or protect the new park, but in June 1872 it purchased Thomas Moran's "Grand Canyon of the Yellowstone," finally finished, for $10,000 and installed it in the Senate lobby, "as if to signify," wrote Stuart Udall in *National Parks of America,* "that a new idea had shouldered its way onto the national stage." It was the first landscape painting to receive such a display on Capitol Hill.

Though inspired by altruism and profit, the architects of the Yellowstone Park Act crafted the legislation for tourism, unaware that it would become an important and historic conservation benchmark. "Yellowstone's awesome natural phenomena," said Sellars, "had inspired a political phenomenon." Amid a blizzard of other bills that season that dealt with land grants, timber and homestead acts, and the General Mining Law of 1872, the Yellowstone Park Act received little public attention. Yet according to historian Aubrey L. Haines, the legislation "completed the evolution of the park idea: from the roots in the Saxon concept of holding village lands 'in common,' through economic and philosophical developments of the early 19th century leading to the scenic cemetery, the landscaped city park, the state park, to arrive at last at the idea of reserving lands 'for the benefit and enjoyment of the people' under federal management.

"This highest development of the park idea, which made its appearance in the creation of Yellowstone National Park, harbored possibilities not immediately apparent. In 1872 the growth of a system of national parks lay unforeseen in the future, and the extension of the matured park concept worldwide was entirely unsuspected."

Still, it had begun. Many decades later, Freeman Tilden, the father of interpretive skills for naturalists in the National Park Service, would reflect on the passage of the Yellowstone Park Act. "That was a wonderful thing," he wrote, "that a hustling, restless, dollar-chasing young nation, with much of its population swarming like locusts over rich virgin land, should have been able to pause to look into the future with such spiritual prudence."

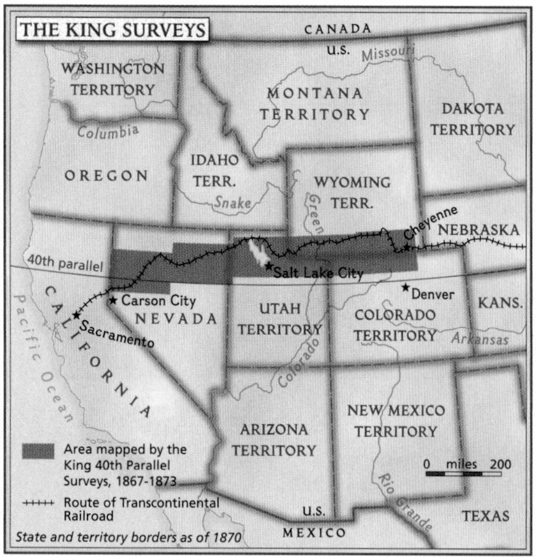

At age 21 Clarence King rode across the country to work for the California Geological Survey. Then he headed the U.S. Geological Survey of the 40th Parallel (above), which followed the route of the Pacific Railroad and produced breathtaking scientific data. The surveys made King (opposite) an admired colleague of Hayden and Powell. He served as director of the U.S. Geological Survey. He later sought his fortune in high stakes mining and lost everything, dying penniless on Christmas Eve 1901 at age 59.

DESPITE ITS HUGE IMPLICATIONS, PASSAGE OF THE YELLOWSTONE PARK Act came and went with relative quiet. The Brooklyn Bridge opened that same year and created a great sensation. The American engineer George Westinghouse perfected the first automatic railroad brake. Thomas Edison, America's greatest inventor, designed the duplex telegraph. And Jules Verne published *Around the World in 80 Days.*

While the British Empire cast its imperialistic net over India and Africa, America set loose a post-Civil War tide of rapacious men who subscribed to the myth of superabundance, believing that wildlife, forests, and minerals in the West were inexhaustible. Roughly 15 million bison still roamed the Great Plains in 1872, and men shot them with long rifles on distant hills as if they were arcade figures in a sporting zoo. Hunters killed one to two million a year and stacked the hides in Fort Worth in rows a quarter mile long. A decade later, fewer than a thousand bison remained, and George Perkins Marsh's prediction of a man-induced desolation appeared inevitable. The old-growth forests began to fall with alarming speed, cut down by loggers who looked at a coastal redwood or sequoia and saw only board feet. Simple blanket-and-burro miners combed the mountains for silver and gold, and staked their claims by the same General Mining Law that would permit heavy metal toxins

During the King Surveys of the 40th Parallel, Timothy O'Sullivan photographed his portable darkroom and equipment wagon in the sand dunes of Nevada's barren Carson Desert. The primary purpose of King's surveys was the hope of establishing a transcontinental railroad route. The same year that O'Sullivan made this photograph, 1867, the United States purchased Alaska from Russia for $7.2 million, roughly two cents an acre.

to poison countless acres of pristine land and miles of streams and rivers. Against this activity, the creation of Yellowstone National Park appeared even more miraculous. "Had the bill been perceived as precedent setting, it would assuredly have received closer scrutiny," wrote Stuart Udall more than a century later. "Fortunately, Yellowstone was conceived not as an example but as an exception. For all anyone in Washington knew, the world's first national park would be its last. In the end, Yellowstone benefited from being one of those rare, why-not? sounds-good-to-me votes legislators sometimes get to cast."

Udall and others point to five traits that made the passage of the Yellowstone Park Act remarkable in the context of its time. First, as a public park it extended democracy to a new level and became another uniquely American invention, like baseball or bluegrass music. Second, the land was set aside, in Udall's words, "not for a year or a decade, but in perpetuum." Third, the land was preserved for nonutilitarian purposes, where trees would be trees, not timber, and animals would be wildlife, not "game," and people would be visitors, not residents. Fourth, while its boundaries formed a near-perfect square with little regard to local topography – slicing across ridge lines and drainage patterns – it was a big square, a prototype for future parks as banks of biodiversity. Fifth, the act proclaimed that here was a place that cannot be improved by man and must remain as it is, the way God made it, sacred in all its beauty, quirks, sunshine, storms, wonders, and wildness. Udall added, "Had the [Yellowstone Park] bill simply accomplished its intended outcomes, it would have been noteworthy. What makes it miraculous is all that it accomplished unintentionally." It would someday inspire an entire park system. It would provide a relatively safe harbor for species of wildlife – bison, elk, beavers, mountain lions, grizzly bears, wolves, and others – in a sea of slaughter. "And certainly," Udall added, "no one intended that the bill would help launch an ethical and moral transition that would lead, inexorably and over time, to a profound shift in the American dialogue with the Earth, a turning from plunder towards stewardship. Here was a place where the nation began to emancipate itself from outdated and ultimately oppressive practices of land use that, had they continued, would have thoroughly and irreparably diminished the productivity of our landscape. To leave Yellowstone wild, we would need to tame ourselves."

ABOUT THIS SAME TIME, JOHN MUIR CAME DOWN FROM HIS MOUNTAINS ready to write and fight; ready to do battle, said one source, "with the enormous conceit that the world was made solely for men." While Washburn and Hayden had explored Yellowstone with taxpayer funds and military escorts, Muir hiked alone in the high country of the Sierra Nevada, free as a bird. He rejoiced in every wild thing. He studied water ouzels and wood rats. He conversed with flowers and trees. He inspected the signatures of glaciers on granite. He said that ice, not catastrophic down faulting, had created Yosemite Valley. And, as if that didn't turn enough heads, including those of the leading geologists of the day, he further suggested that the forests of California could serve no greater purpose than be left standing as God's cathedrals. "Any fool can destroy a tree," he said. To those who argued that a single sequoia could provide enough lumber to build an entire town, Muir responded, "No doubt these trees would make good lumber after passing through a saw mill, as George Washington after passing through the hands of a French chef would have made good food."

Emerson, the wise man of the East, visited Yosemite and met Muir there – Emerson, just shy of 68; Muir, having just turned 33. They had a fine time together, though Muir regarded Emerson's courtiers as too protective and bookish; his "sadly civilized friends," he called them. He urged Emerson to get away from them. "You must not leave so soon," he said. "It is as if a photographer should remove his plate before the impression was fully made." He urged the old man to stay and walk among the big trees. "You are yourself a Sequoia. Stop and get acquainted with your brethren." But Emerson's protectors beckoned him on, and the old man rode away.

What Emerson had written about his entire career – an honorable life acquired through an authentic closeness to nature – Muir himself truly lived. The Maine gale that had chased Thoreau down Mount Katahdin in 1846 and frightened him would have drawn Muir to the summit, where he could embrace its full glory and fury. He knew then, or at least suspected after his time with Emerson, that it was going to take more than minted wisdom to save wild places and create national parks in America. It was going to take activism; bold, glacial-persistent activism.

FOUR IMPORTANT SCIENTIFIC SURVEY EXPEDITIONS HAD BEEN charged with mapping and measuring the Far West at this time. Each had rivaled the others for publicity and annual government funding. With the prestige he received from Yellowstone and his flair for showmanship, Hayden stood above his competition: George M. Wheeler, Clarence King, and John Wesley Powell. A West Point graduate, Lieutenant Wheeler had mapped much of the Great Basin. At one point he led a survey that crisscrossed Nevada, traveling through Death Valley, and nearly lost three men to the 120-degree Fahrenheit heat. King, an effervescent author, poet, explorer, geologist, and politician, spent ten years surveying the 40th parallel from the Sierra

continued on page 194

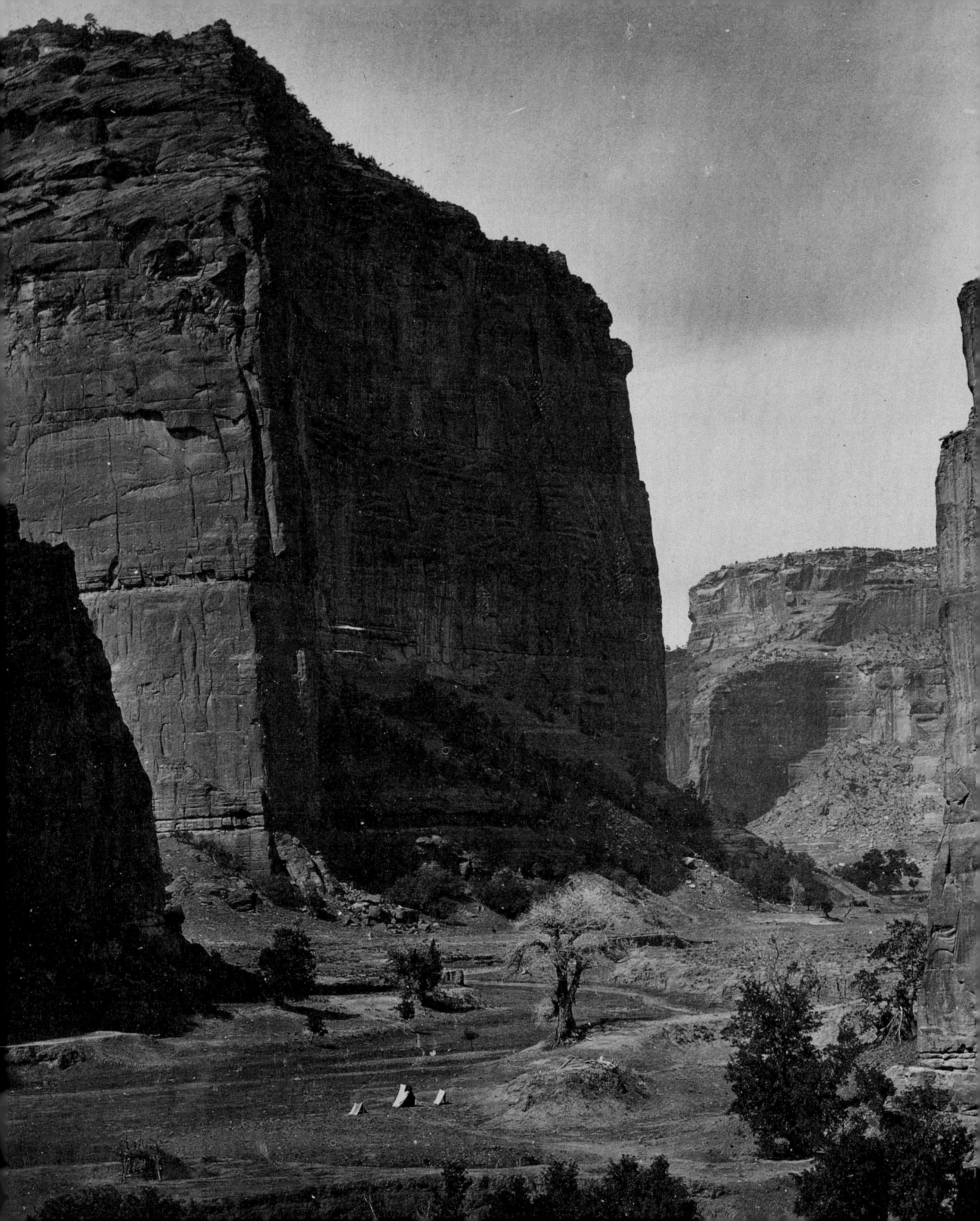

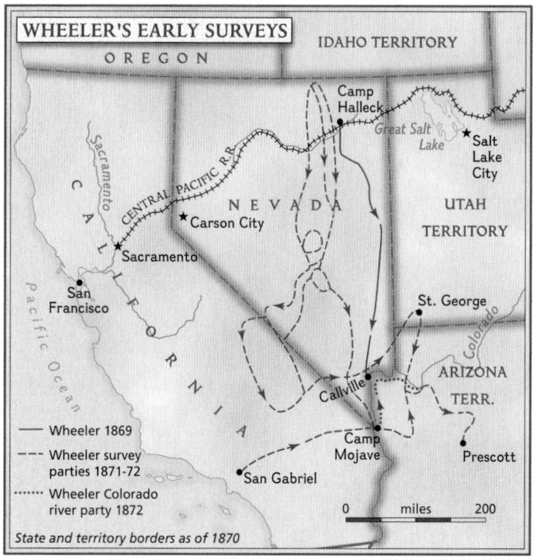

Lt. George M. Wheeler graduated from West Point a little too late to see action in the Civil War. So he made his mark as leader of the U.S. Geographical Survey's West of the One Hundredth Meridian. A rival of Hayden, Wheeler spent three years surveying territory (above) mostly south of King's 40th parallel. In 1871 he explored the desert Southwest, including Arizona's Canyon de Chelly (left). Tragedy struck the expedition when three men were killed by Apache Indians.

In Arizona's Canyon de Chelly, the Wheeler Expedition found enticing Indian cliff dwellings (opposite). Later archaeological research would determine that the abandoned site dates from A.D. *350 to 1300, when occupation suddenly ceased, most likely due to climate change and a collapse of agriculture. Timothy O'Sullivan photographed the abandoned cliff dwellings and an expedition member as he sketched the ruins from across the canyon floor (above). Canyon de Chelly became a national monument in 1931.*

continued from page 189

Nevada to the western slope of the Rockies. He produced a seven-volume report and a textbook on geology, and he gained national attention when he exposed a diamond hoax that saved the fortunes of many would-be investors.

While Hayden explored Yellowstone, Powell made another trip down the Colorado River through the Grand Canyon. This time, according to one account, "he went in style, strapping an armchair to the deck of his boat, the *Emma Dean,* which was named after his wife. From this vantage point he studied the river, gave orders, and, along one of the river's placid stretches, read aloud to his men from Sir Walter Scott's *The Lady of the Lake.*" Powell's Colorado River exploits earned him wide public acclaim, and he made no small overture to Thomas Moran: If you think the Grand Canyon of the Yellowstone is impressive, you should see the Grand Canyon of the Colorado.

In two short years Moran's status among the exploring elite had climbed from that of a beggar to a nationally recognized artist with an open ticket. Hayden invited him on yet another expedition in 1873; he declined and instead found himself in Salt Lake City, where he met Major Powell and the photographer Jack Hillers. They traveled south to the Grand Canyon, and in early August Moran stood on the rim, a view he described as "by far the most awfully grand and impressive scene that I have ever seen...." Again, as in Yellowstone, he sought the best observation points and sketched. To his wife, Mary, he wrote of his travels across the high desert: "The water was thick with a red mud, but was good, and when you want water you are not particular about the color of it. We shot some rabbits and had a game supper. The wolves were howling all around us but they did not come near...."

From his sketches and photographs, Moran produced the "Chasm of the Colorado," a companion painting to his Yellowstone panorama. It fetched the same handsome price from Congress as he had received for the Yellowstone masterpiece, and became what Wallace Stegner called "a Washington fixture, a trophy brought back from the wild West to match the Crow lodges and Sioux war bonnets and the titanotherium bones of the National Museum." It was described as a "brave" picture that one critic said, "...standing before the painting, the first impression is of chaos.... There is no sign of life anywhere – no human interest; not even a bird flecks the sky, nor so much as a lizard crawls on the pitiless rocks. Here and there a few stunted clumps of olive-green sagebrush or rugged mesquite bushes appear to enhance the forlornness of this utter solitude. It is awful."

Powell would have called it accurate, insofar as a painting could be. It was the desert crying out loud, where life is scarce, and water, scarcer. Five years later Powell completed his *Report on Lands of the Arid Regions of the United States,* what one reviewer called "one of the most far-sighted and sobering documents ever issued by the U.S. Government Printing Office.... Powell wrote candidly about the scarcity of water, in the West and the ramifications this unavoidable fact would have for future development. [His] message was not the one railroad promoters and other western boosters wanted heard. Developers of all types, eager to encourage settlement, had long trumpeted the Far West as Nature's garden." Wallace Stegner called the report "revolutionary," as bold as "Powell's plunge down the canyoned river, for it challenged not only the initiative, individualism, and competitiveness...in the American character...but it challenged as well the folklore bred up through generations of frontier farmers in a country of plentiful rain.... As a government scientist, Major Powell was not now defying ignorance. He was taking on vested interests and the vested prejudices by which they maintained themselves."

The American Southwest should not be settled heavily, Powell warned. To do so would invite catastrophe. To live a sustainable life in the desert, people must abide by the laws of the absence of water. They must spread out and listen to the land and live accordingly, like xerophytic plants. He argued for strict limits. He painted no false hopes. His plea for restraint could one day be applied to every overcrowded national park in America. He gave good advice, honest to a fault. And nobody followed it.

Throughout the 1880s the American frontier evaporated under the heat of commerce and growth. Assaults on Yellowstone became commonplace as new industries surrounded it with moneyed people. Politicians attacked it, according to one source, as an "expensive irrelevancy." Chop it up and sell it off, they said. Senator George G. Vest of Missouri replied to these materialists that for the young United States, growing as rapidly as it was, Yellowstone would only increase in value if left alone as "a great breathing place for the national lungs."

In December 1886 the House of Representatives held a floor debate on the merits of building a railroad through the park to reach a nearby mining camp. Representative Payson, a supporter of the railroad, argued: "There is no question of sentiment embraced in the matter, except the merest shadow. No injury can result to any of the objects of natural curiosity there, and the question is presented here whether or not a mining camp of which is believed to be as rich as that of Butte, in Montana, whose output, in my opinion, will be measured by millions of dollars, shall be permitted to have access to the markets of the world by a suitable outlet of this character instead of long tedious, expensive hauls by wagon over mountainous country."

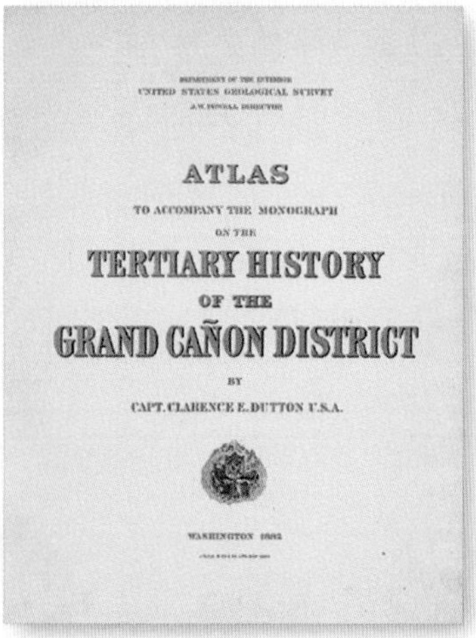

"This is a measure," replied an unconvinced Samuel S. Cox of New York, "which is inspired by corporate greed and natural selfishness against national pride and beauty. It is a shame to despoil this park for mere mercenary purposes, such as running a railroad to these mines, however valuable.... It is a question for the United States, and for all that gives elevation and grace to our human nature, by the observation of the works of physical nature."

Mr. Payson persisted, to which Representative Holman said, "I believe there has been a great deal of interest felt throughout the country in the fact that the park is the final resort and the last shelter of a portion of the great game – buffalo, elk, deer and bear – which at one time occupied in countless numbers the forests, prairies, and mountains of our country. If there are any wild buffalo left in the United States, they are in the park."

Feeling the tide turn, Representative Cox of New York characterized the proposed railroad as the beginning of the end, what he called "the entering wedge. If we authorize this road other railroads will follow....This bill sweeps away the park, if not at once, but in the future, by its being the pioneer. We will stop at no point where we can save this park for our people, unless we stop here and now...."

A geologist, poet, and graduate of Yale who volunteered for the Army at 21, Clarence E. Dutton later served as a senior geologist under the directorship of John Wesley Powell in the U.S. Geological Survey. In 1882 he authored the Tertiary History of the Grand Cañon District, *a monumental piece of work, complete with an atlas (left) and the incomparable illustrations of the Grand Canyon by W. H. Holmes (above).*

"This objection lies in the general condition of the land laws and the rapidly diminishing public domain," added Representative William McAdoo of New Jersey, "which makes it wise to preserve every acre that now belongs to the United States and keep for the present out of the market." Echoing Mr. Cox, McAdoo added, "If this railroad is built other railroads will follow, and the public park will disappear, not into hands of honest and thrifty settlers, but to the insatiate land-grabbers, speculators and corporations."

The vote was not even close. The railroad lost 107 to 65. "Never before," observed Roderick Nash in *Wilderness and the American Mind,* "had wilderness values withstood such a direct confrontation with civilization."

CLEARLY, THE ESTABLISHMENT OF ANY NATIONAL PARK WOULD BE NOT an end in itself but a beginning. Safeguarding the park would become equally difficult, perhaps more so, as people and industry settled around it. The U.S. Cavalry came to rescue Yellowstone in 1886, when vandalism and poaching threatened the park's integrity. In Yosemite, John Muir watched domestic sheep – "hoofed locusts," he called them – trample the high country and threaten irreparable damage to the sensitive alpine ecology. He lobbied for a Yosemite National Park comparable to Yellowstone, saying that the future of Yosemite Valley depended on the future of its surroundings. He reasoned that "the branching canyons and valleys of the basins of the streams that pour into Yosemite are as closely related to it as are the fingers to the palm of the hand." He argued on behalf of Yosemite's watersheds, and always on "the fineness of its wildness."

FOLLOWING PAGES

For five days in June 1899 the Harriman Alaska Expedition explored Glacier Bay, a region made famous by the early adventures and writings of John Muir. In a well-known story from 1880, Muir told of being trapped by crevasses on a glacier with a little dog named Stickeen. As the whimpering dog attempted to cross a thin precipice of ice, Muir exhorted, "Hush your fears, my boy, we will get across safe, though it is not going to be easy. No right way is easy in this rough world. We must risk our lives in order to save them." At the time when Edward C. Curtis made this photograph of Muir Glacier in Glacier Bay, John Muir was fully committed to risk. He believed that nothing less would save wilderness from the destruction of men.

He was not alone. Farmers in California's rich Central Valley said the headwater regions of Yosemite were vital to their irrigation. The Southern Pacific Railroad, seeing the success of the Northern Pacific Railroad in Yellowstone, sought to increase tourism to the Sierra Nevada, and tacitly approved of the park plan. Showing his activist tactics, Muir set aside his rapture and used the same "worthless" argument that Hayden had used nearly 20 years earlier. In a letter to a magazine editor he wrote that none of the finest features of Yosemite "are valuable for any other use than the use of beauty," and in the mountains "not a single valuable mine has yet been discovered in them...a mass of solid granite that will never be used for valuable agriculture."

So it was in the late summer of 1890 that bills providing for Yosemite, Sequoia, and General Grant National Parks slipped quietly through Congress and received little opposition. While Sequoia and General Grant addressed the preservation of magnificent stands of trees and involved smaller amounts of acreage, Yosemite, at five times the size of Sequoia, gained support in part because it was introduced as "reserved forest lands." Secretary of the Interior John W. Noble then decided that Yosemite should be managed as a national park. By then, momentum swept the bill through joint session and over to the White House for signing.

Despite its passage, the bill did not render Yosemite inviolate from populist rhetoric and rooted stakeholders. Sheepmen and private inholders abused the new park with their practices and became such a concern that two years later John Muir founded the Sierra Club to fight for conservation with grassroots initiative. The year after that, in 1893, a young historian named Frederick Jackson Turner delivered his lecture, "The Significance of Frontier in American History," before the American Historical Association in Chicago. Like Muir, Turner hailed from Wisconsin and harbored deep concerns about the disappearance of wildness in America. He noted that every ten years the U.S. Census Bureau had marked the advance of civilization and the retreat of the frontier from east to west across the settled continent. In 1890 the bureau showed the frontier as gone. This disappearance would have a profound impact on the American character, Jackson said. He wondered if the best of

American virtues would disappear with it. "That coarseness and strength combined with acuteness and inquisitiveness; that practical, inventive turn of mind, quick to find expedients...the buoyancy and exuberance which comes with freedom – these are the traits of the frontier, or traits called out elsewhere because of the existence of the frontier."

Would they now disappear, as the frontier had? Would a thoroughly civilized America find herself more and more like Europe and Europeans, the land and people from which she had wanted so desperately to distance herself these past three centuries? Was this the pioneer's paradox, to destroy the very thing he loved?

The get-rich-quick optimism and greed of the 1870s and 1880s had left some citizens of the 1890s feeling robbed of something they could not articulate. Many people lived on wide streets and in fancy homes and saw the American wilderness as something to approach as a vacationer, not a conqueror. They hungered to see the monuments of Yellowstone and Yosemite; to taste the solitude that gave virtue to Leatherstocking and contemplation to Thoreau. Perhaps they suspected that the deep woods that had frightened their grandfathers would someday attract and inspire their grandchildren, if only such places – what few remained – could be preserved forever.

In 1899 Mount Rainier National Park was established, and John Muir, now 61 and with a long white beard, sailed north as a member of the prestigious Harriman Alaska Expedition. A millionaire railroad tycoon, Harriman had fallen ill and been told by his doctors to take a restful sea cruise. He could take along anybody he wished, his doctors said, so long as they were not railroad men. Unable to do anything in a small way, Harriman charted a steamship and filled it with a Who's Who manifest of America's leading scientists, artists, and photographers, as well as a chaplain. It would be Muir's final trip to Alaska, and it filled him with mixed feelings, as did the creation of Mount Rainier National Park.

He had climbed that lofty volcano years ago, the icy summit that was called "St. Peter's of the skies." He lobbied that it become a national park, not just the mountain, which could take care of itself, but the embracing forests and wildflower meadows that surrounded it. Unless this happened, he wrote, "the flower bloom will soon be killed, and nothing of the forests will be left but black stump monuments."

Congress extended its generosity only halfway to Muir and promised the other half to industry. Many of the lands Muir sought to save were excluded. Furthermore, Congress allowed mining and mineral exploration to continue within the park and gave a lucrative land exchange to the Northern Pacific Railroad.

CURTIS

COPYRIGHTED
1899
E.H. HARRIMAN

CURTIS
X225a
COPYRIGHTED
1899
E.H. HARRIMAN

Preservation was thus tailored to fit big business insofar as it would attract revenue and hamstring no future enterprise.

Going to Alaska should have assuaged Muir's concerns, and to a degree it did. But in another way it served to remind him of the vulnerability of the wildest places in North America. The Yukon gold rush of two years before had defiled parts of Lynn Canal and disrupted the way of life of the Tlingits, the native peoples of Southeast Alaska. Muir enjoyed time in Glacier Bay, where he had first explored 20 years earlier and developed many of his theories on glaciation. Harriman wanted to shoot a bear, and Muir did nothing to accommodate him. Finally, the tycoon got a brown bear on Kodiak Island, a small one by Kodiak standards, and Muir was unimpressed. They sailed by majestic coastlines that would one day be part of Glacier Bay, Wrangell St. Elias, Kenai Fjords, Lake Clark, and Katmai National Parks. John Burroughs, a leading nature writer of the day, wrote of the "wonderfully clean air." Henry Gannett, the chief geographer of the U.S. Geological Survey, wrote: "For the one Yosemite of California, Alaska has hundreds. The mountains and glaciers of the Cascade Range are duplicated and a thousandfold exceeded in Alaska.... Its grandeur is more valuable than the gold or the fish, or the timber, for it will never be exhausted. This value, measured in direct returns in money received from tourists, will be enormous; measured by health and pleasure, it will be incalculable."

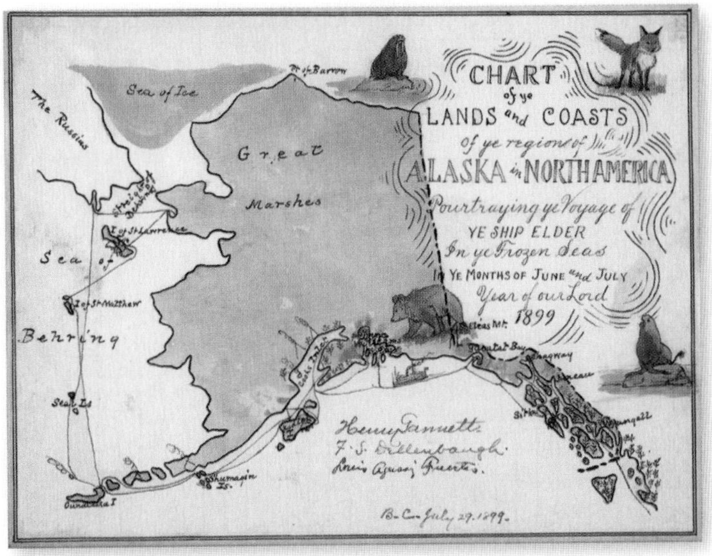

Among the guests on the Harriman Alaska Expedition of 1899 were the "two Johnnies," Burroughs (opposite, top, at left) and Muir. The expedition produced an artful map of its route (above). In Glacier Bay, Edward Curtis photographed two Tlingit seal hunters (opposite, bottom). Curtis would spend much of his life amassing a monumental portfolio of Native Americans that represented the loss of a way of life.

The members of the Harriman Expedition returned with two visions of Alaska. One vision saw it as an unprecedented storehouse of resources – an Alaska for the taking. The other vision saw it as a second chance, an opportunity to do things in moderation rather than with indulgence – an Alaska for the saving. The visions reflected the backgrounds and predispositions of the men who developed them, and so promised a tumultuous future for the last frontier.

The national park system was young then, on the cusp of a new century. But it was a *system*; a grand idea with velocity, perhaps even a little acceleration. Still unresolved was how deep and sustained America's commitment to her parks would be. But John Muir had faith. He had determination. And his most powerful ally would soon come from a place he least expected: the White House.

CHAPTER FIVE

For Our Children's Children

HE CAME FROM THE AFFLUENT SIDE OF NEW YORK CITY, WHERE SERVANTS WORKED ON THE GROUND FLOOR AND THE FAMILY LIVED UPSTAIRS WITH PIANO MUSIC AND A GLASS CHANDELIER AND ROUND-ARCHED MARBLE FIREPLACES EMBRACED BY DARK, RICH WOODS AND OTHER ARCHITECTURAL NICETIES. HIS BROTHER AND SISTERS CALLED HIM TEEDIE, SHORT FOR T. D., HIS FIRST TWO INITIALS. BUT THE REST OF AMERICA WOULD CALL HIM TEDDY, OR T. R., SHORT FOR THEODORE ROOSEVELT. HE SUFFERED FROM BRONCHIAL ASTHMA AS A BOY AND KEPT HIS PARENTS AWAKE MANY NIGHTS WITH SLEEPLESS ADMINISTRATIONS AND WORRY. YET WHILE THIS HANDICAP

A Yosemite Gothic, circa 1880: Tourists pose before a prop of horses and a wagon in this photograph produced by Gustav Fagersteen.

might debilitate or at least discourage most lads, it seemed to fill young Theodore with iron resolve. Fresh air became his best medicine. He soon budded into a serious naturalist and an avid hunter. His uncle, a pioneering conservationist, concerned himself with fish when he wasn't practicing law and educated the boy on the skills of collecting and keying species. His father was a kind and self-effacing man who was loved because of "the sunshine of his affection."

Beyond a stable upbringing, his father gave him many other gifts, including guns and a rowboat and trips abroad. Like John James Audubon, T. R. collected birds and sketched them. In Egypt he engaged in extensive taxidermy, and in the Sahara his asthma vanished. Back in America he continued living with his parents. Soon after he graduated from Harvard, he found the open prairie of the Dakotas much to his liking and built a ranch. Even though he sold the ranch after three years, he would spend much of the rest of his life practicing and extolling the virtues of frontiersmanship. He spoke German and French, and read books like most people drink water. Once during a Dakota winter, when thieves stole his boat, T. R. pursued them down a river through ice and frost and subzero temperatures. He captured the outlaws and for the next six days traveled by boat to bring the bad men to justice. In that time he read *Anna Karenina* from cover to cover, and spoke excitedly about Tolstoy's character development and supple use of language. He traveled by horse and foot on a second leg of the trip, in bitter cold and low on food, and without sleep the last two days. At the end of the journey, when the local sheriff asked him why he had not just shot or hanged the thieves, T. R. responded that the thought had never occurred to him.

He corresponded with the historian Frederick Jackson Turner on his "Frontier Hypothesis" of 1893 and agreed with the Wisconsin scholar that by the 1890s "the frontier had come to an end; it had vanished." According to Roderick Nash in *Wilderness and the American Mind,* "This alarmed Roosevelt chiefly because of its anticipated effect on national virility and greatness. The study of American history and personal experience combined to convince Roosevelt that living in wilderness promoted 'that vigorous manliness for the lack of which in a nation, as in an individual, the possession of no other qualities can possibly atone.' Conversely, he felt the modern American was in real danger of becoming an 'overcivilized man, who has lost the great fighting, masterful virtues.' To counter this trend toward 'flabbiness' and 'slothful ease' Roosevelt in 1899 called upon his countrymen to lead a 'life of strenuous endeavor.' This included keeping in contact with wilderness; pioneering was an important antidote to dull mediocrity."

The dangers of overcommercialization were not lost on the editors at Harper's Weekly, *who in an 1884 issue ran this illustration, "Desecration of Our National Parks." Ten years earlier a Bozeman Montana newspaper had asked in frustration, "What has the Government done to render this national elephant approachable and attractive since its adoption as one of the nation's pets. Nothing." Such opposing ideologies would struggle over the future of the national parks.*

Prior to the establishment of the National Park Service in 1916, the U.S. Army protected the parks from vandalism, poaching, and illegal grazing. Here, a giant sequoia provides a stage for Troop F of the Sixth Cavalry. While the U.S. Army protected the parks, the U.S. Army Corps of Engineers, formerly the topographical corps, planned and built roads in the parks, primarily in Yellowstone.

Roosevelt loved what he called "the silent places...the wide waste places of the earth, unworn of man, and changed only by the slow change of the ages through time everlasting."

In September 1901 Vice President Theodore Roosevelt, then only 42, became the youngest President in the history of the United States after the assassination of William McKinley. According to one of his biographers, historian David McCullough, he was "the first President born and raised in a big city, and the first rich man's son to occupy the White House since William Henry Harrison. He was a well-to-do, aristocratic, big-city, Harvard-educated Republican with ancestral roots in the Deep South and a passionate following in the West, which taken altogether made him something quite new under the sun. As President he was picturesque, noisy, colorful in ways that amused and absorbed the press, worried the elders of his party, and delighted the country."

His critics could hardly call him unqualified, though they did call him many other things, including "that damned cowboy" and a man "drunk with himself." Thomas Edison, an admirer, said he was "the most striking figure in American life." Prior to becoming President, Roosevelt had served as Police Commissioner of New York City, Assistant Secretary of the Navy, and as the flamboyant, bespectacled colonel of the Rough Riders, the "hero of San Juan Hill" in the Spanish-American War. He then became Governor of New York and Vice President. Once in the White House he turned the Presidency into a "bully pulpit." Forever indebted to those things – fresh air and open spaces – that he believed had healed him from a sickly boy into a fireball of a man, he made conservation his cause célèbre.

Time to play hardball, and for good reason. By the beginning of the 20th century the ecological fabric of North America was coming apart at the hands of greedy and corrupt men. In December 1901, only two months after he took office, Roosevelt sent his first Message to Congress, wherein he declared the preservation of the forests to be "an imperative business necessity." This raised more than a few eyebrows, but Roosevelt was just getting started. "The forest and water problems," he said, "are perhaps the most vital internal questions of the United States at the present time."

He appointed the tough-minded Ethan Allen Hitchcock as secretary of the interior, who quickly unearthed a series of buried reports on land frauds from Arizona to Minnesota and from Oregon to Nebraska, involving senators, representatives, judges, land speculators, and syndicates in copper, coal, and timber. Author Linnie Marsh Wolfe wrote in her biography of John Muir, *Son of the Wilderness,* "So it was

On May 15, 1903, John Muir (left) and President Theodore Roosevelt leave Yosemite Valley beneath the granite gaze of Half Dome. While Roosevelt was more at home on a horse, Muir knew Yosemite as a minister knows his church. He appealed to the President to protect Yosemite Valley and the giant sequoias of Mariposa Grove by returning them from the State of California back to federal control as a national park.

LT, *right*, and JOHN MUIR, *left*,

against a formidable host of Goliaths that Theodore Roosevelt and his Secretary strung their bows for that historic warfare against Western 'malefactors of great wealth.' " Many were indicted. Roosevelt offered no apologies. He was just getting started.

While her guide enjoys a cigarette, architect Mary Jane Colter descends a ladder into a kiva at Spruce Tree House, at Mesa Verde National Park in southwestern Colorado. Colter was an avid admirer of Native American architecture and tried to integrate native designs into her own architectural plans. Established in 1906, Mesa Verde National Park was an early creation of the 1906 Antiquities Act, which enabled Presidents to protect areas by proclamation and avoid having to wade through a long legislative process.

Time to go west. "The President is heartily with us in the matter of preserving the forests and keeping out the sheep," wrote C. Hart Merriam to John Muir late in 1901. Merriam was the chief of the U.S. Biological Survey, what would one day become the U.S. Fish & Wildlife Service, and a friend of Muir from summer days on the Harriman Alaska Expedition of two years before. He said that Roosevelt "wants to know the facts...from men like yourself who are not connected with the Government service and at the same time are known and esteemed by the people."

Muir responded, canceling previous engagements to meet T. R. in San Francisco. They traveled by train into the Sierra Nevada, then by stagecoach into the home of the giant sequoias. Nobody had told Roosevelt that he was expected at a banquet in Wawona that first night. He became enraged when he discovered that his luggage had been sent onward. One reporter said, "His jaws snapped together like a coyote, and the flow of language made even the drivers listen with admiring attention."

He boycotted the banquet and camped with Muir among the tall trees, the two men at peace under the great limbs of a living temple. What Emerson had shied away from 30 years before – sleeping on the ground and trusting himself to nature – Roosevelt did with enthusiasm and joy. He was described the next morning as being "as happy as a boy out of school." Also, unlike Emerson, he listened to Muir and not his courtiers. While the main party took coaches into Yosemite Valley, Roosevelt and Muir rode horses up to Glacier Point. At sunset they settled into a fir-fringed meadow to make fresh coffee and cook inch-thick steaks over an open fire. T. R. exclaimed, "Now this is bully." They talked late into the night and awoke the next morning under four inches of new powder snow. "This is bullier yet," T. R. crowed. "I wouldn't miss this for anything."

Dignitaries had gathered in the valley to greet the President, yet nobody knew precisely where he was. Late that afternoon he and Muir and a few other horsemen were spotted riding across the valley, and the crowd rushed forward and cheered. Members of the Yosemite Park Commission had planned yet another hotel banquet for the President, plus an elaborate searchlight show against Yosemite Falls. But T. R. responded, "We slept in a snowstorm last night...just what I wanted. This has been the grandest day of my life." He declined to attend the banquet. Since he had only one night left in Yosemite, he wasn't about to sleep in a soft hotel featherbed imported from San

STEPHEN MATHER

The first director of the National Park Service, Stephen Mather was a wealthy Chicago businessman who made his fortune in borax mining. Born in 1867, he possessed keen political skills and an easy manner with the rich and powerful. His enthusiasm for national parks was unbounded, and he spent much of his own money defending them from critics who said they were at best expensive irrelevancies, and at worst communist enclaves. During his 14 years as director, Mather developed, promoted, and "popularized" parks with new roads, facilities, and concessionaire services. His enduring goal: to increase public enjoyment. He died in 1930, the year after he resigned.

Francisco or anywhere else. Muir suggested that they camp under the towering face of El Capitan and cook one last time over an open fire. When somebody asked about the light show on the waterfall, Roosevelt waved it off as "nature faking."

According to Linnie Marsh Wolfe, "It was all over within an hour. After a brief session by the bridge at the edge of the village, where he spoke to the crowd for ten minutes, shook hands, and cracked jokes, the President mounted his horse and rode on down the street to rejoin Muir. Curses not loud, but deep, were muttered that night. Some of the commissioners and frustrated politicians blamed Muir for seducing the President away from them. In the days that followed, face-saving recriminations swelled into a mighty roar...."

John Muir had usurped the President with nothing more than a genuine closeness to nature. He later told a friend of his night with Roosevelt, "I stuffed him pretty well regarding the timber thieves, and the destructive world of the lumbermen, and other spoilers of the forest."

Roosevelt had bid him farewell, "Good-bye, John. Come and see me in Washington. I've had the time of my life."

Muir never visited the White House.

His influence on Roosevelt was immediate and profound, however. In Sacramento, en route back from Yosemite, the President said that "No small part of the prosperity of California...depends upon the preservation of her water supply; and the water supply cannot be preserved unless the forests are preserved.... I ask for the preservation of other forests on grounds of wise and far-sighted economic policy.... We are not building this country of ours for a day. It is to last through the ages."

Some years later he wrote to Muir, "I always begrudged Emerson's not having gone into camp with you. You would have made him perfectly comfortable and he ought to have had the experience."

Conservation in America at this time pitted two camps against each other: one of utilitarian conservation, the other of strict preservation. Though Roosevelt admired and liked Muir, who was a preservationist, he lived in a strict political world of economic demands and industrial interests, and by the nature of his office he came to endorse the school of utilitarianism. Land reclamation, forestry, and the leasing of public domain to cattle ranchers struck Roosevelt as legitimate and even praiseworthy practices. The conservationists did not agree. What concerned them was the blanket refusal of utilitarian conservationists to approve of the value of scenery as a resource, as something to fill the heart just as a field of wheat would fill the stomach. Utilitarianists countered by saying that to ignore the mining, timber, and any other economic potential of a piece of land, however scenic it might be, was in itself a form of wastefulness.

Beyond religious metaphors, an aesthetic advocate like Muir had no convincing language to reach a typical American urban dweller who might still see the woods and mountains as dark and dangerous places. The Forest Service "resource managers," on the other hand, enjoyed the exalted status of rugged professionals. They were the point guards of a flamboyant new agency that would finally make American forests "productive." Alfred Runte noted in *National Parks: The American Experience*, "only in means, not ends, did utilitarian conservationists break with the pioneer spirit of the nation. As scientists they merely promised America a new frontier of technological innovation and expansion. The conservation of natural resources, as opposed to the establishment of national parks, meant to regulate use rather than totally restrict it."

Foremost among these utilitarianists was Gifford Pinchot, a Yale graduate who traveled to Europe to learn forest management practices in England, France, and Germany. A long-standing trusted advisor to Roosevelt, he returned to America and became the first chief forester of the newly created U.S. Forest Service. Furthermore, Pinchot convinced Congress that the new agency belonged within the U.S. Department of Agriculture, not the Department of Interior, thus cementing as policy his vision of forests as tree farms.

Pinchot's vision deserves illumination as a contrast to the national park idea. He and his legions consigned millions of acres of American wildlands down a path separate from preservation. The forests would not be leveled by independent "thieves," as Muir had feared, but they would be leveled nonetheless, over a long period of time and orchestrated by the federal government, much of it under the clarion call of Pinchot who said, "The first duty of the human race is to control the earth it lives upon."

Utilitarianism was championed by Pinchot as an important ingredient in the recipe to make a better life in America, and so became a tenet of resource management. Muir disagreed. First, he believed that the resource itself, the Earth and all its inhabitants, was the *source.* Again and again he said that the mountains and forests of America offered as much inspiration and salvation as any church, cathedral, or synagogue. He reminded his listeners that when St. Francis of Assisi wanted to be close to God, he didn't go into a building; he went to the mountaintop, where he fasted for weeks. Second, Muir said the best forest management was to let the forest take care

704

Six thousand years ago volcanic Mount Mazama blew its top in the Oregon Cascades and left behind a caldera – Crater Lake – filled with sapphire-blue water. In 1874 Peter Britt took the first photographs of the lake. In this image he photographed his son, Emil, sitting contemplatively above the lake, lost – or perhaps found – in the scenery and the quiet. Established as a national park in 1902, Crater Lake soon sported a cluster of visitor facilities on the crater rim, including a large, rustic hotel, Crater Lake Lodge, that opened to the public in 1915.

of itself. Let it stand as it will and burn when it will. In short, let it be. The best a man could do in an ancient forest was to walk amid it lightly but deeply, filled with respect and restraint. No man could improve it. He could only improve himself by leaving that which he found just as he found it, undisturbed and undefiled.

While some people agreed with Muir, many considered him a crank. Only a crazy man would question the goodness of technology and the proper dominance of the human race on the face of the Earth.

The first decade of the 20th century seemed to many a time of magic. The dreams of Leonardo da Vinci, four hundred years old, came true when the Wright Brothers flew their plane at Kitty Hawk. That same year, 1903, the first coast-to-coast crossing of the American continent by automobile took 65 days. Americans sought independence and personal freedoms in ways not expressed before. While a New York policeman arrested a woman for smoking in public, a couple of years later night-shift work for women was forbidden. In 1905, the same year the U.S. Forest Service was created, a young patent clerk in Switzerland, Albert Einstein, helped to unlock the mysteries of the universe and change the course of history with the publication of his "Special Theory of Relativity."

For hundreds of years the models of Isaac Newton had fitted the Industrial Age and propelled it along in perfect arcs and lines. Machines and clocks, not organisms and ecologies, were the central metaphors of the age. In a struggle over resources and wealth, workers against owners, people had become cogs in their own huge thumping, grinding system, chewing up nonrenewable resources and destroying entire ecosystems as their jobs, like machines, became ever more specialized and repetitive. While Newton's calculus could indeed solve mechanical problems, Einstein's relativity would show that it was meaningless in understanding nature.

Four decades before Einstein, Charles Darwin had rattled people's perceptions of themselves and their world with his work, *On the Origin of Species by Means of Natural Selection.* Now came another revolutionary scientist, a contemporary of Einstein named Sigmund Freud, who explored the human subconscious and expelled reason from its exalted place in human nature. He discovered the central principles of psychoanalysis and the importance of dreams. In the early 1900s he wrote a series of books – *The Interpretation of Dreams, Totems and Taboos,* and *The Psychopathology of Everyday Life* – that again set the western world on its ear. Freud saw every civilized human as a sort of zoo animal constrained by the unseen cages and bars of his or her own society, always in conflict with the changing nature of its pinwheeling culture. Civilization was an arena of struggle between the wishes of the individual and the requirements of society. And while the civilized man would always be pushed to conform to social norms, Freud spoke of the overcivilized man as Roosevelt did, as a somewhat pathetic figure straitjacketed by laws and limitations and rules, a figure who, as long as he remained overcivilized, would never find happiness. "The price of progress in civilization," Freud wrote, "is paid by forfeiting happiness through the heightened sense of guilt.... Men have brought their powers of subduing the forces of nature to such a pitch that by using them they could now very easily exterminate one another to the last man. They know this – hence arises a great part of their unrest, their dejection, their mood of apprehension." Freud was not a conservationist. His wilderness was in the human mind. Like Darwin's and Einstein's, his vocabulary entered mainstream thought and helped to realign relationships, man to woman, man to man, and man to nature.

Muir felt the solution to man finding happiness was simple: Get out of the city. Go back to the woods. Get out of your head and go back to the Earth. Listen to the music in your veins. "Climb the mountains and get their glad tidings...." But things did not go Muir's way. In 1905, the birth year of Einstein's theory of relativity and the Forest Service, Yosemite National Park was reduced in size by more than 400 square miles to release timber and mineral claims to exploitative men who claimed the federal government had "locked up" its valuable resources. In Yosemite Valley, more facilities dotted the meadows. And as if the granite domes and waterfalls were somehow insufficient, a sense of carnivalism arrived. People sought to dress up and costume the parks. One man proposed to cut off the side cascades of Nevada Falls, on the Merced River, where he would create a dam and turn the water into a cataract. Critics howled with indignation, comparing the showmanship to what had happened at Niagara Falls, and the plan vanished.

Another showman, James McCauley, constructed a trail from the valley floor up to Glacier Point, where he later built a rustic hotel and entertained guests by heaving objects over the side to watch them fall to the meadows far below, a suspenseful, dizzying drop of 3,200 feet. A visiting journalist wrote, "An ordinary stone tossed over remained in sight for an incredibly long time, but finally vanished somewhere about the middle distance." A stone wrapped in a colorful handkerchief was dropped and was "visible perhaps a thousand feet deeper." McCauley also threw a large empty box, but even it, viewed with a field glass, "could not be traced to its concussion with the valley floor." He sometimes produced a chicken, a hen that could flutter but not fly. The ladies in the crowd cried with terror, which added to the drama, as McCauley

continued on page 230

Tourism and the Parks

Just as national parks helped to shape tourism in America, tourism has shaped our national parks. Early park legislation codified a strong commitment to public access and enjoyment. Early park managers worked with entrepreneurs and engineers to design roads, lodging, restaurants, campgrounds, and septic systems to provide growing crowds with accommodations. Park boosters exhorted Americans to stay home and "See America First," where the Cascades of Washington and Oregon, for example, possess "mountain scenery in quantity and quality sufficient to make half a dozen Switzerlands." National parks became big business.

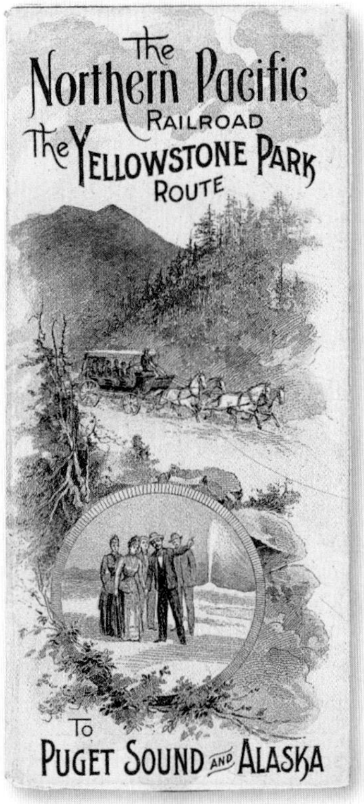

By rail and stagecoach early tourists could visit national parks with all the adventure but little of the adversity that accompanied the saddlesore and footsore explorers who preceded them.

Historian Richard West Sellars wrote in *Preserving Nature in the National Parks* that such development emphasized "the number of miles or roads and trails constructed, the number of hotel rooms and campgrounds available, the number of visitors each year, and the need for continued tourism development. Principally, in an effort to ensure public enjoyment, nature itself would be manipulated in the national parks; to a large extent, natural resource management would serve tourism purposes."

Only by increased visitation could any national park receive additional funding from Congress. In 1914 Mark Daniels, a landscape architect and designer of subdivisions in San Francisco, became the first

OWSTONE—PARK

The new symbol of American independence, the automobile (right) required little time to gear its way into national parks such as Crater Lake. The road into Yosemite's Mariposa Grove, built in 1881, tunneled through the Wawona Tree (above) and received strong publicity.

"general superintendent and landscape engineer" for the national parks. He called for systemic planning and the need for tourism promotion. "Daniels' comments," observed Sellars, "suggested a kind of perpetual motion that would become a significant aspect of national park management, where tourism and development would sustain and energize each other through their interdependence."

By the end of the 20th century, as people flooded into parks by the millions, they began to erode the peace and quiet they came to experience. They crowded the scenery and brought their motor homes, pets, and other belongings. Park managers faced serious challenges, not the least of which was imposing limits and turning people away. The concert hall is full; you are invited to the next performance. For if indeed America's national parks are temples of nature's music, they must have limited seating. Otherwise the only thing visitors will see or hear is each other. It is ironic that the same argument used to promote national parks 100 years ago must now be reversed to save them.

ON CRATER LAKE ROAD
GERKING

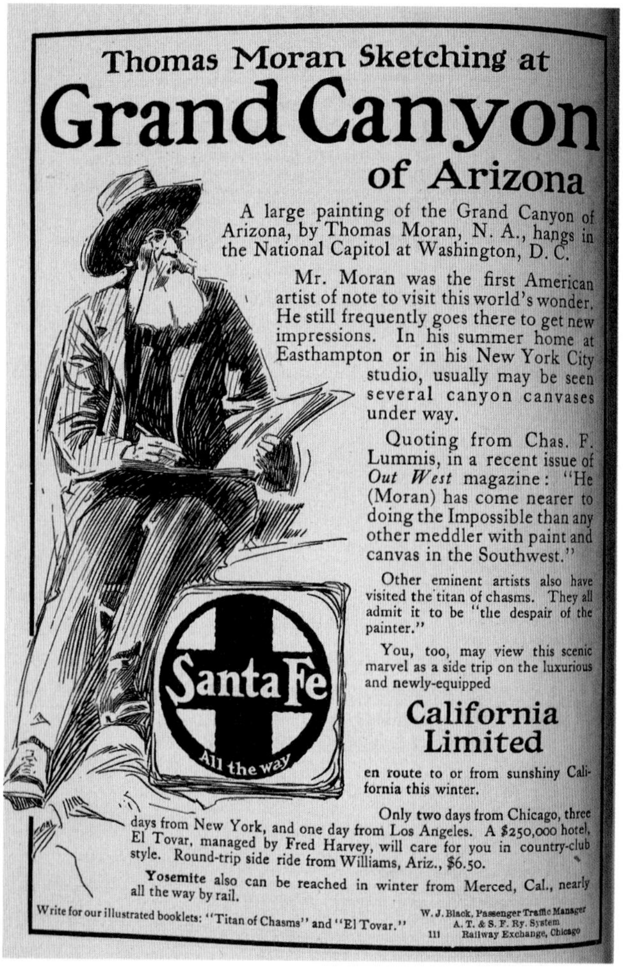

Thomas Moran Sketching at

Grand Canyon

of Arizona

A large painting of the Grand Canyon of Arizona, by Thomas Moran, N. A., hangs in the National Capitol at Washington, D. C.

Mr. Moran was the first American artist of note to visit this world's wonder. He still frequently goes there to get new impressions. In his summer home at Easthampton or in his New York City studio, usually may be seen several canyon canvases under way.

Quoting from Chas. F. Lummis, in a recent issue of *Out West* magazine: "He (Moran) has come nearer to doing the Impossible than any other meddler with paint and canvas in the Southwest."

Other eminent artists also have visited the titan of chasms. They all admit it to be "the despair of the painter."

You, too, may view this scenic marvel as a side trip on the luxurious and newly-equipped

California Limited

en route to or from sunshiny California this winter.

Only two days from Chicago, three days from New York, and one day from Los Angeles. A $250,000 hotel, El Tovar, managed by Fred Harvey, will care for you in country-club style. Round-trip side ride from Williams, Ariz., $6.50.

Yosemite also can be reached in winter from Merced, Cal., nearly all the way by rail.

Write for our illustrated booklets: "Titan of Chasms" and "El Tovar."

W. J. Black, Passenger Traffic Manager
A. T. & S. F. Ry. System
111 Railway Exchange, Chicago

In a 1909 edition of the Fine Arts Journal *(left), the Santa Fe Railroad Company advertised the Grand Canyon by way of the dean of American landscape painters, Thomas Moran, who often visited the site to sketch. Together with the Fred Harvey Company, the railroad built tourist facilities along the canyon's south rim that expanded into a sizable village. In an ambitious ad campaign, photographers were commissioned to create dramatic, hand-colored images (right) to lure American travelers west. Many descriptions of the canyon waxed poetic, such as "Time ceases to exist and the resonating, luminous shapes cast their strange and penetrating reflections upon the soul of the abyss with a delicacy and grace unique."*

To authenticate their postcards from Hawaii's Kilauea Volcano, tourists in 1905 singe them in the furnace-like fissures. Established in 1916, Hawaii National Park was later split into Hawaii Volcanoes National Park, on the big island of Hawaii, and Haleakala National Park, on Maui. As tourism increased over the decades, so did the likelihood of accidents. To discourage visitors from getting too close to the edge of Kilauea's crater, the National Park Service erected at one time signposts with a cartoon: "See Dick and Jane take in the volcano. See Dick and Jane get too close to the edge. See the volcano take in Dick and Jane."

In 1896 William Jennings Bryan, a candidate for President of the United States (below center, with a child on his knee) visited Wind Cave in South Dakota. A so-called "Great Freak of Nature" (right), the cave lacks the wetness typical of other caves and contains calcite boxwood formations. One early entrepreneur complained that "many persons have been unable to visit...on account of inadequate transportation from town." He hoped for a railroad to the area. The cave and surrounding prairie grasslands, rich with wildlife, became a national park in 1903.

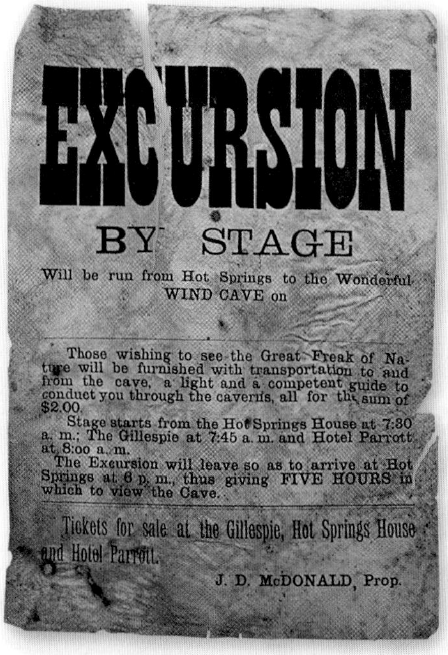

A visit to Hot Springs Reservation in 1870 afforded these ladies a chance to soak their feet in the medicinal waters. Though only four square miles at the time of its creation in 1832, the reservation offered a respite from city life and predated the establishment of Yellowstone National Park by 40 years. Later managed by the U.S. Department of Interior, it became a national park in 1921.

HORACE ALBRIGHT

When illness forced Stephen Mather into a leave of absence as director of the National Park Service, Horace Albright took the helm. Unlike Mather, Albright was not a millionaire. A graduate of Georgetown University Law School, he served as director of the National Park Service from 1929 until 1933, and in that time doubled the number of areas managed by the agency. To avoid a takeover by the Forest Service, he expanded the Park Service into historical battlefield parks and monuments, most of them in the East, giving his agency more responsibility and visibility. In his last 50 years he became a patriarch and spokesman for the Park Service. He died in 1987 at age 97.

continued from page 219

pitched the chicken over the cliff. "With an ear-piercing cackle that gradually grew fainter as it fell," the journalist described, "the poor creature shot downward; now beating the air with ineffectual wings, and now frantically clawing at the very wind...thus the hapless fowl shot down, down, down, until it became a mere fluff of feathers no larger than a quail." And from there "it dwindled to a wren's size," until it "disappeared, then again dotted the sight as a pin's point, and then – it was gone."

After the shock wore off, the women berated McCauley with "redoubled zest," telling him he should be ashamed of himself. The final embarrassment would be theirs, however, when they discovered the chicken went over that cliff again and again, just as they had seen. On their trip back down to the valley floor, the journalist recorded that "...sure enough...we met the old hen about half way up the trail, calmly picking her way home!"

As the years rolled by the chicken-toss graduated into a spectacular firefall. Every night during summer men pushed a huge pile of burning embers off the cliff to satisfy paying crowds far below. The embers fell slowly and glowed bright red with the rushing wind of their descent. McCauley at first blasted off dynamite to accompany the firefall, but by the early 1900s another entrepreneur opted for soft violin music while the embers fell.

Frederick Law Olmsted was in his 80s at this time and near death. A doctor had diagnosed him with infirmity and melancholia. Had he seen the Yosemite firefall, or the tunnels cut through giant sequoias so people could drive cars through them, these antics would have burdened him even more. In the 1860s he had argued against artificiality in the national parks, saying it fixed "the mind on mere matters of wonder or curiosity." Let people in these places see nature on its own terms, he said. Water need not flow uphill to be magic. If a river or a waterfall offers incomplete satisfaction to the viewer, then let that viewer go find a carnival at a state fair, not in a national park. President Roosevelt had effectively echoed Olmsted's sentiments when he called the light show in Yosemite "nature faking."

Yet early caretakers of the national parks persisted in their manipulations, some of which had disastrous ecological consequences.

In *Preserving Nature in the National Parks,* Richard West Sellars noted that "the early mandates for individual parks were not so much the ideas of biologists and other natural scientists, but of politicians and park promoters. There seems to have been no serious attempt to define what it meant to maintain natural conditions. This key mandate for national park management began (and long remained) an ambiguous concept related to protecting natural scenery and the desirable flora and fauna."

Granted, many areas had been grazed, logged, and subjected to mining years before their birth as national parks, and early managers recognized this. To call an area pristine seemed a bit ambiguous. Yellowstone was an exception, due to its remoteness. Yet as early as 1881, nine years after the park had been created, cutthroat trout were taken from waters of abundance and introduced into fishless waters. And eight years after that the U.S. Army introduced non-native brook trout and rainbow trout into the park. The captain in charge, with good intentions but no ecological education, said he hoped such manipulations would allow "pleasure-seekers" to "enjoy fine fishing within a few rods of any hotel or camp." The same sort of thing happened in Yosemite and Crater Lake, also as early as the 1890s.

Sellars noted that park managers in those early days viewed the preservation of natural resources as a choice between two very different paths: one to ignore, the other to manipulate. The former was not easy for problem-solving men who found no virtue in leaving things alone. They simply had to do something. So they did. Small mammals were ignored, as they attracted little interest among visitors. But the second approach, wrote Sellars, "involved extensive interference. Managers sought to enhance the park's appeal by manipulating the conspicuous resources that contributed to enjoyment, such as large mammals, entire forests, and fish populations. Although this manipulation sometimes brought about considerable alteration of nature (impacting even those species of little concern), park proponents did not see it that way. Instead, they seem to have taken for granted that manipulative management did not seriously modify natural conditions – in effect, they defined natural conditions to include the changes in nature they deemed appropriate. Thus, the proponents habitually assumed (and claimed) that the parks were fully preserved."

George Bird Grinnell, the editor of *Forest and Stream* magazine and a co-founder of the influential sportsman's organization, the Boone and Crockett Club, described a panoply of wildlife in Yellowstone and encouraged early visitors to come not just for the geysers, but also for the bison and elk and other large mammals. Here again, park managers practiced manipulation to favor ungulates over the predators that preyed on them. In this way, visitors would not have to "share" desirable elk and bison with wolves, mountain lions (cougars), and coyotes. "Park rangers and army personnel trapped or shot these animals," wrote Sellars, "or permitted others to do so. Yellowstone's predator control program began very early, accelerated when the army arrived,

Seated on granite, John Muir (above) communed with the High Sierra in 1902. For years he fought to save his beloved Hetch Hetchy Valley (opposite, top) from the water barons of San Francisco. He believed that the valley's remoteness would save it. But in fact the opposite was true. With no easy access, Hetch Hetchy had attracted few visitors and no broad constituency and so, in the end, it was flooded (opposite, bottom). In a new world of 20th century politics and shifting allegiances, Muir seemed like an irrational romantic. Since his time, however, that romance has flowered into a deep appreciation of the few wild places that remain, and a bold activism to defend them, every one.

124

In 1908 a group of men, most likely military, posed for a panoramic photo in Yosemite's Mariposa Big Tree Grove. The Southern Pacific Railroad would commission such photographs as part of its promotion. Tourists would arrive in the Sierra Nevada foothills by train and then travel by horseback, coach, or wagon – and later by automobile – into the park.

and continued for decades. Other parks, such as Mount Rainier, Yosemite, and Sequoia, followed suit. Well before the Park Service came into being, predator control had become an established management practice. This effort would ultimately reduce wolves and mountain lions to extinction in most parks."

Still, the worthless argument – the idea that parks were good for nothing else but scenery – persisted into the new century with the creation of Crater Lake National Park in 1902. The proposed area centered around a flooded caldera in the Oregon Cascades and was introduced in Congress as a "very small affair – only eighteen by twenty-two miles." At 9,000 feet in elevation, it contained "no agricultural land of any kind." The spectacular blue lake was 4,000 feet deep, and the surrounding park acreage had been surveyed "so as to include no valuable land." The only objective of the bill, therefore, was to "simply withdraw this land from public settlement [to protect] its great beauty and great scientific value."

Scenic nationalism was not alone in the new family of American patriotism for her natural wonders. It had a sibling, cultural nationalism, that in 1906 contributed to the creation of Mesa Verde National Park to protect Indian cliff dwellings in Colorado. That same year, as souvenir hunters and other vandals hit archaeological sites in the desert Southwest, Congress realized that a better tool was needed for quick and decisive action against such wrongdoers. John F. Lacey, an Iowa congressman and a feisty preservationist, pushed through a bill entitled: "An Act for the Preservation of American Antiquities." Known today as the Antiquities Act, it aimed to

preserve all "objects of historical or scientific interest that are situated upon the lands owned or controlled by the Government of the United States." These new sites, called national monuments, could be created by executive order of the President – no congressional authorization necessary. The Antiquities Act gave the President a swift stick to protect new sites, and Teddy Roosevelt wasted no time in using it. Some would say he abused it.

Over a period of three years, 1906 to 1909, he established Devil's Tower, Chaco Canyon, Muir Woods, Grand Canyon, and Mount Olympus National Monuments. Grand Canyon and Mount Olympus National Monuments covered 800,000 and 600,000 acres respectively. Roosevelt made no apologies for his actions, despite some opposition from people who saw the monuments as perhaps too large and restrictive. The act indeed stated that in "all instances" national monuments should be "confined to the smallest area compatible with the proper care and management of the objects to be protected." The Grand Canyon and Mount Olympus were not objects and were not small. Yet Roosevelt understood how erosion worked in America. Sometimes a generation needed to be rationed in its appetite for consuming wilderness in order to save pieces intact for those who would follow. After his time in Yosemite and Yellowstone in 1903, he had said, "...bits of the old scenery and the old wilderness life are to be kept unspoiled for the benefit of our children's children."

The new monuments were placed under the administration of the Interior,

Just as Nathaniel Langford and Ferdinand Hayden championed the creation of Yellowstone National Park, and John Muir, the creation of Yosemite, George Bird Grinnell fought for years for the creation of Glacier National Park in northwest Montana. The editor of Forest and Stream *magazine who inspired the creation of the National Audubon Society, he and his wife (opposite) spent many glorious days hiking among the alpine wildflowers and glacial topography. Grinnell was a strict preservationist and one of the few men who understood Muir's exaltations about wild nature as a heaven on Earth.*

Agriculture, or War Departments. But in time all would become part of the National Park System. Grand Canyon National Park (established in 1919) and Mount Olympus (established in 1938 and renamed Olympic National Park) would enter the pantheon of great western parks. With their creation as national monuments, Roosevelt set a bold and important precedent. He preserved tracts of land vastly larger than the supporters or opponents of the Antiquities Act ever envisioned.

By the time he left the White House in 1909, the once-upon-a-time asthmatic child had birthed a new age of conservation in America. He had popularized parks, sometimes in spite of technological progress. Under his administration the United States gained some 40 million acres of national forests, 51 bird sanctuaries, 4 national game refuges (the beginnings of the U.S. Fish & Wildlife Service's National Wildlife Refuge System), 16 national monuments, and 5 national parks.

The following year, 1910, the worthless land argument worked again with the establishment of Glacier National Park in northern Montana. It was, said one senator during the park debate, an area "of about 1,400 square miles of mountains piled on top of each other." George Bird Grinnell carefully championed its creation in a series of magazine articles beginning in 1901. Inspired by his friend and conservation colleague John Muir, he did not refute the worthless position. He supported it. He and Muir had sailed together on the Harriman Alaska Expedition and now shared their tactics. They understood the game: Insist that the parks will stunt no economic growth and will, in fact, provide for growth through tourism. Let the frontcountry absorb the crowds, and protect the backcountry at all costs. The backcountry contained habitat, and habitat was the key to maintaining wildlife.

But while Grinnell won his victory in Montana, Muir faced a new threat in California.

Since 1882 the city of San Francisco had searched around the canyons of the Sierra Nevada for a source of fresh drinking water. They found their best prospect in Hetch Hetchy Valley, part of Yosemite National Park since 1890. Muir saw Hetch Hetchy as a little sister to the more famous and developed Yosemite Valley, as beautiful if not as well known. He praised its wildflowers and meadows and open woodlands, and he fought the city of San Francisco with everything he had.

According to Richard West Sellars (and many other park historians), "the national park idea survived and ultimately flourished because it was fundamentally utilitarian." Yet the irony of Hetch Hetchy was how that same position worked against it.

Founded in 1906, the Mountaineers offered alpine outings to its members, including this group in 1915 (right), when more than 50 climbers reached the summit of Mount Rainier. Typical of the growing influence of conservation organizations, the Mountaineers was instrumental in many preservation issues, including the creation of Olympic and North Cascades National Parks. In 1917 visitors wore "tin trousers" — the seats slicked with paraffin — to glissade down the snowy slopes of Mount Rainier (above).

THE MOUNTAINEERS

Rising sentinel-like above the forested Cascades, Mount Rainier commands the horizon in this 1915 stereo photograph. At 14,410 feet, it is the highest of the Cascade volcanoes, only four feet lower than Mount Whitney in California, highest peak in the contiguous United States. John Muir climbed Mount Rainier in 1888 when he was 50. In the forested lower slopes he wrote of "Jubilant winds and waters" that "sound in grand harmonious symphonies."

Its protection from one form of development, tourism, left it vulnerable to another and more serious form of development, dam building and flooding. With no reasonable access, it appeared nonutilitarian, a perfect target to the water barons of San Francisco. They petitioned Secretary of the Interior Ethan Hitchcock, whose sympathies lay with the preservationists, and got nowhere. A few years later they petitioned the new Secretary of the Interior, James A. Garfield, an admirer of Gifford Pinchot, and the permit was approved.

This approval, according to Alfred Runte in *National Parks: The American Experience,* "set the stage for the greatest cause célèbre in the early history of the national park movement in the United States. For preservationists the stakes were especially high. Prior schemes to exclude lands and resources from the national parks, particularly Yosemite, for the most part had been limited to the edges of the reserves. Generally speaking, foothills predominated in these areas; preservationists themselves often shared honest differences of opinion about the suitability of giving national park status to commonplace topography." Hetch Hetchy changed all that. It raised the stakes tenfold. The battle for its future focused not on the fringe of a park but on its very core. The implications were profound, for if Hetch Hetchy could be sacrificed, then preservationists believed every national park would lose an important part of its sanctity that could perhaps never be retrieved.

National parks had become islands of hope for preservationists like Muir and Grinnell, who now, in a widening spirit of Pinchot-minded utilitarianism, had an uphill fight. From the beginning of the Hetch Hetchy debate the burden of proof was theirs. How could they show that the needs of only a couple thousand people who camped on the valley floor and traipsed among the flowers each summer outweighed the needs of half a million thirsty people who lived in the big city? The nation already had one Yosemite Valley, did it not? Besides, a lake in Hetch Hetchy would serve to reflect the surrounding granite walls and double the scenic value.

In the end, John Muir lost. In December 1913 President Wilson signed the bill that authorized the damming of the Tuolumne River and the flooding of Hetch Hetchy Valley. One year later Muir died in a Los Angeles hospital. Some friends said a broken heart contributed to his failing health. He had always been the most lyrical and least politicized voice for the parks, a man who seemed saintly in his exaltations, lark-like, as if waters and storms flowed through him. "Thousands of tired, nerve-shaken, over-civilized people are beginning to find out that going to the mountains is going home," he wrote, "that wildness is a necessity, and that

mountain parks and reservations are useful not only as fountains of timber and irrigating rivers, but as fountains of life."

It was a double blow, first losing Hetch Hetchy, then John Muir. For more than three years park advocates had discussed a national parks bureau that could systematize and better protect the parks and give them a clear sense of mission. Now came a greater sense of urgency. As the Forest Service steamed ahead in search of its identity, it seemed proper that the collective national parks of the United States should also have their own dedicated "service."

In 1912 Secretary of the Interior Walter L. Fisher had exclaimed that the Department of Interior, busy with other tasks, had "no machinery whatever" to deal with national parks. The department sponsored three national conferences that pulled together the brightest minds in the country to discuss matters of transportation, administration, and recreation in the parks. Railroad men attended, as did officials of the American Automobile Association and other similar businesses, plus engineers and landscape architects, all foreshadowing those interests and influences that would shape national parks in the decades ahead.

In June 1916 Robert Sterling Yard, chief publicist of the national parks, wrote an article for *The Nation's Business* magazine entitled "Making a Business of Scenery."

It was time, he said, to follow the examples of Switzerland and Canada and treat each national park in the United States as an "economic asset of incalculable value," but only if managed in a businesslike manner. "We want our national parks developed," he wrote. "We want roads and trails like Switzerland's. We want hotels of all prices from lowest to highest. We want comfortable public camps in sufficient abundance to meet all demands. We want lodges and chalets at convenient intervals commanding the scenic possibilities of all our parks. We want the best and cheapest accommodations for pedestrians and motorists. We want sufficient and convenient transportation at reasonable rates. We want adequate facilities and supplies for camping out at lowest prices. We want good fishing. We want our animal life conserved and developed. We want special facilities for nature study."

Enos Mills poses atop Longs Peak in the Colorado Rockies with eight-year-old Harriet Peters (opposite). Often called the "Father of Rocky Mountain National Park," Mills was an avid climber, photographer (above), and conservationist who lobbied for the area's protection for more than 20 years. It was designated a national park in 1915.

Just two months later, in August 1916, against what one proponent called "hostility" from the Forest Service, the National Park Service Act was signed into law. The statement of purpose in the founding legislation, the Organic Act, was written by none other than Frederick Law Olmsted, Jr., the son who had followed in his famous father's footsteps. Three other men offered unflagging energy and illumination along the way: J. Horace McFarland, a prominent horticulturalist; Stephen T. Mather, a Chicago businessman; and Horace M. Albright, a young lawyer and Mather's assistant during the legislative campaign for the National Parks Bureau. The Organic Act sought to "conserve" scenery, which in a broad sense included preservation as one of its many valid approaches to management. Olmsted's statement declared the fundamental purpose of the parks: "to conserve the scenery and the natural and historic objects and the wild life therein and to provide for the enjoyment of the same in such manner and by such means as will leave them unimpaired for the enjoyment of future generations."

In years ahead people would praise this statement as farsighted and curse it as dichotomous. Yet in its day it made a valuable blueprint. No one disputed the fact that America had come a long way from the King's Forest of Middle Ages England, when good people had nowhere to go to breathe, as equals, the sounds and sights of nature. National parks changed that. Forever.

Ansel Adams, 1941-1942, THE TETONS – SNAKE RIVER, *Grand Teton National Park, Wyoming*

EPILOGUE

The Heart May Be Said to Sing

AT TIMES IT SEEMS LIKE A MIRACLE. IN A COUNTRY WHERE EVERY HOUR IS RUSH HOUR, WE HAVE PLACES TO SLOW DOWN. AMID A DIN OF GADGETS AND MACHINES, WE CELEBRATE THE QUIET. DROWNING IN FACTOIDS AND FASHION, WE REMEMBER THE LANGUAGE OF OUR ANCESTORS, THE MUSIC OF THE WIND, THE HEART-FLUTTERING CALLS OF GEESE, THE HOWLS OF WOLVES. PULLING OFF THE INFORMATION SUPERHIGHWAY, WE STEP INTO THE FOLDS OF NATURE TO FIND MYSTERY AND AUTHENTICITY.

That a nation so fiercely dedicated to capitalism and consumption should set aside 3 percent of its land to celebrate another kind of wealth – a "capital" that fattens no wallet or bank account – is remarkable indeed. Think of it. A mutual fund for all people who invest nothing more than time. No stockbroker needed. Three acres out of every hundred given to the sanctity of nature. Not just nature as a potted plant or a manicured garden, but vast, wild, untrammeled nature that speaks to a new and deeper regard for the larger-than-human world. Not a King's Forest, but a people's park with dew on it, where it's still morning in America, where places exist as they did in the time of Lewis and Clark, of Frémont and Carson, of the Shoshone and the Nez Perce, of the black-footed ferret and the boreal chickadee. This and much more is the gift of our national parks.

An apocryphal story says that an Englishman once commented that national parks were "the best idea America ever had." Better than baseball or bluegrass music or the Bill of Rights is open to debate. But if imitation is the sincerest form of flattery, then America should be flattered. National parks exist in dozens of countries around the world, from India to Peru to Canada to New Zealand to Africa. From mountain meadows to coral reefs, from Arctic coasts to tropical rain forests, national parks today preserve some of the last, best vestiges of wild habitat and human hope on the face of the Earth. They are an invention, a romance, a brake on the wheel of runaway commerce, a departure from a profit-as-a-prophet way of thinking.

Robert Hass, a former U.S. poet laureate who now teaches environmental literature at the University of California at Berkeley, tells his students, "Thoreau read Wordsworth, Muir read Thoreau, Teddy Roosevelt read Muir, and you got national parks." The students take notes as Hass adds, "It took a century for this to happen, for artistic values to percolate down to where honoring the relation of people's imagination to the land, or to beauty, or to wild things, was issued in legislation."

Only by vanquishing wild places did we begin to awaken to what they offered us. Only when we came to bury them did we listen to what they had to say. Now we realize that national parks are important remnants of an America that used to be. They represent not just beauty, but memory, our oldest home, a kinship with the Earth that nurtured us and every other living thing down through the ages. They made us what we are. Lose them, and we lose an important part of ourselves. Every year lives are changed – even saved – in national parks, where people of all colors, sizes, shapes, and ages find something ten times deeper than a postcard or a snapshot. They find a part of themselves they didn't know existed, something they cannot articulate, except perhaps in poetry or music, or in a robust laugh they last heard 20 years ago. Students from around America live and work in the parks every summer, fresh out of college, and from their experiences they develop an ecological conscience. They talk about things "back home," but in truth these wild places are their home. The cyberworld fills them up, but also leaves them empty. As one student said to Robert Hass, "I'm much more bored in the middle of civilization than in the middle of nowhere." Another student, a young Chinese-American woman, wrote in her journal that she didn't feel at home in China because she had been born in the United States. But she didn't feel at home in America either, where she looked different. But out in nature, in the mountains and forests, she felt joyfully at home. She felt challenged yet safe, grounded yet buoyant. "People will learn somehow or another," she wrote in her journal. "They will understand the importance of nature. Maybe not today, and maybe not tomorrow, but one day."

IT HAS BEEN A LONG AND DIFFICULT JOURNEY, THIS MAKING OF THE NATIONAL parks, filled with grand accomplishments and sad shortcomings that mirror our society. It parallels the birth of an American land ethic, and for all the distance covered, the journey has probably just begun. When Stephen T. Mather became the first director of the National Park Service, he wasted little time in adding important acreage to the system. The first park born after the creation of the park service was Mount McKinley National Park in Alaska. For nearly ten years one man, Charles Sheldon, had lobbied to have the area preserved. His chief concern was not protecting the centerpiece of the proposed park, Mount McKinley, but the wildlife, primarily Dall sheep, that fell victim to market hunters. In February 1917 President Woodrow Wilson signed the bill creating the park. Two years later, in 1919, Grand Canyon entered the pantheon of great American national parks.

Under Mather's directorship many other parks were born: Zion, Grand Teton, and Bryce Canyon in the West, but also Acadia, Great Smoky Mountains, Shenandoah, and Mammoth

Cave in the East. These last four were of particular interest to Mather, who wanted to establish a park presence near a sizable and politically powerful population. This would presumably expand the base of interest and help build support for national parks. National parks were a deep economic resource, he said. Too many sightseers went overseas to Europe. It was time to stay home and "See America First."

Yet while early park advocates sought to secure national park status for some places, they also sought to exclude others they regarded as "inferior." They didn't want the National Park System diluted by areas that, according to Horace Albright, "lacked merit." Albright, who later succeeded Mather as director of the National Park Service, said in the 1920s that there were "few worthy candidates for parkhood remaining." Mather even opposed the early creation of Theodore Roosevelt National Park in southwestern North Dakota, amid the colorful eroded badlands that were once home to the former President. He said the country lacked the "quality of supreme beauty required by National Park standards."

"Our national parks system is a national museum," said Robert Sterling Yard, chief publicist for the National Park Service in 1923. "Its purpose is to preserve forever certain areas of extraordinary scenic magnificence in a condition of primitive nature." The preservationists could not agree more. Writing in *Ladies Home Journal* in 1921, novelist Mary Roberts Rinehart echoed Yard's observations when she announced that civilization had "girdled the globe...And, unless we are very careful, soon there will be no reminders of the old West," including, she added, "the last national resource the American people have withheld from commercial exploitation, their parks." The word "park" further concerned Rinehart. "It is too small a name," she said, "too definitely associated with signs and asphalt and tameness."

Yard noted that when people thought of Yellowstone what came to mind were the geysers, which was a "mistake." Yellowstone also contained an incredible canyon. Sounding more like an ecologist than a publicist, he concluded, "were there also no canyon, the scenic wilderness and its incomparable wealth of wild-animal life would be worth the national park." This was a profound statement back when scenic monumentalism – and the patriotism it engendered – was the magnet that pulled most people to their parks.

Ansel Adams, 1941-1942, MOUNT MORAN AND JACKSON LAKE FROM SIGNAL HILL, *Grand Teton National Park, Wyoming*

Yet a growing chorus agreed with Yard. Harold C. Bryant, a cofounder of the Yosemite Free Natural Guide Service, added in 1929, "It is now recognized that [national] Parks contain more than scenery."

While the acreage of the National Park System increased in the early 1900s, enlightenment toward wildlife did not. Few if any natural resource policies changed when the National Park Service was born. Management practices, adopted from the military, remained the same. The first park rangers went so far as to wear Army-style uniforms. Predator control programs were pursued with vigor. Early in his directorship, Stephen Mather reported a "very gratifying increase in deer and other species that always suffer through the depredations of mountain lion, wolves, and other 'killers.' " Blinded by emotions and archaic values that made some species desirable and others not, Mather believed that he was exercising "complete conservation" in the parks. He insisted with unintended irony that the parks were America's "outdoor classrooms"; places that, "in addition to being ideal recreation areas, serve also as field laboratories for the study of nature."

The Park Service developed national parks as if they were theme parks for recreation, not storehouses of genetic diversity. By suppressing fire they unknowingly arrested nutrient cycling and other important aspects of forest and meadow health. Fish populations were manipulated to produce "good fishing" rather than stable lake and stream ecology. Wildlife research remained a low priority until 1929, when a young biologist named George M. Wright used his personal fortune to launch the first professional wildlife research unit within the National Park Service. It was the only Park Service program initiated with private funds, and when Wright died prematurely in an automobile accident in 1936, his programs were eclipsed by other New Deal construction and infrastructure development programs and continued predator control. In 1940 wildlife biologists were moved from the National Park Service into a sister agency in the Department of Interior, the U.S. Fish & Wildlife Service.

In response to the trapping and killing of predators, wildlife biologist Adolf Murie studied coyotes in Yellowstone and wolves in Mount McKinley in the 1940s and concluded that, particularly in Alaska, predators strengthened prey populations by culling out the old, weak, and injured animals. Soon thereafter, in 1949, *A Sand County Almanac* was published. Written by Aldo Leopold, a professor of wildlife management at the University of Wisconsin, the little book birthed a new land ethic and ecological awareness in America. A forest is not a commodity, Leopold said, it is a community to which we all belong as members rather than lords and overseers. Only by careful stewardship and minimal tinkering can we save wild nature and ultimately save ourselves.

In time the predator control programs ended, as did fire suppression. Leopold's oldest son became a professor himself, at Berkeley, where Hass now teaches. "I can remember Dr. A. Starker Leopold on a zoology class field trip in Lake County, California, in 1951," said an observer years later, "telling some of his students that before long fires would be restored to national parks. It seemed a startling and revolutionary idea at the time."

The postwar years after World War II found a growing number of Americans with increasing leisure time and mobility. The interstate highway system was launched. The family vacation and personal automobile became not just dreams but the accoutrements of the common man. And where better to take the family than to a national park. In 1951 Conrad Wirth, a landscape architect, became director of the National Park Service, an agency that remained rigidly enamored of visitor satisfaction in the visual aspects of nature. If Joe and Marge Tourist from Indianapolis found Yellowstone wonderfully scenic, then park managers believed they were doing a good job. "To the untrained eye," wrote Richard West Sellars in *Preserving Nature in the National Parks,* "unoccupied lands can mean unimpaired lands, even where scientists might quickly recognize that human activity has caused substantial biological change. The loss of ecological integrity may have little or no effect on the aesthetics of the general appearance of an area."

The true health and ecological status of any region remained an abstraction to most park managers and tourists alike. Wildlife biologists seldom received a serious audience, let alone adequate funding. The immediate horizon for Wirth (and others like him) was not a new way of ecological thinking, but a tide of construction and development. The National Park Service pursued an idealistic mission that led to great public trust. But it also required constant

continued on page 261

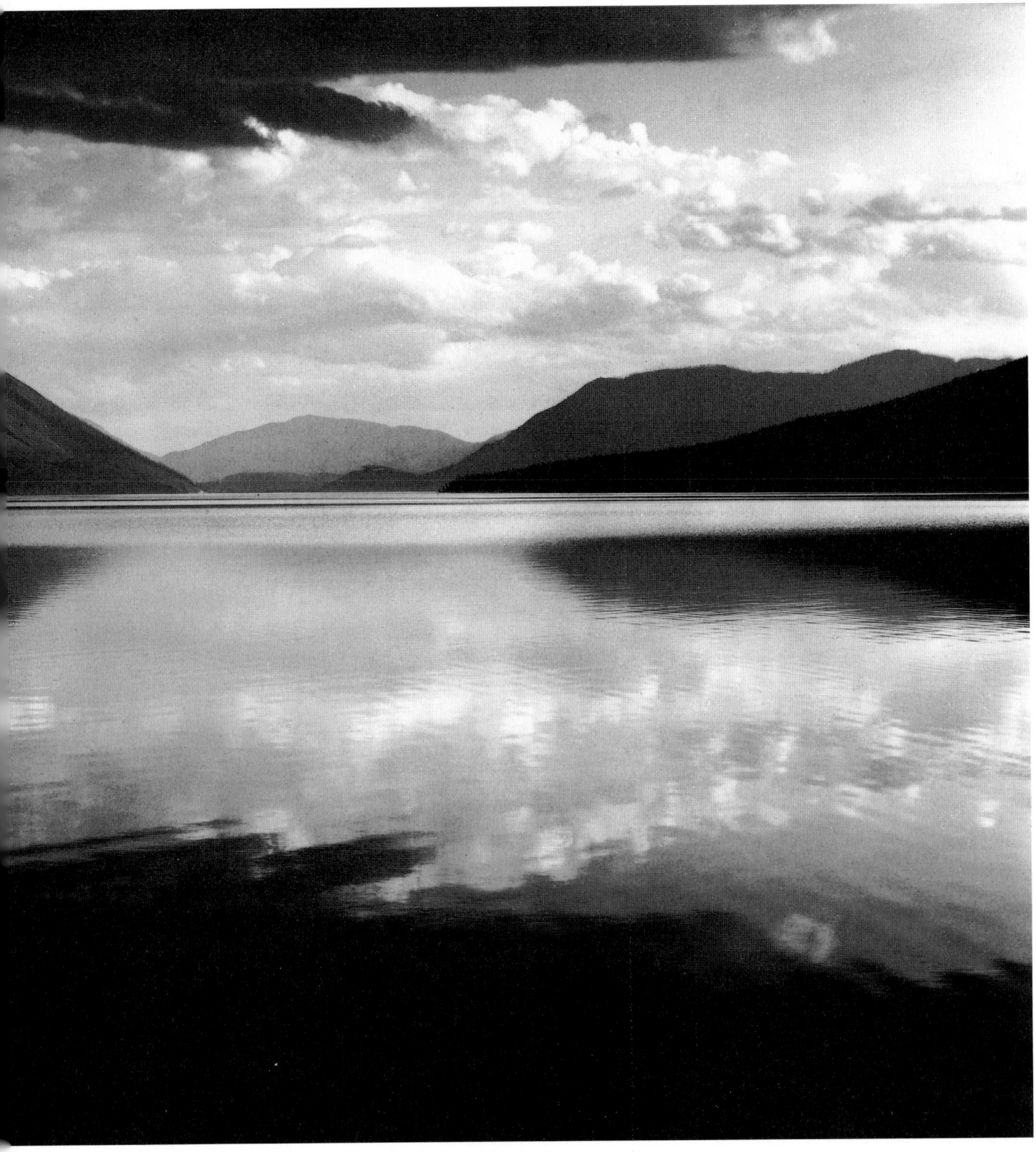

Ansel Adams, 1941-1942, EVENING, MCDONALD LAKE, *Glacier National Park, Montana*

Ansel Adams, 1941-1942, CLOUDS – WHITE PASS, *Kings Canyon National Park, California*

Ansel Adams, 1941-1942, HALL OF GIANTS, *Carlsbad Caverns National Park, New Mexico*

Ansel Adams, 1941-1942, CACTUS AND SHRUBS, *Saguaro National Park, Arizona*

Ansel Adams, 1941-1942, MOUNTAIN TOPS, *Rocky Mountain National Park, Colorado*

Ansel Adams, 1941-1942, CANYON EDGE, *Grand Canyon National Park, Arizona*

continued from page 251

funds from the federal treasury. Other bureaus and agencies, such as the Army Corps of Engineers, the Bureau of Reclamation, and the Forest Service, generated funds for the treasury. Thus funding from Congress became a ceaseless uphill battle for park managers who quickly equated success with the appropriation of dollars. Science meant little to them. And besides, science raised difficult moral issues. In 1956 Wirth wrote to his predecessor, Horace Albright, "Sometimes, I find, Horace, and I am sure you will agree with me on this, that you can get too scientific on these things and cause a lot of harm."

"By the early 1960s," wrote Richard West Sellars, "the [National Park] Service would come under public criticism for its weak, floundering scientific efforts, described in one report as 'fragmented,' without direction, and lacking 'continuity, coordination, and depth.' Moreover, the Park Service would find its management increasingly challenged by conservation groups, and its leadership in national recreation programs seriously weakened, and its control over the parks' backcountry threatened by restrictions in the proposed wilderness legislation, which was gaining support in Congress. These challenges would be mounted in the midst of 'Mission 66,' the Park Service's billion-dollar program to improve park facilities, increase staffing, and plan for future expansion of the system – a highly touted effort to enhance recreational tourism in the parks, and so named because it was to conclude in 1966, the Service's fiftieth-anniversary."

Part of this criticism came from the Leopold Report, a so-called "threshold document" – the first of its kind – that investigated natural resource management by the National Park Service. Produced by the Leopold Committee, a team of scientists under the leadership of A. Starker Leopold, the report concluded that the parks were failing; that park managers must work to create within the parks the "mood of wild America." The report created some tension within the fraternal-minded agency when it called for a "major policy change." The National Park Service, it said, must "recognize the enormous complexity of ecologic communities and diversity of management procedures required to preserve them." Finally, it recommended that scientific research "form the basis for all management programs."

According to David Brower and Ansel Adams of the Sierra Club, the National Park Service was composed of too many hard-hatted road builders and landscape architects, and too few scientists, and for that matter, too few managers with a deep spiritual connection to the natural world. An avid mountaineer and hiker, Brower challenged the Park Service to transcend itself into a more Muir-minded agency. He criticized the spraying of the pesticide DDT in Yosemite and the construction of a new road through Lee Vining Canyon over Tioga Pass into Tuolumne Meadows. It was another place, he said, "sacrificed to the eternal combustion engine." The engine, he said, that never stops.

A talented pianist who surrendered the concert stage for a camera and dark room, Ansel Adams captured the national parks with images that became icons themselves. After Adams's death, Brower would say that "what he saw still exists out there for the most part, and can itself endure if people want it to and make their own personal commitment to keeping wildness alive because they know intuitively that Thoreau was right."

By the end of the 1960s, Redwoods and North Cascades National Parks were added to the system. In the early 1970s America celebrated her first Earth Day, followed by passage of the Clean Water Act, the Clean Air Act, the Endangered Species Act, and the National Marine Mammal Protection Act. Environmentalism had become more than pop culture. It received bipartisan support on Capitol Hill. It became law.

THE NATIONAL PARK MOVEMENT ARRIVED IN ALASKA WITH ALASKA-SIZE debate in the 1970s. President Jimmy Carter used the Antiquities Act with unprecedented flourish to create 56 million acres of new national monuments in 1978. This angered many don't-tread-on-me Alaskans who called it a "land grab" and a "lock up." They were hardly more joyous when two years later Carter signed the Alaska National Interest Lands Conservation Act, which added more than 43 million acres of national parks to the United States. Among the jewels saved: Gates of the Arctic National Park and Preserve at more than eight million acres and Wrangell-St. Elias National Park and Preserve at more than twelve million acres. Mount McKinley National Park, previously two million acres, was enlarged to six million acres and renamed Denali National Park and Preserve.

Since then, many Alaskans have come to see national parks as a good thing, both

Ansel Adams, 1941-1942, OLD FAITHFUL GEYSER, *Yellowstone National Park, Wyoming*

ecologically and economically. The town of Seward, next to Kenai Fjords National Park, now celebrates a park it once opposed. The differences heal slowly, but they do heal. Unlike most parks in the contiguous U.S., those in Alaska embrace vast pieces of geography and entire ecosystems. Hiking in Wrangell-St.Elias, Noel Grove wrote in NATIONAL GEOGRAPHIC magazine, "I can't get over the feeling that I'm the last person on earth. Or maybe the first."

While national parks in their infancy were a come-and-get-it invitation to anybody at anytime, in their adolescence they have become overwhelmingly popular. They struggle to accommodate the pressures put on them by a demanding society. "Parks in Peril" is a common alarm among environmental organizations. Air pollution threatens Yosemite and Grand Canyon and many other parks. Noise pollution has become a serious problem wherever people feel they have the right to drive their cars, trucks, snowmobiles, airplanes, and other devices. Exotic plants and water pollution threaten Everglades National Park in Florida. Overcrowding is epidemic. Most people arrive and leave in a hurry, still strapped to their watches, unable to slow down. The average visitor stay at the South Rim of the Grand Canyon is only 50 minutes. A visitor arrived in Yosemite and told a park ranger, "I only have 45 minutes here, what should I do?' " The ranger replied, "See that rock over there in the sunshine? If I were you, I'd go sit on it and cry. Because if I only had 45 minutes in this place, that's what I would do."

As industry and development have intensified around the parks, and habitats have disappeared, the parks have become ecological islands. Migratory birds and animals come and go, but not all return from the fragmented world outside. Ecologists call this loss "ecosystem decay," the slow erosion of species in a park without the felling of a single tree. The smaller the park, the greater the decay. Since their creation, Bryce Canyon, Lassen Volcanic, and Zion National Parks have each lost about 40 percent of their larger mammal species. Mount Rainier National Park, surrounded by logging clear-cuts, has also lost a considerable number of species.

To counter this trend, scientists now speak in terms of "biotic landscapes," and they search accordingly for solutions. Keeping Yellowstone viable, they say, requires not just the park but also the Greater Yellowstone Ecosystem, a region roughly eight times larger. Beyond that, wild animals need corridors. The Yellowstone to Yukon Conservation Initiative calls for an unprecedented stringing together of preserved lands in the Rocky Mountain region from Wyoming to the Canadian Arctic. Similar proposals exist in the eastern U.S. and in Africa. In Central America biologists from several parks and nations call their proposed corridor *Paseo Pantera,* the Panther's Route, a plan to save the wild cat, based on the Rocky Mountain model to save the mountain lion.

Echoing Emerson, poet Wendell Berry says in *Life is a Miracle,* the "situation calls for language that is not sloganish and rhetorical but rather is capable of reference, specification, precision, and refinement, a language never far from experience or example." What is needed, he adds, is more than the human desire to know, but the desire to "cherish and protect the things that are known, and to know the things that can only be known by cherishing. If we are to protect the world's multitude of places and creatures, then we must know them, not just conceptually but imaginatively as well. They must be pictured in the mind and in memory; they must be known with affection, 'by heart,' so that in seeing or remembering them the heart may be said to 'sing.' "

From scenery to science to spirituality, the American people have found a way to keep alive the places they know, the places they cherish. And when they do, they make music.

In recent years the National Park Service has shown uncommon courage and eloquence in its decisions to do the unpopular thing, but the right thing. Superintendents who can quote Aldo Leopold have let major fires burn in Yellowstone. They have called for the removal of a winter onslaught of snowmobiles. They have reintroduced wolves. In Yosemite, park managers plan to drastically reduce traffic and facilities in the valley that inspired John Muir and Frederick Law Olmsted. In Glacier Bay, where marine conservation is half a century behind terrestrial conservation, the Park Service has taken steps to phase out commercial fishing. The criticism is sometimes intense, it always has been and always will be. Conservation is the brake on the wheel, and preservation the sudden stop. But what a remarkable thing to hear when the engine dies. What a grand and glorious thing when the machine leaves the garden.

It has been said that we do not inherit the Earth from our fathers, we borrow it from our children. In our national parks, if we do things right, we will return it as our fathers found it, and their fathers before them.

North Cascades N.P.
Olympic N.P.
Seattle
WASHINGTON
OLYMPIA
Mt. Rainier N.P.
Glacier N.P.
Portland
SALEM
OREGON
Crater Lake N.P.
Redwood N.P.
Lassen Volcanic N.P.
CALIFORNIA
Reno
CARSON CITY
SACRAMENTO
San Francisco
NEVADA
Yosemite N.P.
Sequoia & Kings Canyon National Parks
Death Valley N.P.
Las Vegas
Channel Islands N.P.
Los Angeles
Joshua Tree N.P.
San Diego
MONTANA
HELENA
Billings
IDAHO
BOISE
Yellowstone N.P.
Grand Teton N.P.
WYOMING
SALT LAKE CITY
UTAH
Great Basin N.P.
Arches N.P.
Capitol Reef N.P.
Zion N.P.
Bryce Canyon N.P.
Canyonlands N.P.
Grand Canyon N.P.
ARIZONA
Petrified Forest N.P.
PHOENIX
Saguaro N.P.
NORTH DAKOTA
Theodore Roosevelt N.P.
BISMARCK
SOUTH DAKOTA
PIERRE
Wind Cave N.P.
Badlands N.P.
CHEYENNE
Rocky Mountain N.P.
DENVER
COLORADO
Black Canyon of the Gunnison N.P.
Mesa Verde N.P.
SANTA FE
NEW MEXICO
Carlsbad Caverns N.P.
El Paso
Guadalupe Mountains N.P.
TEXAS
Big Bend N.P.
AUSTIN
Houston
San Antonio
NEBRASKA
LINCOLN
KANSAS
TOPEKA
OKLAHOMA
OKLAHOMA CITY
Hot Springs N.P.
Voyageurs N.P.
MINNESOTA
ST. PAUL
JEFFERSON CITY
Kobuk Valley N.P.
Gates of the Arctic N.P. & PRES.
ALASKA
Denali N.P. & PRES.
Anchorage
Lake Clark N.P. & PRES.
Wrangell- St. Elias N.P. & PRES.
Katmai N.P. & PRES.
Kenai Fjords N.P.
Glacier Bay N.P. & PRES.
JUNEAU
HONOLULU
Haleakala N.P.
HAWAII
Hawaii Volcanoes N.P.

National Parks Today

Like so many stars in the sky, our national parks make their own constellations across a map of North America. Each offers illumination and opportunities for discovery. While the earliest national parks were established for their scenery and recreational value, more recently they have been established – in some cases enlarged – with attention to biodiversity, ecology, and critical ecosystem size. Collectively, these lands represent a remnant America, a reference point from which everything else in our culture moves away at an accelerating pace. The lands designated as national parks within the National Park System number more than 50 (see map at left), and they are growing. What follows is a colorful compendium of their most important features.

Glacier Bay, Alaska

Notes

Locations listed show sites of park headquaters.

Established date is when the area was officially designated a national park; it may have been protected by the National Park Service under a different designation (e.g., "national monument") or simply "authorized" earlier. The name and boundaries may have changed subsequent to the established date.

Acreage is the total number of acres contained in the national park, rounded to the nearest acre. In Alaska, the adjacent national preserve acreage is also included.

Wilderness is the number of acres of a national park that have been designated as a wilderness area.

Biosphere Reserve and World Heritage Site are both United Nations designations.

Alaska

DENALI NATIONAL PARK AND PRESERVE

McKinley Park, Alaska

- *Established: 1917*
- *Acreage: 4,740,907*
- *Biosphere Reserve*
- *Wilderness: 1,900,000*

The highest mountain in North America, Mount McKinley (20,320 feet) resides here. Wildlife includes grizzlies, moose, and timber wolves. The park is Alaska's most popular, and much of its splendor can be seen from the 85-mile access road that is restricted to buses beyond mile 15.

GATES OF THE ARCTIC NATIONAL PARK AND PRESERVE

Fairbanks, Alaska

- *Established: 1980*
- *Acreage: 7,523,813*
- *Biosphere Reserve (portion)*
- *Wilderness: 7,052,000*

Located north of the Arctic Circle, the park and preserve contain six national wild and scenic rivers, two national natural landmarks, and many jagged mountains. In addition to its aesthetic value, the area is also of great import to scientists. Mostly untouched, the area is known as the ultimate North American wilderness.

GLACIER BAY NATIONAL PARK AND PRESERVE

Gustavus, Alaska

- *Established: 1980*
- *Acreage: 3,224,794*
- *Biosphere Reserve*
- *Wilderness: 2,770,000*
- *World Heritage Site*

The park encompasses several diverse areas, including rocky terrain, lush rain forest, and glaciers. Glacial activity occurs at an accelerated pace here, as evidenced by the 65-mile retreat of one gigantic ice sheet in just 200 years. The bay also supports considerable marine life.

KATMAI NATIONAL PARK AND PRESERVE

King Salmon, Alaska

- *Established: 1980*
- *Acreage: 3,674,530*
- *Wilderness: 3,473,000*

A large population of the protected Alaskan brown bear fish the clear rivers of Katmai for salmon. The park is also known for the 1912 volcanic eruption that earned it the nickname "Valley of Ten Thousand Smokes."

KENAI FJORDS NATIONAL PARK

Seward, Alaska

- *Established: 1980*
- *Acreage: 669,983*

One of the U.S.'s four major ice caps, the 300-square-mile Harding Icefield envelops part of the park. Spilling off the mantle of ice is Exit Glacier, which is accessible by road. The accompanying steep coastal fjords are teeming with puffins, eagles, sea lions, harbor seals, and whales.

Petrified Forest, Arizona

KOBUK VALLEY NATIONAL PARK

Kotzebue, Alaska

- *Established: 1980* • *Acreage: 1,750,698*
- *Wilderness: 190,000*

Adjacent to the Gates of the Arctic, this mix of tundra and boreal forest is often blasted by freezing air. However, ancient sand dunes grace the shores of the Kobuk River. When the climate was more hospitable 12,000 years ago, many animals and humans who crossed the land bridge from Siberia thrived here.

LAKE CLARK NATIONAL PARK AND PRESERVE

Port Alsworth, Alaska

- *Established: 1980* • *Acreage: 2,619,858.*
- *Wilderness: 2,470,000*

Deep in the Chigmit Mountains, black bear and Dall sheep roam the rugged terrain dotted with stands of Sitka spruce. At over 40 miles long, Lake Clark is the largest lake in the park and also the headwaters for spawning red salmon.

WRANGELL-ST. ELIAS NATIONAL PARK AND PRESERVE

Copper Center, Alaska

- *Established: 1980* • *Acreage: 8,323,618.*
- *World Heritage Site* • *Wilderness: 8,700,000*

The park is the largest unit in the National Park System. Three mountain ranges (the Chugach, St. Elias, and Wrangell) converge here to create the continent's largest collection of peaks above 16,000 feet.

American Samoa

NATIONAL PARK OF AMERICAN SAMOA

Pago Pago, American Samoa

- *Established: 1993* • *Acreage: 9,000*

The park includes parts of three volcanic islands in the South Pacific. Unique and endangered plants and wildlife – such as the flying fox fruit bat – make their homes in the tropical rain forests, white sand beaches, and coral reefs.

Arizona

GRAND CANYON NATIONAL PARK

Grand Canyon, Arizona

- *Established: 1919* • *Acreage: 1,217,403*
- *World Heritage Site*

The powerful Colorado River waters carved a deep and colorful canyon, exposing many geological layers to the four million yearly visitors. The park contains 277 miles of the river from Glen Canyon National Recreation Area to Lake Mead National Recreation Area.

Yosemite, California

PETRIFIED FOREST NATIONAL PARK

Petrified Forest, Arizona

- *Established: 1962*
- *Acreage: 93,533*
- *Wilderness: 50,260*

The multitude of fossil plant and animal species identified in this area, including early dinosaurs, indicate that this corner of the Painted Desert was a lush environment over 200 million years ago. Today, large logs of fossilized wood and rainbow-tinted quartz rock can be found throughout the park.

SAGUARO NATIONAL PARK

Tucson, Arizona

- *Established: 1994*
- *Acreage: 91,407*
- *Wilderness: 71,400*

Unique to the Sonoran Desert, the saguaro cactus is a hardy species that can grow to 50 feet in height and weigh over eight tons in its 150-year life span. However, only one in about 40 million seeds will actually survive to maturity. The park also includes five biotic life zones and ancient petroglyphs.

Arkansas

HOT SPRINGS NATIONAL PARK

Hot Springs, Arkansas

- *Established: 1921*
- *Acreage: 5,549*

Initially designated as a reservation in 1832 (40 years before Yellowstone), these springs were a popular health spa destination for the upper class. Many of the buildings on the park property have been preserved in Bathhouse Row. The 47 springs still produce 185,000 gallons a day at 143°F.

California

CHANNEL ISLANDS NATIONAL PARK

Ventura, California

- *Established: 1980*
- *Acreage: 249,354*
- *Biosphere Reserve*

Anacapa, San Miguel, Santa Barbara, Santa Cruz, and Santa Rosa are the islands that constitute the park. Half of its acreage is actually underwater. Over 2,000 species live here, of which 145 are totally unique to the park. Despite their proximity to the heavily populated southern California coast, these islands remain largely undeveloped.

DEATH VALLEY NATIONAL PARK

Death Valley, California

- *Established: 1994*
- *Acreage: 3,367,628*
- *Biosphere Reserve*

This large park is probably best known for Badwater Basin, the Western Hemisphere's lowest elevation at 282 feet below sea level. A gold prospector's elaborate home, Scotty's Castle, is also located nearby. Dotted with curious wildlife, the scenery in this vast desert is spectacular.

Channel Islands, California

JOSHUA TREE NATIONAL PARK

Twentynine Palms, California

- *Established: 1994* • *Acreage: 1,022,976*
- *Biosphere Reserve* • *Wilderness: 429,690*

Two deserts collide within the boundaries of the park: the low, dry Colorado Desert and the high, moist Mojave Desert. The Joshua tree forests are located in the latter (western) portion of the park along with fascinating geological treasures such as Skull Rock. Also, several oases are scattered throughout the park.

KINGS CANYON NATIONAL PARK

Three Rivers, California

- *Established: 1890* • *Acreage: 461,901*
- *Biosphere Reserve* • *Wilderness: 456,552*

Deriving its name from two gaping canyons on the Kings River, the park is dominated by the High Sierra and crisscrossed with many remote trails. Because it shares a lengthy border with Sequoia National Park, the two are managed as one.

LASSEN VOLCANIC NATIONAL PARK

Mineral, California

- *Established: 1916* • *Acreage: 106,372*
- *Wilderness: 78,982*

Between 1914 and 1921, Lassen Peak erupted sporadically. Current incarnations of volcanic activity include hot springs, steaming fumaroles, mud pots, and sulfurous vents. This moderately sized park contains all four types of volcanoes.

REDWOOD NATIONAL PARK

Crescent City, California

- *Established: 1968* • *Acreage: 112,430*
- *Biosphere Reserve* • *World Heritage Site*

An agglomeration of three state parks, this protected area saved thousands of acres of redwoods from lumber companies. These majestic trees grow to heights of over 300 feet during a more than 2,000-year life span. Included in the national park are 40 miles of Pacific coastline.

SEQUOIA NATIONAL PARK

Three Rivers, California

- *Established: 1890* • *Acreage: 402,510*
- *Biosphere Reserve* • *Wilderness: 280,428*

The main attractions at the park are, of course, the towering sequoia trees, which are the world's largest living things. In addition to marveling at these giant beauties, visitors can view areas of former logging where young saplings now grow. The highest peak in the lower 48 states, Mount Whitney (14,494 feet), hugs the park's eastern border.

Mesa Verde, Colorado

YOSEMITE NATIONAL PARK

Yosemite National Park, California

- *Established: 1890* • *Acreage: 761,266*
- *World Heritage Site* • *Wilderness: 677,600*

Thanks to John Muir's determination, Yosemite was one of the nation's first parks. Most of the four million yearly visitors flock to the seven-mile-long Yosemite Valley to gaze at impressive cliffs and waterfalls. Other destinations in this park, which is the size of Rhode Island, include Glacier Point, Mariposa Grove (sequoias), and Tuolumne Meadows.

Colorado

BLACK CANYON OF THE GUNNISON NATIONAL PARK

Gunnison, Colorado

- *Established: 1999* • *Acreage: 20,766*
- *Wilderness: 11,180*

Cut by the slender Gunnison River, Black Canyon's walls are staggeringly steep. Along the 53-mile canyon, the park has three distinct life zones, each with its own flora and fauna: juniper forest, oak flats, and inner canyon. In the late 1800s, a narrow gauge railroad ran through part of the gorge to awe vacationing passengers.

MESA VERDE NATIONAL PARK

Mesa Verde National Park, Colorado

- *Established: 1906* • *Acreage: 52,122*
- *World Heritage Site* • *Wilderness: 8,100*

The park was created to preserve the Anasazi structures within its borders. The area's 4,000 archaeological sites include both mesa-top pithouses and cliff dwellings, dating from A.D. 550 to 1270. It is believed that the Anasazi deserted Mesa Verde during a sustained drought.

ROCKY MOUNTAIN NATIONAL PARK

Estes Park, Colorado

- *Established: 1915* • *Acreage: 265,723*
- *Biosphere Reserve* • *Wilderness: 2,917*

With peaks of more than 13,000 feet and only two hours from Denver, this is one of the most popular national parks. Trail Ridge Road climbs up and over the Continental Divide, providing expansive views of the jagged mountains capped with rock almost two billion years old.

Florida

BISCAYNE NATIONAL PARK

Homestead, Florida

- *Established: 1980* • *Acreage: 172,924*

Most of the protected splendors are found underwater. In fact, the 45 tiny barrier islands (northern Florida Keys) and mangrove shoreline make up only 4 percent of the park. Colorful marine life abounds beneath the surface of the bright blue waters – manatees, coral reefs, sponges, spiny lobsters, and innumerable fish.

Everglades, Florida

DRY TORTUGAS NATIONAL PARK

Homestead, Florida

- *Established: 1992* • *Acreage: 64,700*

So named for its sea turtles by thirsty Spanish explorers, this group of seven islands abounds in both history and biology. A prominent feature is Fort Jefferson, a spectacular stone fortress rendered obsolete before completion. This area, 70 miles west of Key West, is also home to frigatebirds, herons, ospreys, roseate spoonbills, and terns in addition to a variety of marine organisms.

EVERGLADES NATIONAL PARK

Homestead, Florida

- *Established: 1947* • *Acreage: 1,508,607*
- *Biosphere Reserve* • *Wilderness: 1,296,500*
- *World Heritage Site*

Nowhere else in the world do alligators and crocodiles live side by side. Large wading birds and the endangered Florida panther also inhabit the sizable park. The diversity of vegetation in this only subtropical preserve in North America includes mangrove forests, cypress swamps, hardwood hammocks, and sawgrass prairies.

Hawaii

HALEAKALA NATIONAL PARK

Makawao, Hawaii

- *Established: 1916* • *Acreage: 28,350*
- *Biosphere Reserve* • *Wilderness: 19,270*

The park's main attraction is the "crater" atop the dormant volcano Haleakala. This 19-mile-wide, 2,720-foot-deep depression is actually the result of erosion instead of volcanic activity. The other area of interest is the Kipahulu Valley, where spectacular waterfalls and tropical vegetation adorn the gorge and coast.

HAWAII VOLCANOES NATIONAL PARK

Hawaii National Park, Hawaii

- *Established: 1916* • *Acreage: 209,695*
- *Biosphere Reserve* • *Wilderness: 123,100*
- *World Heritage Site*

Kilauea and Mauna Loa are the two active volcanoes protected by the park. Hardened lava, ash fields, cinder cones, and steam vents are reminders of the fury stirring underground. Native Hawaiians leave offerings to the ancient Polynesian goddess Pele at one of the craters. The unscorched areas of the park contain a rich concentration of rare and endangered botanical and ornithological species.

Hawaii Volcanoes, Hawaii

Kentucky

MAMMOTH CAVE NATIONAL PARK

Mammoth Cave, Kentucky

- *Established: 1941* • *Acreage: 52,830*
- *Biosphere Reserve* • *World Heritage Site*

The Mammoth cave system in south-central Kentucky is the longest one on record. Over 350 miles have been mapped, and the full size is not known. The limestone caves lie beneath a sandstone and shale cap that has been penetrated in some places by water. The park offers diversions below ground (200 to 300 feet) and surface trails.

Maine

ACADIA NATIONAL PARK

Bar Harbor, Maine

- *Established: 1919* • *Acreage: 47,738*

The first park east of the Mississippi River, Acadia is the result of individual land donations. Even today, the boundaries are irregular so as to avoid private property. The bulk of the park is on Mount Desert Island, whose dominant features include Mount Cadillac, scattered lakes, rugged Atlantic shores, a lighthouse, and 57 miles of carriage trails.

Michigan

ISLE ROYALE NATIONAL PARK

Houghton, Michigan

- *Established: 1931* • *Acreage: 571,790*
- *Biosphere Reserve* • *Wilderness: 132,018*

The 45-mile-long island in the middle of Lake Superior is a true wilderness. Arriving by boat, visitors must carry all of their supplies in and out of the park. Many are rewarded with a glimpse of a hare, beaver, fox, moose, or endangered gray wolf.

Minnesota

VOYAGEURS NATIONAL PARK

International Falls, Minnesota

- *Established: 1975* • *Acreage: 218,054*

Tucked up against the Minnesota-Ontario border, this North Woods park has over 30 lakes and 900 islands. The resident northern pikes, walleyes, eagles, loons, and wolves provide diversion for pleasure boaters and campers alike. The park is named for the French-Canadian fur trappers who traversed these waters in birch-bark canoes.

Carlsbad Caverns, New Mexico

Montana

GLACIER NATIONAL PARK

West Glacier, Montana

- *Established: 1910*
- *Acreage: 1,013,572*
- *Biosphere Reserve*
- *International Peace Park*
- *World Heritage Site*

As many as 50 glaciers are interspersed among the rugged Rockies of northwest Montana. Clear, cool glacier-fed streams and lakes serve as drinking pools for gray wolves, grizzlies, and other animals. Brilliantly colorful wildflowers line the valley floors.

Nevada

GREAT BASIN NATIONAL PARK

Baker, Nevada

- *Established: 1986*
- *Acreage: 77,180*

Despite its name, the park is actually rippled by mountains such as Wheeler Peak. The "basin" refers to a much larger area in which all rivers flow inland. Inside the park, Lehman Caves is a labyrinth of limestone ornately decorated with bizarre stalactites and aragonite crystals. Above ground, 3,000-year-old bristlecone pines thrive.

New Mexico

CARLSBAD CAVERNS NATIONAL PARK

Carlsbad, New Mexico

- *Established: 1930*
- *Acreage: 46,767*
- *World Heritage Site*
- *Wilderness: 33,125*

Underground lies a honeycomb of 85 known caverns, including Lechuguilla Cave, the nation's deepest (1,567 feet). Carved out of limestone in a Permian-age fossil reef, the caves contain many formations with names like pearls, beards, rusticles, and chandeliers. Carlsbad is also home to the migratory Mexican free-tailed bats in summer.

North Dakota

THEODORE ROOSEVELT NATIONAL PARK

Medora, North Dakota

- *Established: 1947*
- *Acreage: 70,447*
- *Wilderness: 29,920*

The park honors President Theodore Roosevelt's extraordinary contributions to conservation in America. Besides preserving part of his Elkhorn Ranch, it also protects a chunk of the badlands. In this isolated park, bison, deer, elk, and pronghorn roam against a backdrop of horizontally striated cliffs and a meandering river.

Great Smoky Mountains, Tennessee

Ohio

CUYAHOGA VALLEY NATIONAL PARK

Brecksville, Ohio

- *Established: 1974* • *Acreage: 32,853*

Local Native Americans named the river Cuyahoga, which means "crooked." The park follows a 22-mile section between Cleveland and Akron, guarding the area from development and providing a recreational outlet for locals. The Erie & Ohio Canal Towpath Trail is the park's principal historic landmark.

Oregon

CRATER LAKE NATIONAL PARK

Crater Lake, Oregon

- *Established: 1902* • *Acreage: 183,224*

About 7,700 years ago, Mount Mazama of the Cascade Range erupted, forming a caldera where its peak had been. The blue Crater Lake fills this 1,932-foot-deep basin. The average annual snowfall is 45 feet, and the air is so clean that visibility of 100 miles is common.

South Dakota

BADLANDS NATIONAL PARK

Interior, South Dakota

- *Established: 1978* • *Acreage: 242,756*
- *Wilderness: 64,250*

Mixed grass prairie mingles with sharp buttes and spires in this rugged park. Its ancient fossil beds hold clues to the evolution of several land mammal species. The endangered black-footed ferret was reintroduced here. The sites of the 1890s Sioux Ghost Dances are also within its boundaries.

WIND CAVE NATIONAL PARK

Hot Springs, South Dakota

- *Established: 1903* • *Acreage: 28,295*

The origin of the unusual calcite boxwood formations remains one of the biggest mysteries of Wind Cave. The powerful gusts that rush through the cavern's entrance contribute to its dryness. Above ground, the prairie meets the ponderosa. Wildlife viewing in the open grasslands is excellent.

Tennessee

GREAT SMOKY MOUNTAINS NATIONAL PARK

Gatlinburg, Tennessee

- *Established: 1934* • *Acreage: 521,621*
- *Biosphere Reserve* • *World Heritage Site*

Most visitors see the park from the crowded scenic highway that bisects it. However, the 800 miles of hiking trails are the best way to experience the thousands of species of densely packed northern and southern flora. The water and hydrocarbons exuded by the multitude of leaves create the "smoke," now contaminated with harmful pollution particles.

Arches, Utah

Texas

BIG BEND NATIONAL PARK

Big Bend National Park, Texas

- *Established: 1944* • *Acreage: 801,163*
- *Biosphere Reserve*

Where the Rio Grande abruptly changes direction is an area known as Big Bend. A 118-mile section of the river forms the park's southern border. With mountains and canyons of various origins, this section of the Chihuahuan Desert is topographically interesting. Heavy rains can inundate the normally hot and dry landscape with flash floods.

GUADALUPE MOUNTAINS NATIONAL PARK

Salt Flat, Texas

- *Established: 1972* • *Acreage: 86,417*
- *Wilderness: 46,850*

Reaching 8,749 feet, this wall-like desert mountain range was an underwater reef long ago. That ancient inland sea was also responsible for the formation of nearby Carlsbad Caverns. Apaches made this area home until prospectors came in search of the legendary Guadalupe gold.

Utah

ARCHES NATIONAL PARK

Moab, Utah

- *Established: 1971* • *Acreage: 79,979*

Hundreds of natural rock arches are the dominant features in the park. Other products of erosion such as windows, pinnacles, and spires also abound. Carved out of vertical slabs of colorful red sandstone, many formations appear otherworldly. The park also has a petroglyph attributed to the Ute Indians.

BRYCE CANYON NATIONAL PARK

Bryce Canyon, Utah

- *Established: 1928* • *Acreage: 35,835*

The park boasts several horseshoe-shaped areas populated with eerie rock spires called "hoodoos." Covering six square miles, Bryce Amphitheater is the most impressive of these – particularly at sunrise. Water is still carving out formations in the limestone, mudstone, and sandstone.

CANYONLANDS NATIONAL PARK

Moab, Utah

- *Established: 1964* • *Acreage: 337,598*

Adjacent to the Glen Canyon Recreational Area, the park is where the Green River flows into the Colorado. The rivers slice the park into districts: Island in the Sky (high mesa), The Needles (red-and-white pinnacles), and The Maze (confusing navigation). No roads directly connect the regions so as to preserve the abundant backcountry.

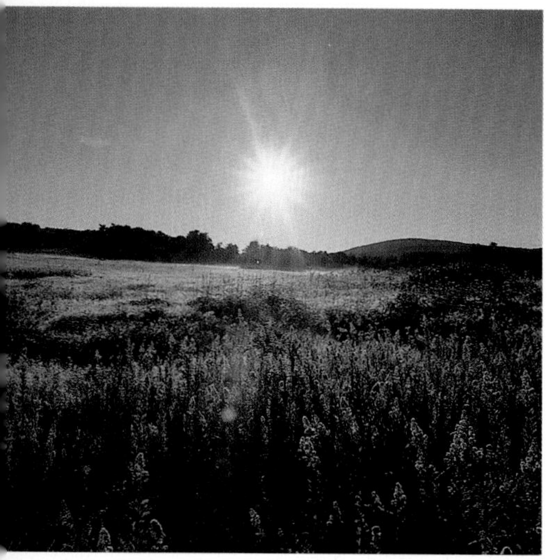

Shenandoah, Virginia

CAPITOL REEF NATIONAL PARK

Torrey, Utah

• *Established: 1972* • *Acreage: 244,392*

Waterpocket Fold, a sandstone uplift with intense coloring, runs the length of the park. Iron in different chemical states provides the pigment for the sedimentary rock of the reef's exposed faces. Frémont Indian rock art and an old Mormon settlement are also within the park's borders.

ZION NATIONAL PARK

Springdale, Utah

• *Established: 1919* • *Acreage: 146,592*

The central feature is the deep Zion Canyon. Here, the Virgin River carved its way through layers of ancient sand dunes stacked by wind. The smaller Kolub Canyons are in the park's northwest section. Sheer cliffs with horizontal stripes are common throughout, some of which drop 3,000 feet.

Virginia

SHENANDOAH NATIONAL PARK

Luray, Virginia

• *Established: 1935* • *Acreage: 198,182*

• *Wilderness: 79,579*

The park is a 105-mile, north-south slice of the Blue Ridge Mountains in western Virginia. Skyline Drive follows the length of it, crisscrossed by many trails and paralleled by the Appalachian Trail. Settlers lived and worked on this land long before it became a park, unlike most in the park system.

Virgin Islands

VIRGIN ISLANDS NATIONAL PARK

Cruz Bay, U.S. Virgin Islands

• *Established: 1956* • *Acreage: 14,689*

• *Biosphere Reserve*

Covering most of the island of St. John, the park is a Caribbean paradise complete with white sand beaches and coral reefs. Sugar plantations dominated the 19-square-mile island in the 18th and 19th centuries when Denmark controlled it. Today, lush subtropical vegetation blankets the rolling hills that sprout from the turquoise sea.

Washington

MOUNT RAINIER NATIONAL PARK

Ashford, Washington

• *Established: 1899* • *Acreage: 235,613*

• *Wilderness: 228,480*

Twenty-five glaciers radiate from Mount Rainier like spokes on a pinwheel. The mountain, a dormant volcano, is the tallest in the Cascade Range (14,411 feet). With its rocky waterfalls, wildflower meadows, and abundance of hiking trails, the park is a favorite among the residents of nearby Seattle.

The Tetons, Wyoming

NORTH CASCADES NATIONAL PARK

Sedro Woolley, Washington

- *Established: 1968*
- *Acreage: 504,781*
- *Wilderness: 634,614*

Steep vertical peaks and scattered glaciers permeate this section of northern Washington State. Ross Lake National Recreation Area (Skagit River) bisects the park into a North Unit and a South Unit. Large mammals such as mule and black-tailed deer, black bears, mountain goats, mountain lions, and bobcats roam the entire area.

OLYMPIC NATIONAL PARK

Port Angeles, Washington

- *Established: 1938*
- *Acreage: 922,651*
- *Biosphere Reserve*
- *Wilderness: 876,669*
- *World Heritage Site*

The park covers a significant portion of the interior Olympic Peninsula plus three distinct ecosystems: 60 miles of Pacific shoreline, glacier-capped mountains, and temperate rain forest. The park also boasts eight plants and five animals unique to Mount Olympus, which glaciers once completely isolated.

Wyoming

GRAND TETON NATIONAL PARK

Moose, Wyoming

- *Established: 1929*
- *Acreage: 309,993*

Because they do not have foothills, the Tetons are uniquely dramatic. The park encompasses most of this jagged range and the reflective lakes that flank it, as well as the broad, flat sagebrush valley known as Jackson Hole. The Snake River winds its way across the park, attracting thirsty animals at sunset.

YELLOWSTONE NATIONAL PARK

Yellowstone National Park, Wyoming

- *Established: 1872*
- *Acreage: 2,219,791*
- *Biosphere Reserve*
- *World Heritage Site*

The level of geothermal activity in the park, including the geyser Old Faithful, is unmatched anywhere on Earth. Yellowstone also has the distinction of being the very first national park. It now also serves as a refuge for animals that once roamed the West in abundance, such as bears, bison, coyotes, eagles, elk, moose, and more.

The Society and America's National Parks

BY PAUL PRITCHARD

NO OTHER AMERICAN INSTITUTION, PUBLIC OR PRIVATE, CAN LAY GREATER CLAIM TO THE SPIRIT OF America's national parks than the National Geographic Society. For while the debate simmers about which individual first uttered the words "national park," the Society made the words into incredible experiences for generations – visually, virtually, and for a few, experientially.

Look at the depth and breadth of the 33 individuals assembled in 1888 who formed the Society. They included explorers Adolphus Washington Greely and John Wesley Powell, naturalist William H. Dall, and meteorologist Edward E. Hayden. Their lives represented their commitment to understand the elements that went into the parks – nature, anthropology, and history. Powell's expedition into the Grand Canyon rivaled the 1871 expedition into Yellowstone. The Society's founding fathers' charge was "organizing a society for the increase and diffusion of geographical knowledge." They not only asked "why," they also sought to spread this knowledge as part of their "egalitarian ideal."

The Society's magazine early on picked up the spirit of the parks. Authors like L. F. Schmeckebier piqued the interest of readers in visiting the budding park system. His 1912 article about 11 national parks was written four years before the National Park Service was created. No doubt, it helped build the public support necessary to bring the parks together under one agency, the National Park Service.

In addition to spreading its message in the magazine, the Society has also played a financial role in the protection of our national parks. When, in 1916, huge thousand-year-old sequoias in the heart of Sequoia National Park were threatened by the timber industry, the Society contributed $20,000 to round out the necessary Congressional appropriation to save them. This effort included the General Sherman Tree, a 275-foot-tall sequoia – the world's largest living thing, with a circumference of 103 feet.

The Society has also fostered a dynamic learning world that explores, records, and relates the experience to the observer. The continuing flow of books, documentaries, articles, interactive materials, and educational programs by the Society has provided more information and stimulated more awareness about the idea of national parks than any other similar source. As the founding president of the Society, Gardiner Greene Hubbard, said, the purpose of the Society is to "diffuse the knowledge so gained...so that we may all know more of the world upon which we live." His ideals are a cornerstone upon which rest the words of park naturalists, park researchers, and park interpreters to this day.

ACKNOWLEDGMENTS

The author and staff of *An American Idea: The Making of the National Parks* wish to thank the many individuals, groups, and organizations mentioned or quoted in the book. We also wish to acknowledge the following people: John Baston, kayak guide with Alaska Discovery; Marylou Blakeslee and Kevin Richards, Glacier Bay National Park and Preserve; Bill Bonner, National Geographic Society Archive Collection; William E. Brown, National Park Service historian (retired); Barbara Brownell, National Geographic Society; Lyn Clement, proof reader; Tom DuRante, National Park Service; Carol Edwards, USGS; Joe McGregor, USGS; the board and staff of the National Park Trust; Robin Remp, proof reader; Justin Smith, musician and carpenter in Gustavus, Alaska; Gilbert Stucker. In addition, we want to thank the archives of the following national parks for their assistance in gathering the photographs: Crater Lake, Denali, Glacier, Haleakala, Hawaii Volcanoes, Lassen Volcanic, Mount Rainier, Mesa Verde, Rocky Mountain, Sequoia and Kings Canyon, Wind Cave, Yellowstone, and Yosemite.

NOTES ON CONTRIBUTORS

A former ranger at Glacier Bay, Denali, and Katmai National Parks, KIM HEACOX was a member of the National Park Service's Prince William Sound Oil Spill Task Force in 1989. The author and photographer of many books, this is his fourth title with National Geographic. His first novel, *Caribou Crossing*, published in 2001, is a political thriller about the Arctic National Wildlife Refuge. He lives in a small town in Alaska with his wife, Melanie, three sea kayaks, two guitars, one African drum, and a warm blanket of friends and neighbors.

JIMMY CARTER, as 39th President of the United States, worked tirelessly to protect our natural resources for future generations. During his administration, the Alaska National Interest Lands Conservation Act added millions of acres to the National Park System, more than doubling its size at that time. To this day he remains an important spokesperson on behalf of national parks. He currently serves as Chairman of the Carter Center (http://www.cartercenter.edu) and is the author of 15 books.

PAUL PRITCHARD is president and founder of the National Park Trust. His career spans three decades of park management, public leadership, and conservation writing. This is Paul's second book for the National Geographic Society on parks.

ADDITIONAL READING

Readers may wish to consult the National Geographic Index for related articles and books. The following titles may also be of interest:

Brooks Adkinson, ed., *The Selected Writings of R.W. Emerson* (1992); Stephen E. Ambrose, *Undaunted Courage* (1996); Nancy K. Anderson, *Thomas Moran* (1997); Wendell Berry, *The Unsettling of America* (1977); David Brower, *For Earth's Sake* (1990); Joseph E. Ellis, *American Sphinx* (1997); Dana Nadel Foley, *Celebrating Wild Alaska* (2000); Garraty & Gay, ed., *The Columbia History of the World* (1981); Bil Gilbert, *The Trailblazers* (1973); Goetzmann & Sloan, *Looking Far North* (1990); Al Gore, *Earth in the Balance* (1992); Noel Grove, *NGS Atlas of World History* (1997); Bernard Grum, *The Timetables of History* (1991); Aubrey L. Haines, *Yellowstone National Park: Its Exploration and Establishment* (1974); Aubrey L. Haines, *The Yellowstone Story*, (1977); Daniel Halpern & Dan Frank, ed., *The Nature Reader* (1996); Garrett Hardin, *The Tragedy of the Commons* (1968); Kim Heacox, *Visions of a Wild America* (1996); Bhyh C. Herndl & S. Brown, ed., *Green Culture* (1996); Leo Marx, *The Machine in the Garden* (1964); David McCullough, *Mornings on Horseback* (1981); Frederick Merk, *Manifest, Destiny and Mission in American History* (1966); Stephanie Mills, ed., *In Praise of Nature* (1990); Roderick Nash, *Wilderness and the American Mind* (1967); David Roberts, *A Newer World* (2000); Kenneth Roberts, *Rabble in Arms* (1947); Alfred Runte, *National Parks: The American Experience* (1979); Alfred Runte, *Yosemite: The Embattled Wilderness* (1990); Witold Rybczyski, *A Clearing in the Distance* (1999); Scott Russell Sanders, *Wilderness Plots* (1983); Roberts Sayre, *Henry David Thoreau* (1885); John Sears, *Sacred Places* (1998); Richard West Sellars, *Preserving Nature in the National Parks* (1997); Bill Sherwonit, ed., *Denali, A Literary Anthology* (2000); Herbert F. Smith, *John Muir* (1965); Wallace Stegner, *Beyond the Hundredth Meridian* (1992); Henry David Thoreau, *Walden and Other Writings* (1992); Keller & Turek, *American Indians and National Parks* (1998); Stewart & James Udall, *National Parks of America* (1993); Herman J. Viola, *Exploring the West* (1987); Keith Wheeler, *The Railroaders* (1973); James Wilson, *The Earth Shall Weep* (1998); Linnie Marsh Wolfe, *Son of the Wilderness* (1973).

INDEX

Boldface indicates illustrations.

ILLUSTRATIONS CREDITS

NGP= National Geographic Photographer

Cover, Southern Oregon Historical Society; **1,** Museum of New Mexico; **2-3,** Library of Congress, Georgraphy and Map Division; **5,** Library of Congress, Prints & Photographs Division, Neg. LC-USZC4-4698; **6,** Library of Congress, Prints & Photographs Division, Neg. LC-USZ62-097312; **11,** Library of Congress, General Collection; **12-13,** Museum of Fine Arts, Boston. Gift of Martha C. Karolik for the M. and M. Karolik Collection of American Paintings, 1815-1865. Reproduced with permission.; **20 (left),** Fine Arts Museums of San Francisco, Museum Purchase, M. H. de Young Art Trust Fund 46.13; 20 (center), Library of Congress, Rare Book Division; 20 (upper right), Oregon Historical Society, Neg. OrHi 977; 20 (low right), , Yosemite Museum, National Park Service; **21 (upper),** Library of Congress, Geography & Map Division; **21 (center),** Dept. of Interior Museum; **21 (low),** Library of Congress, Geography & Map Division; **22,** British Museum; **25,** Library of Congress, Geography and Map Division; **26-27,** Library of Congress, Geography & Map Division; **30-31,** Library of Congress, Prints & Photographs Division, Neg. LC-USZC4-4596; **32-33,** "Wadsworth Atheneum, Hartford. Purchased from the Artist before 1950"; **35,** Library of Congress, Prints and Photographs Division; **36-37,** Washington University Gallery of Art, St. Louis; **39,** Library of Congress, Rare Book Division; **40-41,** Library of Congress, Rare Book Division; **43 (upper),** Library of Congress, Geography & Map Division, photo by Joseph H. Bailey; **43 (low),** Library of Congress, Geography & Map Division; **44 (upper),** Library of Congress, Rare Book Division; **44 (low),** Missouri Historical Society; **45,** Yale Collection of Western Americana, The Beinecke Rare Book and Manuscript Library; **48-49,** Library of Congress, Rare Book Division; **50-51,** Library of Congress, Rare Book Division; **52,** Library of Congress, Rare Book Division; **53,** Library of Congress, Rare Book Division; **54,** Library of Congress, Prints & Photographs Division, Neg. LC-USZ62-8222; **56-57,** Library of Congress, Rare Book Division; **58,** Library of Congress, Rare Book Division; **60,** American Museum of Natural History, Courtesy Department of Library Services, Neg. no. 1822(5), Photo by Logan; **61 (upper),** Library of Congress, Rare Book Division; **61 (low),** Library of Congress, Rare Book Division; **62,** Library of Congress, Rare Book Division; **64-65,** Joslyn Art Museum, Omaha, Nebraska; **70 (left),** Library of Congress, Prints & Photographs Division, Neg. LC-USZ61-361; **70 (right),** Library of Congress, Rare Book Division; **74,** Library of Congress, Prints and Photographs Division; **74-75,** Allen Memorial Art Museum, Oberlin College, Gift of Charles F. Olney 1904, photograph by John Seyfried; **76,** Fine Arts Museums of San Francisco, Museum purchase, M.H. de Young Art Trust Fund, 46.13; **77,** The Warner Collection of Gulf States Paper Corporation, Tuscaloosa, Alabama; **78-79,** New Britain Museum of American Art; 80 (left), Library of Congress, Prints & Photogrpahs Division, Neg. LC-USZ62-36388; **80 (right),** Library of Congress, Rare Book Division; **81,** The New York Public Library; **82-83,** The Cleveland Museum of Art, Mr. & Mrs. Willaim H. Marlatt Fund, 1965.233; **86,** The Library of Congress, Prints & Photographs Division, Neg. LC-USZ62-107578; **87,** Library of Congress, Geography and Map Division; **88-89,** Library of Congress, Rare Book Division; **90-91,** Library of Congress, Rare Book Division; **93 (upper),** Library of Congress, RareBook Division; **93 (low),** Library of Congress, Prints and Photographs Division; **94,** Library of Congress, Prints & Photographs Division, Neg. LC-BH8301-137; **95,** Library of Congress, Prints & Photographs Division, Neg. LC-USZ62-068112; **96-97,** Bishop Museum; **99,** Oregon Historical Society, Neg. OrHi 977; **100-101,** Library of Congress, Prints & Photographs Division, Neg. LC-USZ62-8185; **102,** National Archives, Still Picture Branch; **104,** Oakland Museum of California; **108-109,** Library of Congress, Rare Book Division; **112,** Library of Congress, Prints & Photographs Division, Neg. LC-USZ62-41049; **112-113,** Library of Congress, Prints & Photographs Division, Neg. LC-USZ62-24182; **114-115,** National Cowboy Hall of Fame and Western Heritage Center; **118,** Yosemite Museum, National Park Service; **119,** Putman Foundation,Timken Museum of Art, San Diego, CA, 1864; **120-121,** Bierstadt, Albert (1830-1902). Indians in Council, California. Circa 1872. Oil on canvas. Gift of Marvin J. and Shirley F. Sonosky in memory of Harryette Chon. Smithsonian American Art Museum, Washington, DC/U.S.A.; **121,** California Historical Society, Photographer Eadweard Muybridge: N-15685; **122,** National Park Service, Frederick Law Olmsted National Historic Site, Olmsted Family Photographs; **124-125,** The New York Public Library; **126,** Library of Congress, Prints & Photographs Division; **129,** Yosemite Museum, National Park Service; **130-131,** Library of Congress, Prints & Photographs Division, Neg. LCUSZC4-836; **132,** Yosemite Museum, National Park Service; **133 (upper),** Library of Congress, Prints & Photographs Division, Neg. LC-USZC4-2911; **133 (low left),** Huntington Library; **133 (low right),** Huntington Library; **135,** National Archives, Still Picture Branch, Neg. 79-BC-166; **138,** Bruce Dale; **139,** National Archives, Still Picture Branch, Neg. 57-PS-71; **140 (low),** Library of Congress, Prints & Photographs Division; **141,** Library of Congress, Prints & Photographs Division; **142-143,** Library of Congress, Prints & Photographs Division; **144,** Library of Congress, General Collection; **145,** National Archives, Neg. 57-PS-618; **146-147,** National Archives, Neg. 57-PS-431A; **152,** National Park Service, Yellowstone National Park, Photograph © Board of Trustees, National Gallery of Art, Washington, DC; **154,** National Archives, Neg. 77Q329-30; **155,** National Archives, Neg. 57-HS-1112; **157,** Merrill G. Burlingame Special Collections, Montana State University Libraries, Bozeman; **158-159,** National Archives, Neg. 57-HS-288; **161 (low),** U. S. Geological Survey and National Geographic Society Collection; **162,** National Park Service, NGS Image Collection; **164,** American Antiquarian Society, NGS Image Collection; **165,** U. S. Geological Survey, W. H. Jackson, #1184,; **166-167,** National Archives, Neg. 57-HS-1180; **168-169,** National Geographic Society and U. S. Geological Survey Collection; **172,** Library of Congress,, Prints & Photographs Division, Neg. LC-USZ62-043469; **172-173,** National Park Service, Yellowstone National Park, Photograph © Board of Trustees, National Gallery of Art, Washington, DC; **174 (left),** Library of Congress, General Collection; **174 (upper right),** National Park Service, Yellowstone National Park; **174 (right center),** Library of Congress, General Collection; **174 (low right),** National Park Service, Yellowstone National Park; **175,** National Park Service, Yellowstone National Park, Photograph © Board of Trustees, National Gallery of Art, Washington D. C.; **176-177,** Department of the Interior Museum; **178 (upper),** The Library of Congress, Prints & Photographs Division, Neg. LC-USZC4-3251; **178 (low),** Library of Congress, Rare Book Division; **179,** Library of Congress, Prints & Photographs Division, Neg. LC-USZC4-3249; **180-181,** Department of the Interior Museum; **181,** East Hampton Public Library; **185,** Bancroft Library, University of California, Berkeley; **186-187,** Library of Congress, Prints & Photographs Division, Neg. LC-USZC4-4649; **190-191,** Library of Congress, Prints and Photographs Division; **192,** Library of Congress, Prints & Photographs Division, Neg. LC-USZC4-3874; **193,** National Archives, Still Pictures Branch; **196,** Library of Congress, Geography & Map Division; **196-197,** Library of Congress, Geography & Map Division; **200-201,** Library of Congress, Prints & Photographs Division; **202 (upper),** Library of Congress, Prints & Photographs Division, Neg. LC-USZ62-36760; **202 (low),** Library of Congress, Prints & Photographs Division; **203,** Library of Congress, Manuscript Division; **204,** Yosemite Museum, National Park Service; **207,** Library of Congress, Prints & Photographs Division, Neg. LC-USZ62-122812; **208,** National Park Service, Harpers Ferry Center, Historic Photographic Collection; **210-211,** California Historical Society, FN-26182; **212,** Mesa Verde National Park, National Park Service; **214,** Library of Congress, Prints & Photographs Division, Neg. LC-USZ62-3863; **216-217,** Southern Oregon Historical Society, Neg. 724; **220,** Library of Congress, Prints & Photographs Division, Neg. LC-USZC4-4169; **220-221,** Library of Congress, Prints & Photographs Division, Neg. LC-USZC4-1938; **222,** Library of Congress, Prints & Photographs Division, Neg. LC-USZ62-097301; **222-223,** Southern Oregon Historical Society, Neg. 5379; **224,** Library of Congress, General Collection; **224-225,** William L. Kopplin Collection, Photographer: William E. Kopplin; **226-227,** Bishop Museum; **228 (upper),** Wind Cave National Park, National Park Service; **228 (low),** National Archives, Still Picture Branch, Neg. 48-RST-5D-1; **229,** National Park Service, Harpers Ferry Center, Historic Photographic Collection; **230,** National Park Service, Harpers Ferry Center, Historic Photographic Collection; **232,** Library of Congress, Prints & Photographs Division, Neg. LC-USZ62-52000; **233 (upper),** Yosemite Museum, National Park Service; **233 (low),** Yosemite Museum, National Park Service; **234,** Library of Congress, Prints & Photographs Division, Neg. LC-USZ62-121148; **234-235,** Library of Congress, Prints & Photographs Division, Neg. LC-USZ62-121149; **235,** Library of Congress, Prints & Photographs Division, Neg. LC-USZ62-121150; 237, Glacier National Park Archives, National Park Service; **238,** National Archives, Still Picture Branch; **238-239,** Special Collections Division, University of Washington Libraries, Neg. UW18747; 241, Washington State Historical Society, Tacoma; **242,** Enos Mills Cabin Collection; **243,** Enos Mills Cabin Collection; **244-245,** National Archives, Still Picture Branch, Neg. 79-AA-G01; **249,** National Archives, Still Picture Branch, Neg. 79-AA-G07; **252-253,** National Archives, Still Picture Branch, Neg. 79-AA-E06; **254-255,** National Archives, Still Picture Branch, Neg. 79-AA-H16; **256,** National Archives, Still Picture Branch, Neg. 79-AA-W07; **257,** National Archives, Still Picture Branch, Neg. 79-AA-N01; **258-259,** National Archives, Still Picture Branch, Neg. 79-AA-M11; **260,** National Archives, Still Picture Branch, Neg. 79-AA-F24; **263,** National Archives, Still Picture Branch, Neg. 79-AA-T22; **268,** David Alan Harvey, NGP; **269,** Walter Meayers Edwards; **270,** David Alan Harvey, NGP; **271,** James P. Blair; **272,** William Albert Allard, NGP; **273,** David Alan Harvey, NGP; **274,** David Alan Harvey, NGP; **275,** David S. Boyer; **276,** David Alan Harvey, NGP; **277,** Walter Meayers Edwards; **278,** Richard S. Durrance; **279,** David Alan Harvey, NGP.

An American Idea: The Making of the National Parks

Kim Heacox
Foreword by Jimmy Carter
Paul Pritchard, *Consultant*

PUBLISHED BY THE NATIONAL GEOGRAPHIC SOCIETY

John M. Fahey, Jr., *President and Chief Executive Officer*
Gilbert M. Grosvenor, *Chairman of the Board*
Nina D. Hoffman, *Executive Vice President*

PREPARED BY THE BOOK DIVISION

Kevin Mulroy, *Vice President and Editor-in-Chief*
Charles Kogod, *Illustrations Director*
Barbara A. Payne, *Editorial Director*
Marianne R. Koszorus, *Design Director*

STAFF FOR THIS BOOK

Barbara A. Payne, *Editor*
Margaret Johnson, *Illustrations Editor*
Bill Marr, *Art Director*
Carl Mehler, *Director of Maps*
Joseph F. Ochlak, *Map Research*
Matt Chwastyk, *Map Production*
Roxie France-Nuriddin, *Researcher*
R. Gary Colbert, *Production Director*
Lewis Bassford, *Production Manager*
Janet A. Dustin, *Illustrations Assistant*
Corinne Mercedes, *Editorial Assistant*

MANUFACTURING AND QUALITY CONTROL

George V. White, *Director*
Vincent P. Ryan, *Manager*
Phillip L. Schlosser, *Financial Analyst*

Library of Congress Cataloging-in-Publication Data

Printed in the U.S.A.

Composition for this book by the National Geographic Society Book Division. Printed and bound by R.R. Donnelly & Sons, Willard, Ohio. Color separations by Quad Graphics, Martinsburg, WV. Dust Jacket printed by the Miken Co., Cheektowaga, New York.